Obama and Kenya

Ohio University Research in International Studies

This series of publications on Africa, Latin America, Southeast Asia, and Global and Comparative Studies is designed to present significant research, translation, and opinion to area specialists and to a wide community of persons interested in world affairs. The series is distributed worldwide. For more information, consult the Ohio University Press website, ohioswallow.com.

Books in the Ohio University Research in International Studies series are published by Ohio University Press in association with the Center for International Studies. The views expressed in individual volumes are those of the authors and should not be considered to represent the policies or beliefs of the Center for International Studies, Ohio University Press, or Ohio University.

Executive Editor: Gillian Berchowitz

Obama and Kenya

CONTESTED HISTORIES AND THE POLITICS
OF BELONGING

Matthew Carotenuto and Katherine Luongo

Ohio University Research in International Studies
Global and Comparative Studies Series No. 15
Ohio University Press
Athens

To obtain permission to quote, reprint, or otherwise reproduce or
distribute material from
Ohio University Press publications, please contact our rights and permissions
department at (740) 593-1154 or (740) 593-4536 (fax).
www.ohioswallow.com

Printed in the United States of America

The books in the Ohio University Research in International Studies Series
are printed on acid-free paper. ∞ ™

26 25 24 23 22 21 20 19 18 17 16   5 4 3 2 1

Library of Congress Cataloging-in-Publication Data

Names: Carotenuto, Matthew, author. | Luongo, Katherine, 1975– author.
Title: Obama and Kenya : contested histories and the politics of belonging /
    Matthew Carotenuto and Katherine Luongo.
Description: Athens : Ohio University Press, 2016. | Series: Ohio University
    research in international studies, global and comparative studies series ;
    no. 15 | Includes bibliographical references and index.
Identifiers: LCCN 2016006262| ISBN 9780896802995 (hc : alk. paper) | ISBN
    9780896803008 (pb : alk. paper) | ISBN 9780896804920 (pdf)
Subjects: LCSH: United States—Relations—Kenya. | Kenya—Relations—United
    States. | Obama, Barack—Family. | United States—Politics and
    government—2009– | Kenya—Politics and government—2002– | Group
    identity—Kenya.
Classification: LCC E183.8.K4 C37 2016 | DDC 327.7306762—dc23
LC record available at http://lccn.loc.gov/2016006262

To Mama Ethan
and
Marie and Mary Ann

Contents

Illustrations

Acknowledgments

Scholarship is often a solitary, even lonely, endeavor, but in writing this book we are fortunate to have been inspired by our shared passions for Kenya and its history and to benefit from each other's approaches to and support in writing and editing.

Kate extends her heartfelt thanks to Matt for his unstinting enthusiasm for and faith in this project. One could not hope for a better collaborator and friend. Matt shares Kate's thoughts and knows that without her shared critique and insight, this book would not have been possible.

While only two names appear on the cover of this book, many colleagues and friends deserve special thanks for their long-term support for an idea born out of casual conversations more than a decade ago.

Our former PhD advisers, John Hanson and David William Cohen, deserve special thanks for their thoughtful critiques and continued professional and personal support long after graduation. The foundational scholarship on Luo history and identity produced by E. S. Atieno Odhiambo and David William Cohen was never far from our minds when writing this book. Their many years of collaboration and friendship serve as a model and inspiration for us. Matt would also like to thank his longtime mentor and friend Don Wright. With origins in his lowly undergraduate years, Don's encouragement and model he set as a teacher and scholar continues to drive Matt's work today.

During our initial dissertation fieldwork year together, Dan Branch, Nic Cheeseman, Gabrielle Lynch, and Gez McCann provided great breaks from the archives and a collaborative scholarly community. Their own excellent work informs this book in many ways.

A number of scholars and colleagues from around the world read drafts and provided important critiques along the way. Derek Peterson, David William Cohen, and Frederick Cooper all provided important insights on Kenya and all things colonial as well as judicious advice and warm encouragement as this book took shape. Bruce Berman enthusiastically supported our vision at a key moment. Brett Shadle, Paul Ocobock, Julie MacArthur, Nate Plageman, Liz McMahon, Hannington Ochwada, Jim Brennan, Caterina Pizzagoni, and many others helped flesh out ideas and shape this book through lively discussions and with their own scholarship and supportive friendship. Many thanks go to Gillian Berchowitz, who supported our project from its inception, and to Ohio University Press. We would also like to thank the anonymous reviewer whose careful, astute critiques and imaginative suggestions helped us to refine the project even further.

In Kenya, the staff at the Kenya National Archives (KNA) have been incredibly accommodating and resourceful over the years. Richard Ambani, Peterson Kithuka, and Evanson Kiiru always make the KNA search room a welcoming space and lend their expertise and passion for research to scholars from around the world. In Western Kenya, Martin Adero Metho and Amos Odhiambo helped with early interviews. Atieno Adala was Matt's first Dholuo teacher and welcomed us into both her family home and her family history. Henry Adera deserves special mention for his long-term dedication to this project. From archival research to oral interviews, Henry is a formidable researcher himself and provided key advice and support with translation and analysis while bouncing around Nyanza in our little Maruti.

Our students and colleagues at St. Lawrence and Northeastern provided important support in the halls and classrooms. Ryan Deuel and Bill Johnson helped us flesh out some important ideas in concise and accessible ways. The staff at the St. Lawrence Kenya Semester program made Nairobi a home-away-from-home and continues to produce some of our greatest student critics. St. Lawrence GIS staff Carol Cady and Dakota Casserly produced the maps for this book, and St. Lawrence student, now alumna, Emma Burr created key images.

We are grateful to the several institutions that have directly supported our research. Our dissertation research was funded by Fulbright-Hays fellowships. We have also been supported by our home departments and institutions. Fellowships at the Cambridge University Centre for Research in the Social Sciences and Humanities, the Princeton University Shelby Cullom Davis Center for Historical Studies, and the Library of Congress John W. Kluge Center provided time away from teaching and collegial venues in which to write. Special thanks go to Professor Philip Nord at the Davis Center and Mary Lou Reker at the Kluge. We are also grateful to the audiences at the Harvard University Weatherhead African Studies Seminar and to the Boston University African Studies seminar for their feedback on early iterations of this project.

Finally, without our families none of this would have been possible. Our parents have always been supportive of our work, no matter how far it took us from home. Without their dedication to us to follow our passions in life, Kenya would have remained merely an idea in our minds. Jolene (Mama Ethan), believed in this project from the beginning, allowed us the space to conduct research, and shared many of our experiences at home and abroad. Without her support Matt would never have been able to keep up, and he attributes his continued professional and personal growth to her support and dedication to their family. And a special thanks to Ethan, whose birth and early years grounded our scholarly focus. He always welcomed Daddy home with a hug and games after long hours of research and writing, putting what is most important in life into perspective.

For Kate this project has been both a pleasure and a lifeline in difficult years. Marie Luongo and Mary Ann Jordan deserve special thanks for their selfless support and generous compassion that made life possible in too many ways to count. Peter Luongo and Sharon Luongo Naioti have also been important sources of support. Ann Terry and Meghann Terry Kirk were ever only a text message away and provided invaluable help and necessary levity at key moments over two years. John and Elise Glynn made their home Kate's home in every way at a critical time; she is grateful that it remains so. In both New York and France, Frederick Cooper and Jane Burbank have provided much-needed cheer, kind support, and excellent cooking. Nahomi Ichino, Nina Sylvanus, Tim Brown, Donna McKean,

Diane Damphousse, Sana Aiyar, and Priya Lal have each been present at important moments and in important ways. Carol-Ann Farkas, Charissa Threat, and Lane Summers have truly been Kate's "sisters."

With the historical roots of this project dating back more than a decade, we have said good-bye to some dear friends and family throughout this journey. We continue to draw inspiration from their legacy and in part dedicate this book to their memory.

Abbreviations

AU	African Union
CMS	Church Missionary Society
CORD	Coalition for Reform and Democracy
DC	district commissioner
ECK	Electoral Commission of Kenya
FORD	Forum for the Restoration of Democracy
GEMA	Gikuyu, Embu, and Meru Association
GES	Global Entrepreneurship Summit
IBEAC	Imperial British East Africa Company
ICC	International Criminal Court
IDP	internally displaced person
KADU	Kenya African Democratic Union
KANU	Kenya African National Union
KAR	King's African Rifles
KAU	Kenya African Union
KCA	Kikuyu Central Association
KNA	Kenya National Archives—Nairobi
KPU	Kenya People's Union
KSH	Kenya shilling (the national currency)
LCE	Luo Council of Elders
LDP	Liberal Democratic Party
LLC	Luo Language Committee
LUTATCO	Luo Thrift and Trading Corporation
MDC	Movement for Democratic Change

MOU	memorandum of understanding
MP	member of Parliament
NAMLEF	National Muslim Leaders Forum
NARC	National Rainbow Coalition
NDP	National Development Party
ODM	Orange Democratic Movement
PC	provincial commissioner
PNU	Party of National Unity
RIAT	Ramogi Institute of Advanced Technology
UNDP	United Nations Development Programme
UNESCO	United Nations Educational, Scientific, and Cultural Organization
YKA	Young Kavirondo Association

Charting the Obama and Kenya Story

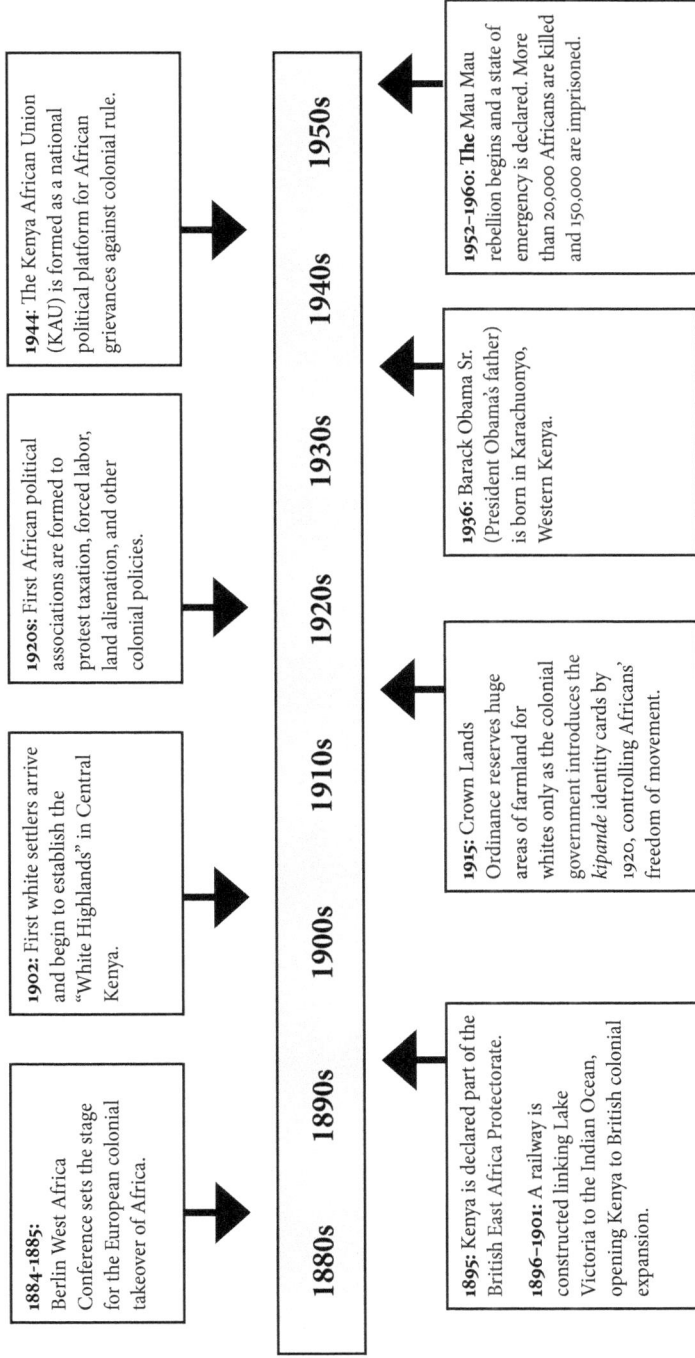

1884–1885: Berlin West Africa Conference sets the stage for the European colonial takeover of Africa.

1902: First white settlers arrive and begin to establish the "White Highlands" in Central Kenya.

1920s: First African political associations are formed to protest taxation, forced labor, land alienation, and other colonial policies.

1944: The Kenya African Union (KAU) is formed as a national political platform for African grievances against colonial rule.

1895: Kenya is declared part of the British East Africa Protectorate.

1896–1901: A railway is constructed linking Lake Victoria to the Indian Ocean, opening Kenya to British colonial expansion.

1915: Crown Lands Ordinance reserves huge areas of farmland for whites only as the colonial government introduces the *kipande* identity cards by 1920, controlling Africans' freedom of movement.

1936: Barack Obama Sr. (President Obama's father) is born in Karachuonyo, Western Kenya.

1952–1960: The Mau Mau rebellion begins and a state of emergency is declared. More than 20,000 Africans are killed and 150,000 are imprisoned.

| 1880s | 1890s | 1900s | 1910s | 1920s | 1930s | 1940s | 1950s |

1960s

1959: Barack Obama Sr. leaves Kenya to study at the University of Hawaii.

1961: Barack Jr. is born in Honolulu.

1964: Barack Obama Sr. returns to Kenya.

1963: Kenya wins independence from British rule. Jomo Kenyatta becomes Kenya's first president, with Oginga Odinga as vice president.

1966: Odinga forms the opposition Kenya People's Union (KPU) party and is removed from the VP office.

1970s

1969, 1975: Key political assassinations of Tom Mboya and J. M. Kariuki mar the second decade of Kenya's independent government.

1978: Jomo Kenyatta dies in office, and Daniel arap Moi becomes Kenya's second president.

1980s

1982: A coup attempts to overthrow the Moi government; Raila Odinga and other opposition leaders are imprisoned. Kenya becomes a one-party state. Barack Obama Sr. dies in an automobile accident.

1988: Barack Obama Jr. visits Kenya for the first time.

1990s

1992: First multiparty elections since the 1960s. Barack Obama Jr. visits Kenya for the second time with fiancée Michelle Robinson.

1997: Moi wins Kenyan presidential election for the third time.

2000s

2002: Mwai Kibaki is elected as Kenya's third president.

2004: Barack Obama is elected to the US Senate.

2006: Barack Obama visits Kenya during an official tour as a senator from Illinois.

2007: Mwai Kibaki wins against challenger Raila Odinga in a controversial reelection marked by widespread postelection violence.

2008: Barack Obama Jr. elected President of U.S.

2010s

2010: A new constitution is passed in Kenya via a national referendum.

2011: Uhuru Kenyatta, son of Kenya's first president, is indicted by the International Criminal Court (ICC) for crimes related to the 2007–2008 postelection violence.

2012: Barack Obama Jr. is reelected as US president.

2013: Uhuru Kenyatta defeats Raila Odinga in a peaceful yet contentious election.

Map 1. Kenya (St. Lawrence University GIS Program: Carol Cady, Dakota Casserly, and Sean Gannon, 2015).

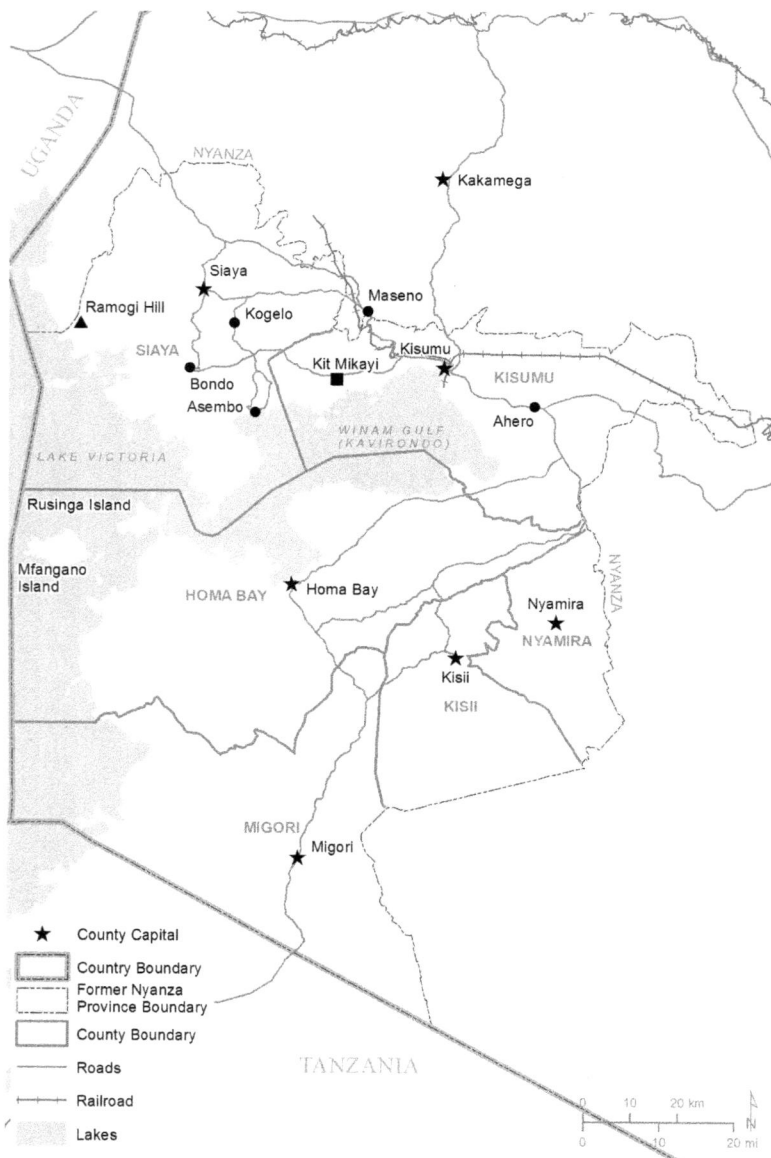

Map 2. Western Kenya (St. Lawrence University GIS Program: Carol Cady, Dakota Casserly, and Sean Gannon, 2015).

Introduction

Obama and Kenya in the Classroom

In 2008 we witnessed the global flood of attention directed toward Kenya as the world aimed to better know and understand the complex heritage of Barack Obama Jr.— the Hawaiian-born son of a white woman from the American Midwest and a black man from East Africa. The Obama and Kenya connection, an important theme in the explosion of biographies that accompanied the election of the first African American president of the United States, sparked a number of debates in classrooms around the globe. As a wide variety of authors of varying credentials and political stripes scrambled to write the story of the Obama family and attach it to *American* history, simplified and boldly inaccurate narratives about Kenya's past and present began to proliferate. *Obama and Kenya* critically challenges and corrects these depictions, showing how Kenya's past and present are relevant not only to African history, but to American and world histories. This book also provides a contemporary space for students of history and African studies to examine how both popular and scholarly narratives often refract analysis of the past through the lens of contemporary political discourse.

Kenyan history is certainly not something the average student or "history buff" encounters regularly on the shelves of the local bookstore or while flipping through documentaries on the History Channel. If one does stumble upon literature or media concerning Kenya, the stories these sources tell tend to range widely in tone, evidence, perspective, and bias. For instance, scholars note that up until Kenya's tumultuous 2007–2008 election season, much of the journalistic writing on Kenya had typically characterized the country as "an island of peace and economic potential in a regional sea of stateless chaos (Somalia), genocide (Rwanda), mad dictators and child soldiers (Uganda), and a decades-long civil war (Sudan),"[1] thereby contrasting Kenya with its more fractious and problematic neighbors. Other sorts of popular accounts drew heavily on colonial nostalgia, making Kenya out to be a romantic world of tented safari camps and sundowner cocktails. In both cases, the ever-present threat of "tribal" violence simmers below the surface of an otherwise idealized Kenya. As *Obama and Kenya* argues throughout, such prevailing stereotypes fit broadly with the way Africa is typically depicted in popular discussions about the continent's histories, cultures, and politics. It shows how these stereotypical representations have driven debates about Obama's connection to the continent and about Kenya's place not simply in African history, but also in *world* history.

As American scholars teaching African history and world history courses in the United States, we regard challenging stereotypes and correcting misinformation about Africa as essential parts of our pedagogy and as central to equipping students with key skills in historical analysis. Most students come to our classes with little or no exposure to African history, and if they have learned about Africa in high school, it has been principally through the lens of African American history or via the history of European imperialism. While they might have learned a smattering of facts, for instance, that American slaves originally came from West and Central Africa in the 1600s or that Europeans "carved up the continent" at the Berlin Conference of 1884–1885, students often complain that they have rarely, if ever, had the chance to examine African history from *African* perspectives or to learn about how African actors have engaged in global historical events and processes. *Obama and Kenya* provides a critical space in which to do both.

Introductory discussions in our classes about *what* we know about Africa and *how* we know it stimulate rich debates about not only the legacy of racism and ethnocentrism in American high school curriculums but also the stereotypes about Africa to which American students have frequently been exposed through film, literature, and popular media. These discussions are also useful in opening a dialogue about the politics of who writes the histories we encounter both inside and outside of the classroom and how African voices and experiences, if presented at all, are often framed as only marginally important in the context of world history.[2] *Obama and Kenya* uses the story of an American president and his Kenyan roots to ask larger questions about historical representations of Africa and the ways both Africans and non-Africans have drawn on a US president's personal and political biographies to tell very particular stories about the world's second-largest continent. For teachers and students of African and world history, *Obama and Kenya* speaks to global discourse about Africa today and to key themes in the continent's history over the last one hundred years. In doing so, it analyzes the political work these representations have done and continue to do in Kenya and abroad.

Focusing on contested narratives of British colonialism in Kenya and the challenges of building a national identity after independence in 1963, we explore how the Obama family is represented in relation to histories of Kenya's colonial era and the early decades of independence, paying close attention to how Kenyan voices have debated this relationship in oral, written, and digital form. With Barack Obama Jr's political rise taking place firmly in the digital age, the story of Obama and Kenya provides a unique opportunity to analyze how Africans debate the past in a variety of forums and how access to political and social discourse has changed over time. Primary sources, ranging from social media to political cartoons to tourist advertisements, are now available at the click of a mouse and form a key part of a growing body of digitized archival material in African history.[3] We have compiled a number of these digitally available primary sources on a companion website (obamakenya.org). *Obama and Kenya* and obamakenya.org highlight these useful resources so that readers can scrutinize primary sources themselves, hone their own skills in histori-cal analysis, and further grasp how Kenya's contested histories speak to broader issues in Africa and world history.

The history of Kenya over the last century offers an important case study in both African history and world history. Given its location in East Africa, Kenya's history is often absent from the broader secondary school curriculum in the United States, which typically focuses on the histori-cal geography of the Atlantic slave trade and its significance to African American history. However, Kenyan history from the precolonial era forward offers countless examples of transnational connections, which speak broadly to comparative studies of European imperialism and the global history of trade and cultural interaction in the Indian Ocean world. Kenya's colonial experience, in which development occurred through massive land grants to a small coterie of white settlers who displaced Africans from their homes and turned them into squatters, resonates potently with the histories of other settler colonies from Zimbabwe to Algeria.

Among the movements for independence from colonial rule that swept the continent in the mid-twentieth century, Kenya's anticolonial struggle is the key exemplar of African resistance through violent insurrection. The Mau Mau rebellion—as Kenya's complex anticolonial contest is known—which motivated the British to throw the military might of their waning empire against the Kenyan rebels, the Land and Freedom Army, was also frequently invoked by participants in the burgeoning American civil rights movement.[4] With the advent of independence in the 1960s, Kenya wrestled with the legacies of colonial rule while negotiating Cold War tensions and the challenges of local development. As in many African nations struggling to develop after decades of colonial neglect, Kenya's economy failed to take off, thus driving a new wave of migration abroad in search of better opportunities for work and education. Kenyan migrants of this era included the father of a future US president.

Critically analyzing Kenya's colonial experience and the challenges the new nation faced after independence offers students of African history and world history a great deal of thematic, topical, and factual information to bring to bear in an array of comparative contexts. While many popular narratives of Obama and Kenya recount a profoundly simplistic view of the country's past and present, the contested histories and the politics of belonging in Kenya cannot be distilled into a simple, single story about the son of an African "goat herder."[5] Further, discussions of the diverse symbolism and meaning of the Obama presidency should not be confined to the American history classroom, as the connection between Obama and Kenya provides a powerful personalized account through which students can debate critical issues that have shaped Africa's place in the world for much of the last one hundred years.

Obama and Kenya is divided into two parts that both serve to introduce readers to the Obama and Kenya connection more broadly and that provide more focused examples of the ways in which diverse audiences have woven Obama into particular African stories and themes. Part 1 begins by exploring the origins of Kenya's fascination with Obama. The authors' personal accounts of conducting research in Kenya during the 2004 US elections underscore the complexity of Kenya's politics of ethnicity and how the roots and relevance of Obama's connections to East Africa reveal a deeper window into representations of Kenyan history from colonial times to the present. Chapter 2 builds on this introduction and familiarizes the reader with key themes that have dominated the last one hundred years of Kenyan history: colonialism, ethnicity, regionalism, migration, and electoral politics. We introduce the unfamiliar reader to the fractious worlds of colonial and postcolonial Kenya where the politics of belonging—of race, class, ethnicity, or other forms of social identity—often work to shape historical realities. In doing so, we briefly explore the dominant myths about the country and contrast them with the realities of Kenyans' lived experiences. Here the goal is not just to narrate a series of past events, but rather to draw close attention to how myths and realities operate in constant tension with each other in reconstructions of Kenya's contentious histories.

Chapter 3 situates Obama in the regional history of the Luo community to reveal how a US political figure has fit into local Kenyan understandings of the nation's diverse social and cultural landscape. Obama's unlikely rise to the top of the political order in the United States was regarded by many Kenyans specifically as the ascendancy of a *Luo*, rather than more generally as that of an American of Kenyan or African descent, and revived specific debates about the failures of a number of Luo politicians to achieve similar feats in East Africa. Here *Obama and Kenya* returns to the question of the saliency of ethnicity in Kenya's political history and examines how the framework of contemporary ethnic identities, assembled by specific historical actors beginning in the colonial era, has impeded the development of an inclusive Kenyan national identity after independence.

Part 2 of *Obama and Kenya* shows how the past and the present are intimately connected in the ways local Kenyan and international audiences have debated the Obama and Kenya connection since 2004. Chapters 4 and 5 take the story of Obama and Kenya to the United States and then back to Kenya to show how Obama's political opponents in the US and his supporters in Kenya have made sense of the US president's Kenya connection by reinvigorating stereotypes and creating new, yet highly erroneous, narratives of Kenya. In doing so, we address the important issues of when and how to "trust" primary and secondary historical sources. Offering a nuanced look at the myth and reality of popular writings about Kenya, *Obama and Kenya* examines what happens to Kenya's image abroad when the country's history is used as a political commodity, and what happens to the politics of rural development at home when tourists imagine the Obama family's homestead in Western Kenya as a global historical monument.

In chapter 6, we return to the question of the political utility of historical representation using the lens of twenty-first-century electoral politics. This chapter examines global representations of Kenya's hotly contested December 2007 presidential election and its violent aftermath, which drew upon well-worn, ahistorical clichés about ancient tribal rivalries. The text then turns to the presidential elections of March 2013, which again revived the familiar portrayal of Kenya as a nation filled with "tribal gangs" roaming the forests and ready to unleash the savage violence of the past. The chapter also addresses how the election pitted Uhuru Kenyatta, son of Kenya's first president, and Raila Odinga, son of Kenya's first vice president, against each other in a contest many Kenyans viewed as part of a historic struggle of regional and dynastic family politics. As the political discourse clearly showed, the legacy of colonialism was a regular point of reference in this high-stakes political contest, where particular narratives of the past were often evoked on the campaign trail and even among pundits abroad. Picking up where chapter 6 leaves off and focusing on the Obama administration's reactions to the 2013 elections, chapter 7 explores the ways in which the administration has or has not engaged with Africa since 2008. Returning briefly to the continent-wide celebrations of Obama's victory in 2008, the chapter asks how African expectations for the Obama presidency have aligned with American policy and practice. The epilogue focuses on Obama's official state visit to Kenya in July 2015, analyzing both how the first such visit by a sitting US president was figured in the two countries and the issues that Obama, as the first *Kenyan* American president, was uniquely positioned to address.

Part I

Obama and Kenya

1

Discovering Obama in Kenya

The seeds for this book were sown in the multitude of places we visited and the variety of voices we encountered as eager graduate students fumbling through our dissertation fieldwork across Kenya's diverse landscape in 2004. As we read through stacks of dusty files at the Kenya National Archives (KNA), conducted interviews along the rocky shores of Lake Victoria, and engaged in more casual debates in the bustling cafés and nightclubs of Nairobi, Kenya's energetic, cosmopolitan capital city, we never imagined that ten years later our multifaceted research experiences would lead us to write a book about the place of an American president in the history of Kenya.

While in the last decade we have engaged in countless conversations about and collected many examples of the local and global significance of Barack Obama's ties to Kenya, one episode at an American embassy event in Nairobi pointed to a need for and shaped the vision of our book. Fortunate to be supported by Fulbright fellowships through the US Department of Education, we received formal invitations in the fall of 2004 to attend an exclusive celebration that takes place in the early morning hours only once every four years during the first week of November—an Election Day breakfast held by the American embassy in Nairobi. Flattered to be invited to a special gathering at the posh Nairobi residence of the then US ambassador to Kenya, William Bellamy,[1] excited about whom we might meet, and like all graduate students pleased by the prospect of a free meal, we luckily landed at what must have been the very bottom of an exclusive invite list that included much of Kenya's political elite.

On the morning of November 3, with Kenya some eight hours ahead of eastern standard time, much of the diplomatic and expatriate American community in Kenya had been up all night, tracking the election returns in the US presidential race. Having followed the campaign all fall as we completed our research projects on colonial and postcolonial Kenyan history, we, too, had stayed up, bleary-eyed and eager for the results. Focused mainly on the presidential race between Republican incumbent George W. Bush and his Democratic challenger, John Kerry, we had paid little attention to a more minor contest in the midwestern state of Illinois that had already begun to overshadow the presidential race for many Kenyan audiences.

Unaware of the singular moment that would unfold that morning, we left the congested confines of Nairobi's central business district during the predawn hours to make our way to the ambassador's residence in the leafy suburb of Muthaiga. Heading out of the city center during the ritual tussle of Nairobi's hectic morning commute, we escaped the brunt of the daily bumper-to-bumper line of packed buses, overflowing *matatu* (van taxis), and commercial traffic that Kenyans simply refer to as "the jam." Turning off the main highway not too far from downtown, we entered a tranquil suburban relic of the colonial past. Now a mixed bastion home to international aid workers, diplomatic personnel, and Kenya's political elite, the tony neighborhood of Muthaiga has roots dating back to the early twentieth century, complete with the golf outings and colonial cocktail parties that made up the days of Britain's privileged white settler class.[2] Like many of the homes and businesses, the US ambassadorial residence still reflects the imposing architecture and manicured style of the British colonial past and is hardly visible behind the razor wire–topped walls and guarded gates that dot one of Nairobi's most exclusive neighborhoods.

Arriving just before six in the morning, we waited in the long security line along with an array of impeccably dressed guests to be welcomed to the traditional American election party, already off to a lively start despite the hour and the fact that US media outlets more than seven thousand miles away had yet to finalize the tally of votes cast the day before. Clearing the armed security and entering the residence, we were struck by the chatter expressing the broad Kenyan interest in the US elections as well as the lavish spread of food and the numerous satellite televisions scattered across the living room, veranda, and pristine gardens of the residence compound that displayed real-time CNN election results.

Mixing in this unfamiliar world, we tentatively scanned the slew of guests and noticed faces familiar to us from the pages of the Kenyan press, including influential members of the international diplomatic corps and a sampling of Kenya's political elites. Spotting figures ranging from then official government spokesperson Alfred Mutua to then minister for the environment Kalonzo Musyoka, we spent the next few hours sipping tea and trying to make awkward small talk with a sea of parliamentarians, permanent secretaries, and other government officials who operate high above the daily lives of the everyday Kenyans, the *wananchi* as they are known in Kiswahili, and certainly outside the sphere of the average US graduate student.

In our awe of the overall gathering that day, one group of Kenyan politicians stood out from the rest and instantly captured our attention. Entering amid an entourage of supporters, the Luo leader Raila Odinga was clearly a visible star among this elite group of "Big Men." Hailing from Siaya, the Western Kenyan county that was also the birthplace of Barack Obama Sr., Odinga has been a fixture in Kenyan politics at the national level since the 1980s. Son of Kenya's first vice president, Oginga Odinga, and scion of one of Kenya's most prominent political dynasties, by 2004 Raila, as he is popularly called, was known in local circles as the edgy political dissident and exile from the 1980s who had risen to represent Nairobi's Langata Constituency in Parliament in the 1990s and was easily the most recognizable politician from Kenya's relatively small but politically important Luo community. That day, however, Raila was not flying the metaphorical flag of Kenya's political opposition, but he was instead sporting a wide American flag tie set off by a large Obama pin stuck prominently to the lapel of his pricey suit. His entourage was similarly, though less flamboyantly, kitted out in visible support for the United States broadly and Obama particularly.

While it was not unusual for guests to demonstrate their support for the American electoral process during a gathering at the US ambassador's home, we were immediately struck by hów Raila exhibited fervent enthusiasm for a relatively unknown senatorial candidate from Illinois, Barack Obama. In the months leading up to the November election, Matt Carotenuto had fielded an increasing number of questions from Kenyans about this "Obama fellow" during his fieldwork near Raila's home areas in Western Kenya. Word had gotten around that the Democratic candidate campaigning to represent Illinois in the US Senate was in fact the son of the same Barack Obama Sr. who was born in the 1930s not far from Raila's hometown close to Lake Victoria in the Western Kenyan county of Siaya. Some nine years older than Raila, Obama Sr., a onetime government employee and midlevel technocrat, had died tragically in an automobile accident in Nairobi in 1982.[3] Though successful in his own right, Obama Sr. was certainly not of the same political pedigree or elevated achievement as Raila, yet, in Western Kenya, a strange sense of dynasty had nonetheless begun to emerge around Barack Obama Jr., the US senatorial candidate whose ties to Kenya generally and to the history of the Luo community particularly had been seized upon by Luo people in the months leading up to the American elections. However, it was not until the lopsided victory of Obama Jr. over his Republican challenger in Illinois was declared that we began to witness the significance of this US electoral victory to international relations and to "Big Man" politics in Kenya.

Called long before the presidential race, the senatorial victory of Barack Obama Jr. drew the most dramatic response from the Kenyan guests of any election results announced that morning. A sporting cheer and rounds of overwhelming applause led by Raila's group erupted when CNN declared Obama the winner.[4] However, instead of simply joining politely in the applause celebrating the election of a junior senator with paternal ties to Kenya, Ambassador Bellamy made his way straight for the Odinga contingent and began shaking Raila's hand boisterously as if the Kenyan politician's own brother had been elected. In congratulating Raila, first among the cream of the Kenyan political elite present at the party, and doing so in such a public space, Ambassador Bellamy, who drew some subtle stares from various other Kenyans at the gathering, seemed to imply that Obama's victory was not something to be celebrated by the wananchi across Kenya but something belonging more narrowly to a particular region and ethnicity; a particular victory for Western Kenya and for the Luo.

Congratulating Raila first was a bold diplomatic move to make that morning during an event billed as nonpartisan—both American *and* Kenyan political temperatures were running high in 2004—and inspired a number of important initial questions about the significance of the Obama-Kenya connection in both local and global political circles. Was Bellamy's hearty handshake in response to a Democratic victory merely a nod to the Democratic leanings of the party guests? The traditional, friendly straw poll conducted by the embassy that morning had revealed that attendees overwhelmingly favored Democratic nominee John Kerry's candidacy for president. Or was the ambassador perhaps simply trying to cultivate a personal relationship with one of Kenya's most important political figures regardless of how alienating this may have been to those in the audience who resided at the opposite end of the political spectrum from Raila?

These questions carry weight in large part because in the interpenetrated worlds of international affairs and global commerce, Kenya is an important strategic ally and trading partner of the United States and of many other Western nations. The country borders the "hot zones" of the Horn of Africa and northern Uganda and South Sudan, while its principal port at Mombasa serves as the economic gateway to many of the markets of Eastern Africa, spanning Uganda and Rwanda to Ethiopia and South Sudan. After the US embassy in Nairobi was bombed by Al-Qaeda in 1998, killing 213 Kenyans and American diplomatic staff, Kenya became one of the American government's chief allies in the growing "war on terrorism." The United States expanded its embassy, already the largest American embassy in Africa and the second-largest American embassy in the world, into a huge fortresslike compound not far from the ambassador's residence.[5] Nonetheless, even taking into consideration the importance of the US diplomatic relationship with Kenya, the ambassador's acknowledgment of Raila's "special relationship" with Obama spoke to more than US-Kenya ties forged over terrorism and trade. Rather, as social historians of twentieth-century Kenya, we recognized that Bellamy's gesture, and the awkward smiles of the other Kenyan guests that followed it, was a testament to the widely acknowledged and broadly accepted purchase of ethnic politics and regionalism in contemporary Kenya, formations with deep roots in the colonial past.

Over the coming weeks and months, we watched closely as a steady stream of politicized popular discourse, occurring informally in Kenyan homes and workplaces and on the pages of the local press, about the connection between Obama and Kenya generally, and Obama and the Luo particularly, began to flow. Indeed, over the weeks and months that followed his election, Senator Barack Obama was publicly celebrated as a "son of the soil" of Kenya in public discourse, but in other debates at home and abroad, his Kenyan roots were firmly being replanted in Kenya's western regions, casting him first and foremost as a member of the minority Luo community, who make up just over 10 percent of the population.[6] "Obamamania," as Kenyans came to refer to the celebration of Obama's rise, began to grip the nation in late 2004. T-shirts and commemorative songs written about the junior senator from Illinois began to be seen and heard on the streets of Nairobi and in the Western Kenyan city of Kisumu even before Obama gained widespread national appeal in the United States.[7]

Obamamania reached a fever pitch four years later with the next round of American presidential elections in 2008. Importantly, what we came to glean over several years of research sparked by the ambassador's enthusiastic congratulations offered to Raila was how the story of Barack Obama Jr. and his Kenyan heritage has been used by numerous political actors in Kenya and abroad to frame narratives of Kenya's history that have both perpetuated common Western stereotypes about Africa and helped to reinforce the contentious politics of ethnicity rooted in Kenya's colonial history. These narratives of Kenya's past engendered by the Obama-Kenya connection have held world historical significance, contributing to the shape of contemporary electoral politics both in the United States and in Kenya. For political actors in both Africa and the United States, the Kenyan roots of an American president (read and complicated through the lens of identity politics in two very different contexts) have offered ample resources with which to envisage their own localized concerns and to market narratives of Africa's past to distinct audiences. Further, viewed through the prisms of race and ethnicity and refracted through politicized understandings of Kenya's past, the story of Obama and Kenya has been interpreted not simply as an American political story but as an event of national political import in Kenya *and* a historical moment of global significance. For political actors and audiences in Kenya, the United States, and an array of places and spaces around the world, the targeted telling of the Obama and Kenya story has transformed the Kenyan past into a sort of political currency, a situation that, as Dane Kennedy argues, "highlights the polemical power of history and the complex array of politically and morally freighted meanings that inform its practice."[8]

As historians of Kenya, we trace the impact and meaning of these interwoven histories of Kenya and the Obama family after more than a decade of historical and political entrepreneurship aiming to capitalize on the Obama-Kenya connection. Depictions of this connection, found in productions as diverse as best-selling political biographies and amateur histories, have influenced the ways in which multiple publics around the world conceive Kenya's past and present, and also point to the increasingly digital methods and means through which local and global histories are both produced *and* consumed. Indeed, Obama's political ascendancy created a unique space in which African history was debated in real time by global audiences who read, wrote, blogged, chatted, and tweeted about the significance of the Obama family's place in the history of Kenya, and the place of Africa in world history more generally.

Throughout this book we identify and break down the dominant narratives about Kenya's colonial past and postcolonial present in order to dispel some of the stereotypes of and misunderstandings about Kenya's history that the Obama story has rekindled and fanned. Using a variety of sources, from archival records and oral interviews to the popular press and amateur histories, we analyze how Obama's Kenyan roots, and the histories associated with them, have been interpreted by and for a range of local and international audiences. From Obama's political supporters in East Africa to his opponents abroad, examining the ways in which local and global audiences have interpreted Obama's connection to Kenya can tell us not only about how Kenya's past and present (and Africa and its place in the world more generally) have been represented since the early twentieth century, but also about the social, political, and material significance of these representations.

Placing Obama and His Kin in the Contested Story of Kenya

Constructing a history of Kenya through the story of an American president's paternal heritage is certainly not an easy task, and it is one we take on with great caution and with the goals of clarification and correction. Kenya is a large country, bigger than France and nearly the size of Texas.[9] Spanning the equator, its landscape represents many points across the environmental spectrum. A thin, tropical band runs along the Indian Ocean, while vast savanna grasslands with variable and often unreliable rainfall patterns dominate more than 70 percent of the country's interior. Much of the northern region of Kenya, extending to the borders with Somalia, Ethiopia, and South Sudan, consists of sparsely populated terrain suitable mainly for pastoralism due to the semiarid climate and history of underdevelopment in the area. In fact, when traveling from the capital city to northern towns like Garissa, Wajir, Marsabit, or Lodwar, one is often greeted with the wry question "How is Kenya?"—a query reflecting both the sharp physical divide between the dry, sparsely peopled North and the more fertile, more densely populated regions of the country, and the historical divide in development created by policies dating back to the colonial era that have favored the rest of the country to the expense of the North.[10]

Over much of the last century, the southern-central and western regions of Kenya have been most intensely marked by colonialism and its legacies and have dominated colonial and postcolonial politics. From Mombasa to Kisumu, the stories of the Obama family and Kenya span these regions, revealing the broader history of Kenya's colonial past and illustrating the postcolonial political and socioeconomic challenges that have shaped Kenya since it gained independence from Britain in 1963. Rising to an average of more than five thousand feet in many places, the temperate and densely populated regions of Central Kenya form the economic engine of the country's largely agriculturally based economy, in which tea, coffee, sugarcane, and other cash crops are grown alongside subsistence staples like maize and wheat throughout rural areas. Cutting a swath through the center of the country is the Great Rift Valley, flanked by magnificent escarpments, volcanic massifs, and the snowcapped highest peaks of Africa, Mount Kenya and Mount Kilimanjaro. To the west, the country is bounded by the craggy beaches of Lake Victoria, the source of the Nile

Figure 1.1. Famed Kenyan critique of Obamamania from renowned East African cartoonist GADO (Godfrey Mwampembwa). *Daily Nation*, June 10, 2008.

River and the historical home of Kenya's Luo-speaking populations and of Obama's kin and ancestors.[11]

While the flora and fauna of Kenya's countryside have long fascinated visitors, the demographic history of Kenya reflects dramatic changes similar to those of neighboring countries in regard to migration patterns and to the related economic prospects of the wananchi. With a population of just over eight million in 1960, by 2013 Kenya had swelled to more than forty million citizens, a quarter of whom now reside in urban environments.[12] In fact, the Kenyan government projects that by 2030 its population will exceed sixty million, with more than half of the wananchi making the move from the countryside to the city.[13] Even the casual visitor to Nairobi cannot miss the effects of this change as a construction boom involving large-scale infrastructure projects dominates both the high-rise cityscape of downtown Nairobi and the sprawling suburbs of the greater capital's three million–plus residents.

Just as the map of Kenya reflects a great deal of environmental and demographic variability, its cultural landscape is equally diverse. With a fast-growing population speaking more than forty different languages, no one linguistic or cultural group represents a majority of the population.[14] Like most African countries, Kenya's history as a nation-state does not start with the founding of an ancient African kingdom or empire, but instead begins with the story of how late nineteenth-century British imperialism and African resistance to it carved out the borders of the Kenya Colony from among people whose cultures, connections, and histories extended far beyond colonial boundaries. Even a casual observer cannot help but notice evidence of Kenya's long-standing global connections residing side by side with the vestiges of colonial rule from the saltwater shores of the Indian Ocean to the freshwater beaches of Lake Victoria.

For example, visiting Mombasa, Kenya's second-largest city and an urban center of note for more than a millennium, one is struck by the muezzin's call to prayer, so familiar in the predominantly Muslim, Kiswahili-speaking areas of Kenya's coast, echoing over the fortified walls of Fort Jesus, erected by the Portuguese in the late 1400s, and across a port where international cargo vessels and dhows, a type of lateen-sail vessel used in the region for a thousand years, both ply the waters. Unsurprisingly given the region's deep cosmopolitan connections, inhabitants of the Kenyan coast, both past and present, have imagined their distinct "Swahili" religio-cultural identity as intimately linked with the experiences of other Indian Ocean communities from the Middle East to Indonesia.[15] Yet, the Swahili Coast is not the only region of Kenya where identity has been imagined through webs of cultural and linguistic connections constituted by long-standing patterns of migration and trade.

Heading west to the freshwater coast of Lake Victoria, where Kenya borders Tanzania and Uganda, one arrives in the port city of Kisumu. In the home of Kenya's Luo community, the paternal kin of Barack Obama, one encounters traders from around the Lake Victoria basin mingling on the beaches, wolfing down grilled tilapia and *ugali*, a thick maize meal porridge, at long picnic tables while chatting in a mixed lingua franca of English, Kiswahili, and Luo as Swahili hip-hop from Tanzania competes with Congolese Lingala and local Benga and Ohangla beats. In this region, too, connectivity and a sense of distinct linguistic-cultural identity stretch deep beyond present-day commerce, back centuries to the migrations of people from along the Nile up to northern Uganda and down to South Sudan who belonged to groups related in language and practice to Kenya's Luo community. Here in Barack Obama's ancestral home, colloquially called "Luoland," many Luo signal as much affinity for other Nilotic-speaking groups as they do for their fellow Kenyans nationwide.[16]

In sum, the vignettes presented above point to the book's key themes—the complex narratives that make up Kenya's history and how the politics of belonging create sometimes competing notions between national and local identities. As *Obama and Kenya* shows, there is no one story of what it means to be Kenyan. Rather, identities are historical, flexible, multilayered, and crosscutting. As such, any claim to the existence of a definitive "Kenyan" identity or to a singular Kenyan history is fraught with inaccuracy and bias. Here we also want to caution readers about the politics of language broadly used in the debate about Obama and Kenya and direct them to pay close attention to the politics of one loaded term, "tribe," which can have disparaging connotations, but is also widely employed by Africans themselves. In Western discourse, "tribe," "tribal," and "tribalism" have often been used to dismiss Africans as primitive, primordial. Such usage does not reflect how African communities figure their own identities along tribal lines.

As much as this book is about unpacking the contested histories that Obama's East African roots underscore, it is also an exploration into the local politics of belonging in Kenya. Many popular outside accounts frame the complex history of ethnic identity in Kenya with simplistic and static terms like "tribe" and use pejorative adjectives like *tribal* and *tribalism* to describe everything from cultural beliefs to political conflict. Like many students in our classes, we, too, agree that these words carry political weight in contemporary discourse that perpetuates understandings of African identities as "uncivilized," "primitive," and "timeless." As the term "tribe" fails to capture the ways Kenyans have historically debated ethnicity as constantly changing, contingent, and negotiated, we reject the term in our own analysis and treat the Obama and Kenya connection as much more complicated than a simple story about the son of a "Luo tribesman" from Kenya hewing to his "tribal" heritage.[17]

Given Kenya's fascinating environmental and cultural diversity, it is not surprising that the country and its people have inspired the production of numerous historical narratives. However, these works often deliberately fail to embrace Kenya's complexity, instead simplifying or skewing Kenya's multifaceted past to fit with particular social and political agendas. Since the earliest days of British imperial expansion in the late nineteenth century, Western audiences have been bombarded by scenes of majestic wild landscapes where heroic beasts are pitted against noble yet "savage" Africans. Further, literary and cinematic representations of a glamorous colonial life of sundowner cocktails and lion hunts abound, and films like the Oscar-winning *Out of Africa* have long helped to perpetuate romanticized images of the colonial period with the civilizing zeal of the "white man's burden" lurking as a dangerous subtext.

While contemporary representations are perhaps more subtle than the popular accounts of the colonial era, Kenya's past has long been narrated as the history of a wild environment brought into the "developed" world through colonial expansion targeted to serve European interests. For instance, when Frederick Lugard, a famous British colonial official and architect of imperial policy across much of the continent, wrote about *The Rise of Our East African Empire*, he cited the Earl of Rosebery's now famous speech, delivered at the Royal Colonial Institute in 1893, which argued that the British were "engaged in 'pegging out claims for the future.' . . . We have to consider what countries must be developed either by ourselves or some other nation and we have to remember that it is part of our responsibility and heritage to take care that the world, as far as it can be moulded by us, shall receive the Anglo-Saxon and not another character."[18]

Written in an era of colonial expansion and violent repression of African resistance across the continent, Lugard's book argued that colonial policy in East Africa should keep with the nineteenth-century paternal logic of social Darwinism and scientific racism wherein African subjects would be expected to adopt the "three C's": Christianity, civilization, and commerce. Lugard argued:

> The essential point in dealing with Africans is to establish a respect for the European. Upon this—the prestige of the white man—depends his influence, often his very existence, in Africa. If he shows

by his surroundings, by his assumption of superiority, that he is far above the native, he will be respected, and his influence will be proportionate to the superiority he assumes and bears out by his higher accomplishments and mode of life. In my opinion—at any rate with reference to Africa—it is the greatest possible mistake to suppose that a European can acquire a greater influence by adopting the mode of life of the natives. In effect, it is to lower himself to their plane, instead of elevating them to his. The sacrifice involved is wholly unappreciated, and the motive would be held by the savage to be poverty and lack of social status in his own country. The whole influence of the European in Africa is gained by this assertion of a superiority which commands the respect and excites the emulation of the savage.[19]

Throughout the colonial period, this racist and ethnocentric view of Euro-African relations dominated how the story of Kenya was told, and historians have noted how these early, popular narratives have clouded the more complex story of Kenya's colonial past and postcolonial present. For instance, David Anderson, in his seminal work on the anticolonial Mau Mau rebellion of the 1950s that ultimately led to Kenya's independence in the early 1960s, notes that the rhetoric of popular, colonial accounts of the Mau Mau period differed little from the racist language of nineteenth-century writers like Lugard. Citing a 1955 best-selling novel about the well-known Mau Mau rebellion, Anderson highlights American author Robert Ruark's warning to readers: "To understand Africa you must understand the basic impulsive savagery that is greater than anything we civilized people have encountered in two centuries."[20]

Remaining largely unchallenged and even promoted by popular accounts produced throughout the colonial period, such stereotypical representations, as many African authors and scholars have long complained, have continued to be firmly perpetuated in print and on film long after the end of colonial rule. Painting Africans as marginal players in world historical events, these enduring stereotypes have long shaped the way many outside audiences have been introduced to and encouraged to think about Africa's past. For instance, Kenyan author Binyavanga Wainana quipped in his 2005 satirical instructional essay, "How to Write about Africa," that to sell books in the contemporary global market, authors needed to treat the continent "as if it were one country. It is hot and dusty with rolling grasslands and huge herds of animals and tall, thin people who are starving. Or it is hot and steamy with very short people who eat primates. Don't get bogged down with precise descriptions."[21]

Boiling down complex historical events like Kenya's Mau Mau rebellion into simplistic accounts of savage violence or racial conflict is part of what Nigerian author Chimamanda Adichie argues is the "Danger of a Single Story" of Africa.[22] While such stories are most typically found in popular literature, Africanist scholars have had to combat similar Eurocentric and stereotypical readings of the past—sometimes even coming from the academy—since professional, scholarly study of Africa took off in the 1960s. For example, scholars have challenged the views of world-renowned Oxford historian Hugh Trevor-Roper, who argued throughout much of the 1960s that the only issues worth exploring on the African continent were those that pertained to "the history of Europe in Africa," dismissing the rest as "the unedifying gyrations of barbarous tribes in picturesque but irrelevant corners of the globe."[23]

Such blatant stereotyping and biased accounts cannot be ignored when analyzing how the political rise of Barack Obama has been depicted and the broader ways a global audience has interpreted his connections to Kenya. For many of his political opponents in the United States, Obama's Kenyan heritage has provided key fodder with which to attack his political legitimacy through marketing stereotypical readings of African history and politics, renewed with the aim of linking Obama's American political identity to erroneous accounts of "tribal" violence and anticolonial insurrection. However misplaced these analyses may be, they nonetheless have been crystallized in best-selling books and through documentary films since 2004 that have shaped global interpretations of both presidential elections in the US and contemporary Kenyan politics and history.[24]

An attention to the political uses of history also returns us to the congratulatory scenes we witnessed at the US ambassador's residence in 2004. Here African political actors like Raila Odinga were actively trying to claim Obama as their own and market personal ties to his paternal heritage for their own political gain. In keeping with a long past of local patriotic history writing that often distills complex genealogies and local histories into simple narratives for political gain, Raila and others performed their historical commemoration that day with the celebrations of Obama's Kenyan and Luo heritage. Shortly after, similar representations began to appear on the shelves of Nairobi's bookstores and on the pages of Kenya's popular press.

Scholars argue that such narratives of Kenyan history belong to a deep genealogy of regional ethnography and hagiography by way of which African "entrepreneurs [have] sifted through history and summoned political communities into being" by focusing on heroic and often uncritical narratives of the past.[25] For instance, combing the publications and memoirs of Africans from the colonial period, one can often find histories of linguistic communities framed as mythical celebrations of romanticized traditions from a static and unchanging precolonial past. These texts were often authored by African colonial elites who sometimes elevated the role of important men, demonized all Europeans, and failed to critically examine the internal conflicts over gender, class, and generation that long predated the arrival of British colonial rule in the region.[26]

Thus, in endeavoring to claim Obama as their own, Raila and the Luo politicians by his side in 2004 treated the moment of the election party as an opportunity to display a certain version of the Kenyan past so as to promote the political significance of the Luo community and to demonstrate how the importance of this local ethnic identity—"Luoness"—transcended the boundaries of Kenya. It was of no concern to Raila or others that Obama himself did not identify as Kenyan or Luo, because they read his background through a distinctly Kenyan lens and not through the matrix of the mixed African American heritage that Barack Obama had spoken of so widely in his career as a US politician.[27] Raila and his supporters were simply drawing upon strategies long used by African actors across the continent to reshape and market ethnic or regional identities for a variety of social, economic, and political reasons. These actions have consistently challenged notions that African ethnicities are static "tribal" identities rooted in the distant past. Indeed, scholars and Africans alike now regard ethnicity in Africa as a much more fluid category, one that can even act like corporate identity with a brand/image that is carefully managed, reimagined, and constantly marketed by both elite and local actors.[28] For his part, Ambassador Bellamy may have also fallen into a trap of promoting a different stereotypical version of Kenya's politics of belonging. By congratulating Raila, he was publicly confirming the victory for the Luo community and displaying an interpretation of Kenyan politics in a way that many Western journalists and other commentators might simply and uncritically dismiss as "tribalism" by another name.

Obama and Contemporary Kenyan Histories

Obama and Kenya is very much a Kenyan story, where the actual actions, feelings, and statements of the American president, while not insignificant, play only a minor role in structuring the debate about ethnic identity and the complex politics of belonging. Obama's political ascendancy in the United States has stirred up various controversies about Kenya's past from the colonial era to the present day, and provides a critical space in which to examine how representations of African history have been constructed and politicized throughout much of the twentieth century and how these representations have done important "work." In popular sources about the president and in the explosion of Obama biographies, Kenya's past and politics are sometimes treated as peripheral or are typically very much distorted to fit within the publication's political bent. Few scholars have yet to take up the intertwined discourses about Obama, Kenya, and history, and until now no book-length study—scholarly or otherwise—has examined how Obama's ascendancy to the "highest office in the land" has shaped the telling of Kenyan or African histories in a global context.[29]

Unlike those Africans living in the era of the late nineteenth-century colonial administrator Sir Frederick Lugard, Africans in the twenty-first century have channels at their disposal to fight back against politicized readings of their own histories and to generate real-time input to the contemporary twenty-four-hour media cycle of political commentary and historical debate. Thus, as much as *Obama and Kenya* is grounded in traditional sources—archival documents, oral interviews, and material culture—the book aims to examine the ways in which historians of contemporary Africa can add digital resources and other nontraditional source material to their analytical tool kits.[30] While the United States Library of Congress has begun archiving blogs and tweets, and our own students debate complex issues with friends daily through social media forums and in other digital venues, we privilege the increasing number of African voices in the digital world who participate in debates about the Obama and Kenya connection in real time.[31] We also pay close attention to how African voices in the digital age are consumed abroad, as global debates about Obama since 2004 have cited African news media and even transcripts of debates on the floors of Kenya's Parliament now freely available online. In evaluating these new sources, it is important to ask how the digitized data we consume are produced and if the phenomenon is promoting greater equality in global discourse or simply providing new media to perpetuate long-standing inequality.

To fully understand the Obama and Kenya connection, we must take a broad historical look at Kenyan history and its representation in a variety of media. This history predates the 2004 election and even the 1961 Hawaiian birth of Barack Obama Jr. It begins in the colonial past and weaves its way through the story of Luo migrations from the colonial period and histories of how members of the Obama family and other Kenyans experienced the challenges of life under British colonial rule. The story also extends into the turbulent period of decolonization and independence and examines how different political actors have narrated this contested period to corrupt and claim ownership over Kenya's struggle for independence and the postcolonial challenges of nationhood.

2

Representations of Kenya

Myth and Reality

Figure 2.1. *Theodore Roosevelt, Three-Quarter Length Portrait, Standing Next to Dead Elephant, Holding Gun, Probably in Africa.* Photo by Edward Van Altena, 1909, http://www.loc.gov/pictures/item/2002709191/.

Barack Obama was not the first president of the United States whose connections to Kenya shined an international spotlight on the country. A century before the inauguration of the first African American president, one of Obama's predecessors was busy making plans for an extended tour of East Africa. Just three weeks after leaving office in 1909, Teddy Roosevelt set sail for an expedition in British East Africa cosponsored by the Smithsonian Institution.[1] An avid hunter and naturalist who as president had established five national parks, Roosevelt, together with his son Kermit, felled game to be mounted for exhibitions at the Smithsonian in Washington, DC, and the Museum of Natural History in New York. The expedition carried home hundreds of hunting trophies (including nine lions, thirteen rhinoceroses, and twenty zebras) and romantic tales of a rugged yet opulent life on safari, introducing American households to people, places, and things with which they were almost wholly unfamiliar.[2]

Arriving in the ancient port city of Mombasa on Kenya's Swahili Coast in late April after almost a month at sea, Roosevelt's extravagantly outfitted party—their entourage included 250 porters, and Roosevelt's tent had a bathtub—set off on an extensive safari, making a circuit through Kenya, Uganda, Congo, and into Sudan that took nearly a year to complete. The expedition was widely covered in the press, and Roosevelt had been commissioned by *Scribner's* magazine beforehand to document his travels for the princely sum of $50,000 (an amount equivalent to roughly 1.3 million in 2014 US dollars).[3] His serialized accounts of the expedition were later compiled and published as *African Game Trails*. A best seller by all standards, the book provides an important window into how Kenya was popularly marketed to American and international audiences more than a century ago.

Most directly, Roosevelt's expedition stimulated interest in big game hunting and helped to designate Kenya as the premier site for a safari. As Edward Steinhart writes, "Even after the construction of the Uganda railroad, travel to and within East Africa remained both arduous and expensive. Only the wealthiest European and American aristocrats could make the excursion for the purpose of shooting big game."[4] Such travelers, he points out, "laid the basis for the growth of Kenya's modern tourist industry."[5] We would add that the safari experiences recounted in print by travelers like Roosevelt, complete with luxurious trappings and outdoor adventure, have contributed strongly to the elite character of tourism in Kenya that continues to center on the recreation of the interpenetrated worlds of the white hunter and the colonial settler.[6]

More abstractly, set against backdrops of dramatic natural beauty, Roosevelt's descriptions of the flora, fauna, and people that he encountered on safari offer insights into the roots of enduring, exoticized stereotypes about Africa and the lasting effects of such representations on Kenya. The foreword to *African Game Trails* reflects the triumphant zeal of an explorer, the scientific curiosity of a naturalist, and the latent racism of the early twentieth-century American. Focusing on what he saw as the untamed nature of both African landscapes and Africans, Roosevelt recounts:

> In these greatest of the world's great hunting-grounds there are mountain peaks whose snows are dazzling under the equatorial sun; swamps where the slime oozes and bubbles and festers in the steaming heat; lakes like seas; skies that burn above deserts where the iron desolation is shrouded from view by the wavering mockery of the mirage; vast grassy plains where palms and thorn-trees fringe the dwindling streams; mighty rivers rushing out of the heart of the continent through the sadness of endless marshes; forests of gorgeous beauty, where death broods in the dark and silent depths. . . . The dark-skinned races that live in the land vary widely. Some are warlike, cattle-owning nomads; some till the soil and live in thatched huts shaped like beehives; some are fisher-folk; some are ape-like naked savages, who dwell in the woods and prey on creatures not much wilder or lower than themselves.[7]

Coming a quarter century after the "Scramble for Africa," during which the European powers carved up Africa following the Berlin Conference, Roosevelt's expedition took place as the mysterious "dark continent" was becoming increasingly knowable through the processes of colonization and when discourses about the imperial nations' "civilizing mission" in Africa were in full flower. Accordingly, Roosevelt's prose, bolstered by his authority as a former president, helped cement images of Kenya as an exotic locale inhabited first by spectacular flora and fauna and populated second by "dark skinned races" whose "primitive" lifestyles rendered them stuck in almost primeval time.

Roosevelt was not alone in depictions of the landscapes and lifestyle he found in Kenya as both exotic and static. Rather, *African Game Trails* was typical of its genre; travelers' accounts of the period rarely acknowledge the sweeping political, social, and economic changes wrought by colonialism (and African engagement with them) or the violence (and African resistance to it) that accompanied the imposition of British rule. Such incomplete representations of Kenyan culture and history invite the following questions: What might have *Kenyans* thought of the ways in which their experiences were described in works like *African Game Trails*? How has outsiders' "ownership" of history and control over representations affected Kenya's social, economic, and political trajectories from the early twentieth century forward? In what ways and in what contexts have Kenyans narrated their own stories and represented themselves? What have these competing histories accomplished?

With these questions in mind, this chapter focuses on the complexities of the colonial experience, the myths surrounding it, and the work that competing discourses about Kenya's colonial past continue to perform into the present day—not simply in Kenya, but globally as well. Indeed, writing about his long discussions with a local historian in Western Kenya during his 1988 visit, Obama recalls being admonished, "The worst thing that colonialism did was to cloud our view of our past."[8] Accordingly, a primary goal of this chapter is to sharpen understandings of Kenya's colonial past and its relationship to the present. We turn next to one of the most enduring and powerful tropes, or common themes, about Kenya—Kenya as a "white man's country."[9]

Creating the Colonial Landscape: The (Un)Happy Valley of the "White Man's Country"

By the time Roosevelt made his journey, the colonization of Kenya[10] figured as the domain not just of the "white hunter" but of the white settler. In the swath of fertile land that extended from the slopes of Mount Kenya to escarpments hugging the Great Rift, with its volcanic lakes, to the plains of

Laikipia that composed the White Highlands (so called because they were lands alienated, or officially given over to white settlement and ownership), Africans were progressively turned off the lands they had inhabited and worked for generations. They were expelled to "native reserves," islands of agriculturally poor lands demarcated along tribal lines, or they were allowed for a time to "squat" on white farms, exchanging their labor for the right to reside on settler lands and to retain a small fraction of the crops they produced.

This realization of Kenya as a "white man's country" had its deep roots in an African adventure undertaken a little more than a decade before Roosevelt's epic safari by another young man of prominent family and considerable means, Hugh Cholmondeley, Lord Delamere.[11] In 1896, accompanied by an entourage that included teams of Somali bearers, a professional photographer, and two hundred camels, Delamere, who reputedly coined the term "white hunter," embarked on a far-ranging safari that led him more than one thousand miles throughout Somaliland and concluded ultimately in Central Kenya.[12] The lush landscape captured Delamere's imagination, and a few years later, shortly before British East Africa became the Kenya Colony and Protectorate in 1905, he returned as a settler, taking up a ninety-nine-year lease on one hundred thousand acres near the Mau Plateau that he pledged to spend £5,000 developing over a period of five years.[13]

Working from his vast Equator Ranch and as a chief figure in the settler lobby in Nairobi, Delamere threw his energy into the development of Kenya as a "white man's country." Chairing an official land commission in 1905, Delamere advocated that the initial development of the highlands be undertaken by wealthy, elite émigrés with large land grants. He was able to entice an array of his aristocratic contemporaries to emigrate from Britain, and in what became known as the "Happy Valley"[14] of the White Highlands, they created a microcosmic world of privilege and decadence that has endured in romanticized, popular imagination as being "authentically Kenyan." This was a world seemingly composed of "sundowner" cocktails, usually gin and tonic, taken outdoors every evening as the equatorial sun dropped out of the sky; of vast farmhouses dripping with bougainvillea and staffed by black servants in white *kanzu* (long robes); of months spent on safari and of regular black-tie balls at the tony Muthaiga Club or Norfolk Hotel in Nairobi. Yet, the reality of the Happy Valley included seedier elements of widespread substance abuse—the visiting Prince of Wales was notoriously offered cocaine at a dinner party—and scandalous adultery: "Are you married or do you live in Kenya?" was a popular joke in interwar Britain.[15]

The world of the Happy Valley endured in popular imagination not only after many of its denizens succumbed to dissolution, bankruptcy, and scandal, but even after the end of British rule in 1963. The area was chronicled at the time by white settlers, most notably Baroness Karen von Blixen-Finecke. Known by the nom de plume Isak Dinesen, her famous memoir, *Out of Africa*, begins with the lilting line, "I had a farm in Africa at the foot of the Ngong Hills."[16] Nostalgia for the dramatic and glamorous aspects of this colonial milieu was reinvigorated in the mid-1980s with the release of the film version of *Out of Africa*, based on Blixen's memoir and starring Meryl Streep and Robert Redford, which in turn stimulated a spate of books and media productions romanticizing the settler lifestyle.[17] This nostalgia for a romanticized British colonial past and its vast marketability even inspired a new Ralph Lauren fragrance, Safari, its print campaign mirroring the aesthetics of *Out of Africa* and making India Hicks, granddaughter of the last viceroy of India, its primary face.[18] Yet, notably absent from these scenes set in Kenya's upcountry "islands of white" are black Kenyans and their experiences of British colonialism. Missing, too, are any indications of conflict between the colonizers and the colonized or of the inherent violence of the colonial project overall.[19] It is to these topics that the remaining sections of this chapter turn.

Colonial Rule: Conquest, Bureaucracy, and "Tribal" Imaginaries

Popular representations of the White Highlands would seem to suggest that the British arrived in Kenya and immediately took control of the country and its people without incident. But the reality of the coming of colonialism and the imposition of British rule was much more complicated—and violent. The first British boots on the ground in Kenya were not those of "great white hunters" or settlers like Delamere, but rather those of explorers and missionaries who traversed East Africa in the Victorian era.[20] They were followed by members of the Imperial British East Africa Company (IBEAC). As we noted above, the British had come into possession of Kenya through the "Scramble for Africa." Indeed, a popular anecdote of the late Victorian era highlighting the arbitrary nature of the scramble held that Queen Victoria ceded Mount Kilimanjaro, thereby shifting the border between British East Africa and German East Africa, to her grandson, the future Kaiser Wilhelm II of Germany, because she had two mountains—Mount Kenya and Mount Kilimanjaro—and he had none.[21]

At the Berlin Conference of the mid-1880s, the imperial powers agreed that in order for one country's claim to an African territory to be recognized by the others, the claiming country had to show that it had "effectively occupied" the territory, that is, set up some form of rudimentary administration that would facilitate free trade and free transit in the territory. By the late 1880s, the British government had set up the IBEAC, the concessionary company "chartered to occupy Britain's sphere of influence," that is, to see to economic and administrative development of the British East African territories.[22] By the late 1880s, the IBEAC was sending ivory caravans from the Swahili Coast through Kenya to Uganda, and by the 1890s had begun the violence-ridden process of conquering and subduing the area's African populations. British officials often referred to this process as "pacification," which resulted in "punitive" expeditions against any active resistance. For instance, in the Nandi-speaking regions of Western Kenya, British "pacification" from 1890 to 1906 resulted in the deaths of thousands of Nandi warriors as well as cattle seizures that decimated the pastoralist community's herds.[23] However, at the same moment the IBEAC was cementing itself militarily with such punitive missions, its economic power was waning. The Foreign Office took over direct control of Kenya, establishing the East Africa Protectorate in 1895 and taking charge of building a railway from the coast to Lake Victoria, while many of the "company men" stayed on as the first British administrators.[24]

In ruling Kenya, the British were confronted with two central, interrelated problems: their numerical inferiority vis-à-vis African populations and the incredible diversity of African communities, or "tribes" as they called them. The system of governance known as "indirect rule" addressed both of these problems. Developed by Lord Frederick Lugard, chief British administrator in Nigeria, indirect rule was a co-optive model of administration based on African institutions and managed by African leaders under the oversight and authority of British administrators.[25] Outsourcing day-to-day administration to specially designated African functionaries dealt with the inability of the slim ranks of British officials to be everywhere at once in the districts under their authority, and indirect rule had the added advantage of being cheap. To borrow Sara Berry's famous phrase, indirect rule was meant to enable "hegemony on a shoestring" and institutionalize a political, racial, and social hierarchy.[26]

Implementing indirect rule required the work of imagination and invention. British authorities had a "mental map" in which Kenya's diverse and numerous ethnic groups were neatly divided into easily discernible "tribes," with particular expectations attached to them. "Tribes," as Brett Shadle points out, "were in the colonial imagination discrete collections of people attached to unique cultural, political, and societal norms, ruled by strong chiefs."[27] Even if African communities did not assert "tribal" identities, Shadle's statement brings us to the second layer of invention—the creation of African institutions and offices where none had existed before or had been present in significantly different forms. In many instances, the British introduced hierarchical political organization into ethnic groups that were acephalous, or "without a head," or which located and exercised authority through councils typically composed of elders. As one 1909 administrative report neatly summed up, "The prestige of the chiefs is in the process of being created in most cases."[28] The introduction of indirect rule and the tribal imaginings that accompanied it had far-reaching consequences in East Africa. Images of the British administrator in a pith helmet and the loyal, submissive African chief in "tribal dress" emerged, like those of the white hunter and the settler baron, as avatars of colonial rule.[29] Indirect rule was also part of the politics of "divide and conquer," as British policy and practice hardened flexible webs of ethnic affiliation and affinity into distinct, cemented "tribal" categories, and subsequently parceled out power and privilege to favored "tribes" whom they deemed more "advanced" or "evolved." This (re)imagining of fluid ethnicities into fixed tribes mobilized Victorian views of European history and contemporary notions of scientific racism. As John Iliffe explains, British officials believed that "every African belonged to a tribe, just as every European belonged to a nation. The idea doubtless owed much to the Old Testament, to Tacitus and Caesar, to academic distinction between tribal societies based on status and modern societies based on contract, and to postwar anthropologists who preferred 'tribal' to the more pejorative word 'savage.'"[30]

This view of the African as inherently "tribal" not only shaped colonial policy and practice, but also transformed the ways in which Africans reckoned their own identities and conceived of "self" and "other," "us" and "them." While the ethnic boundaries of many communities were ossified through this process of "inventing" tribes out of ethnicities, entirely new "umbrella" groups, such as Kalenjin, Abaluhya, and Mijikenda, were also formed out of amalgamations of smaller groups and imagined as discrete cultural communities for the first time.[31] Overall, from the top down, British policies "invented tribes," but Africans worked to shape and manage these identities throughout the colonial period.

Local politics, upended by a model of colonial rule that introduced new offices and often filled them with young men who would have been on the outside of conventional precolonial power structures, came to be deeply inflected by "tribal" identifications and interests. As amply illustrated by the Luo embrace of Obama that forms the core of this book, ethnic affinities continue to drive Kenyan politics, while "tribalism" has remained the central trope used in characterizing politics in Kenya from the colonial era into the present day.[32] The effects of indirect rule and "tribal imaginaries" were not confined to the social and political arenas, but also profoundly reshaped economic life in Kenya. The next section turns to living and laboring and law in colonial Kenya and the myth of the "dutiful native."

Creating Markets and Compelling Labor: Settler Violence and the Myth of the "Dutiful Native"

The alienation of African lands to white settlement was carried out through a series of laws that created two side-by-side systems of landholding in Kenya. The Crown Lands Ordinance of 1902 solved the problem of who "owned" land in Kenya, rendering all land not "physically occupied by local people" free for white settlement. The 1915 Crown Lands Ordinance further alienated land for whites only. Acquiring massive estates, settlers were quick to enhance their prestige as landed colonial aristocrats, with Africans realizing that many settlers had little desire to increase productivity. By 1920, more than three million acres of Central and Western Kenya's best farmland was owned by European settlers, with just 5.6 percent of this land under cultivation.[33] As settler and author Elspeth Huxley summed up in her biography of Lord Delamere, "The government had a certain obligation to the European farmer. They had deliberately invited him into the country to sink his capital and make his home there. . . . They had, therefore, an obligation to help him obtain native workers."[34] Further, an important element of the colonial project was the integration of commodities produced on settler farms—especially precious arabica coffee—into world markets, and the wide-scale plantation agriculture necessarily demanded vast numbers of laborers.

The introduction of a colonial cash economy, together with the implementation of a colonial tax system and land alienation, compelled Africans to enter wage labor markets. For example, the Native Hut and Poll Tax Ordinance (No. 2) of 1910 taxed individuals and their dwellings, putting an unfair tax burden on polygynous African families. Each wife was required to have her own home, which the British pejoratively labled a "hut." Africans' efforts to resist this tax resulted in lifestyle changes that forced societies to break long-standing cultural taboos in order to avoid the punitive tax system. An administrative report from the early twentieth century noted a decline in tax revenues "owing to the fact that people have broken up their huts and placed more than one wife in a hut."[35] Such heavy annual tax demands payable only in cash drove black Kenyans to the colonial labor market, forcing them off the reserves and onto settler farms and into emerging urban centers to labor for wages. In turn, pass laws regulating the registration of African males were introduced in 1920. The *kipande*, or pass, permitted black Kenyan men to leave the reserves for employment and served to regulate the quality, quantity, and flow of the African workforce.[36] Following the model of another settler colony—South Africa—Kenya was spatially segregated along racial lines, particularly in urban areas. White settlers and officials regarded Africans at best as temporary instruments of labor that could be removed from white areas when they were no longer needed, and as sources of dangerous dissolution at worst. For example, a 1926 report produced by Kenya's Native Affairs Department quoted the 1921 South African Native Affairs Commission: "A town is a European area in which there is no place for the redundant native who neither works nor serves his people but forms the class from which professional agitators, slum landlords, liquor sellers, prostitutes and other undesirable classes spring. The exclusion of these redundant natives is in the interests of Europeans and natives alike."[37]

Once African laborers were employed at low wages and in generally poor conditions on settler farms or in urban centers, their employers were free to treat them as they saw fit. Settlers saw transforming Kenyans, whom they regarded as shiftless and work-shy, into "dutiful natives" as both economically necessary and central to their "civilizing mission." "Evidence given to the Native Labor Commission of 1912–1913," Shadle writes, "revealed that many settlers believed violence to be integral to labor relations," and noted that white settlers could mete out corporal punishment to their laborers with virtual impunity.[38] Propagandist British discourse, in contrast, portrayed African servants and laborers as simple, obedient, and docile subjects; grateful for the benevolent paternalistic embrace of their colonial masters.[39]

Coercion was not confined to settler enterprises. While taxation created much-needed revenue for the colonial state, programs of forced labor—presented under the guise of "communal" labor—compelled Kenyans to work without wages on light infrastructure-development projects. These programs had a secondary objective of drawing Kenyans out of the reserves and into the greater colonial labor pool. In some instances, colonial officials went so far as to coercively procure "communal" labor to serve the needs of individual settlers.[40]

Settler violence and colonial coercion were in many cases met by African resistance. Kenyans used "foot dragging, dissimulation, desertion, false compliance, pilfering, feigned ignorance," the well-known "weapons of the weak," to counter burdensome and violent compulsions to colonial labor.[41] They also countered the violent discipline of colonial economic order through supernatural and spiritual means. For example, the colonial administration was forced to acknowledge that the consistent brutality of a white settler toward his Kenyan workers had been a factor in the outbreak of a prophetic possession movement that had severely impeded the collection of tax and the procurement of labor in the region southeast of Nairobi. A King's African Rifles (KAR) patrol dispatched from the capital was eventually able to exert a "quieting effect" over the area.[42] By the 1920s such politically inflected outbreaks of prophetic or spiritualist activity were hardly unusual. Relatedly, decades of missionary activity had led to the establishment of various African churches that interpreted and translated the Christian message in accordance with local belief structures, often clashing with European conceptions of morality and of scriptural and doctrinal interpretations. The leaders of these new African churches mobilized the "politics of the pulpit" to contest colonial rule. Colonial administrators were quick to interpret (and dismiss) supernaturally based forms of political expression in racist and ethnocentric ways. For instance, in 1929, a district commissioner (DC) reporting on the Nomiya Luo Mission, and independent Africans churches more generally, explained:

> This class of thing is met with throughout Africa, where mission influence has been at work for some time. To my mind it is but a clear indication that the natives are unable to embrace the Christian religion as presented to them. As long as they are under the immediate influence of the European Missionary they are stimulated but as soon as they became so numerous or scattered that the influence can be but a shadow they search about and work out for themselves some of the Bastard Christianity more suited to their mental and social development. . . . My experience in South Africa taught me that it is a mistake to think these movements will die out. I am inclined to think this one is no exception and is on the increase.[43]

The DC's comments both reflected the discriminatory character of white minority rule and foreshadowed the rise of African resistance. As Kenyans increasingly mobilized not only supernatural but also political strategies to contest the power of the colonial state in the 1930s and 1940s, religion and ethnicity provided key spaces in which black Kenyans debated sociopolitical life under colonial rule as African resistance began to segue into desires and demands for independence. The next section of this chapter turns to Kenya political movements, the anticolonial Mau Mau rebellion, and the (ethnic) dilemmas of rule in independent Kenya.

Politics and Revolution in Colonial Kenya: From Migration to Mau Mau to Nationhood

The reshaping of identities and economies that accompanied colonial rule simultaneously brought about significant social and political transformations in the lives of many Kenyans. In Central Kenya, for example, land alienation did not simply displace Kikuyu people but severely disrupted a complex system of tenancy called *githaka*, which allocated land and organized landholding along clan and generational lines as well as importantly providing for the integration of outsiders into Kikuyu communities.[44] In Western Kenya, Luo people, far from the settler farms of the White Highlands, were compelled to migrate in search of wage labor. As in Kikuyu areas, this economically driven displacement challenged notions of property and belonging that revolved around the *dala*, or Luo homestead.[45] These ruptures around land and labor, and the social transformations that accompanied them, together with the emergence of coteries of mission-educated Kenyans, drove African politicization that was skewed along regional and "tribal" lines. By the 1920s, Kikuyu- and Luo-speaking communities had established political organizations—the Kikuyu Central Association (KCA) and the Young Kavirondo Association (YKA)—concerned with the promotion of their respective material interests and the articulation of what it meant to be "Kikuyu" or "Luo" in rapidly shifting colonial landscapes.[46]

Yet, even as African politicization continued to expand and accelerate over the next two decades, whites settlers and many colonial administrators still clung to the idea that they were enacting a "civilizing mission" for the benefit of Africans mired in "tribal" primitivity and that governance should remain exclusively the domain of whites. These racist and paternalistic ideologies were well entrenched by the 1940s, and many colonialists in Kenya and in Britain believed that diverse "tribes" would never be capable of uniting under any banner of Kenyan nationalism. For example, a 1943 Colonial Office memorandum on political affairs in Kenya reiterated the dominant view:

These tribes speak different languages and have entirely different social customs. Many of them are in a very primitive state and it is not possible to envisage the time when they will become sufficiently united as a whole, speaking a common language and having trust in elected leaders from their own tribe or still less of another tribe. It would be very much easier to make a united Europe under the domination of Germany than to make a united Kenya under the domination of the Maasai. The conception of a central self-government elected by these primitive tribes is simply not within practical politics.[47]

Five years later, marginalized Kikuyu had begun a campaign of violent rural action—including labor strikes, arson, and maiming of farm animals. By the early 1950s, such violence was steadily rising and increasingly politicized, organized through a network of oathing. This movement emerged into a full-scale rebellion known as Mau Mau, which gave rise to an enduring representation of Kenya as a space in which tribal atavism and savage violence always simmered below the surface of social and political life.[48] Colonial political propaganda and the Western media portrayed the rebellion as a race war that pitted families of peaceful white farmers against African "terrorists," as a contest of primitive African "savagery" versus white, modern "civilization," and overlooked the brutality of the colonial and complex violence of decolonization in settler colonies like Kenya.

The rebellion took the shape of an insurgency carried out by the Land and Freedom Army, a disparate guerrilla force of landless Kikuyu supported in varying degrees by Kikuyu who pledged (on pain of death and not always voluntarily) to simply keep silent or to actively assist the fighters with intelligence and supplies. As Mau Mau action escalated and violence intensified, the colonial governor declared Kenya in 1952 to be under a state of emergency, which lasted nearly a decade. While it retained its anticolonial character and targets, Mau Mau further developed into a civil war between supporters of the guerrillas and those Kikuyu who had benefited from indirect rule—namely Kikuyu chiefs and headmen—and other Kikuyu loyalists or "home guards."[49] In the protracted course of the rebellion, the British effectively dehumanized individual Kikuyu, interning a substantial proportion of the adult male Kikuyu population (and thousands of women) in interrogation camps that were often established on settler lands and run with wide-ranging brutality, sometimes by settlers deputized by the colonial state. In the end, as David Anderson notes, only thirty white settlers died during Mau Mau, while at least 20,000 Kikuyu were killed, with an additional 150,000 imprisoned in internment camps.[50]

While political leaders of various "tribes"—most notably the Kikuyu politician Jomo Kenyatta—were accused of organizing the rebellion, convicted in kangaroo courts, and sentenced to long terms of imprisonment, Kenya, outside of Nairobi and the White Highlands, was largely untouched by the violence of the rebellion.[51] In Kikuyu areas, however, the British threw their military might at the insurgency, bombarding the forests around Mount Kenya with fighter planes, calling in regiments from Britain, and importing counterinsurgency experts from other parts of their empire. They also set in motion a potent propaganda machine that militarized the "civilizing mission," portraying the colonial forces as defenders of law and order and the Kikuyu as "terrorists" who had lost their collective sensibility and veneer of civilization.[52] This characterization and image was picked up by international press organizations, including the *New York Times*, and quickly imported into Western popular culture through Mau Mau–era films such as *Simba*, which opens with a white settler being hacked to death by a Kikuyu with a *panga* (machete); and *Safari*, which follows the exploits of a great white hunter as he tracks a Mau Mau "terrorist."[53] Ultimately the British were able to put down the rebellion, but the protracted and bloody nature of Mau Mau showed them that Kenya had become ungovernable. Kenya's independence was negotiated at a series of talks in London, and Kenya became independent in 1963, with Jomo Kenyatta as president and Oginga Odinga, the foremost Luo cultural and political leader, as vice president.[54]

The experience of Kenya in the years immediately following independence was that in some ways, rule can be harder than revolution. In the new world order of the Cold War, Kenya positioned itself as the solid capitalist bulwark in Eastern Africa and Kenyatta as the foil to its socialist counterpart, President Julius Nyerere of Tanzania. Its domestic politics were quickly riven along "tribal" lines, as within a decade the authoritarianism of colonialism was superseded by a single-party state dominated by Kenyatta's Kenya African National Union (KANU) party at the expense of any political opposition. As Tom Mboya, a leading Luo politician, lamented explicitly of Kenya and implicitly of the Luo experience a few months before his assassination in 1969, "In less than a decade of independence our enemies have too often been given the opportunity to point a finger at our tragedies; our friends have sadly drawn attention to our shortcomings and we ourselves must feel frustrated at the non-realisation of our dreams and aspirations. We have found ourselves in a critical and hostile world which insists on perfection where Africa is concerned—despite the fact that none of the older nations have themselves achieved such perfection."[55]

Using the history of the Obama family as a lens, the following chapters of this book attend to Mboya's lament, showing how the complex realities of nationhood and the complicated work of representation have shaped Kenya's trajectory over the last fifty years. The vestiges of settler society and the racial and class hierarchies of colonial rule are still visible in contemporary Kenya. Indeed, many *wananchi* (Kenyan citizens) wondered to what extent settler impunity had actually dissipated after Tom Cholmondeley, the great-grandson of Lord Delamere, was not prosecuted for shooting an undercover black game ranger on the Delamere ranch in 2005 and found guilty only of manslaughter for shooting an alleged poacher on his property the next year.[56]

The colonial legacy of Mau Mau, settler society, and violence has loomed large over both popular and scholarly representations of Kenya. For instance, the scope and scale of the torture and abuse carried out against suspected Mau Mau supporters has become clear only as archival documents have been released and scholars have interviewed survivors.[57] Claims that Obama's paternal grandfather, Hussein Onyango Obama, had been interned and tortured as a Mau Mau rebel spiked American and British interest in the rebellion.[58] Most pointedly, however, in the summer of 2013, the British foreign secretary acknowledged and apologized for the torture of Kikuyu during the Mau Mau and announced that elderly Kikuyu survivors who brought suit against the British government for abuses committed against them during the rebellion would receive several million pounds in reparations.[59]

The presidency of Jomo Kenyatta from 1963 to 1978, and the 2013 election of his son, Uhuru Kenyatta, to Kenya's highest office, has continued to fuel a long-standing attention to the histories of Central Kenya and the

Kikuyu community. Shaped in many cases by popular accounts of the glamour of the White Highlands and the savagery of Mau Mau, political and social accounts of Central Kenya dominate depictions of the country as a whole. In contrast, by focusing on Luo people, places, and things—including the heritage of the first African American president of the United States and representations of his background—we challenge the dominant nationalist narrative of Kenya's sociopolitical history, popular myths of the country's past, and depictions of its political present. Using the history of the Obama family as a lens, the coming chapters offer a critical inquiry into the representations of and work done by ethnicity and by related notions of "belonging" from the early twentieth century forward.

3

The Obama Family

Ethnicity and the Politics of Belonging in Kenya

There's your ordinary house in Nairobi. And then there's your house
in the country, where your people come from. Your ancestral home.
Even the biggest minister or businessman thinks this way. He may
have a mansion in Nairobi and build only a small hut on his land in
the country. He may go there only once or twice a year. But if you ask
him where he is from, he will tell you that that hut is his true home.
So, when we were at school and wanted to tell somebody we were
going to Alego, it was home twice over, you see. Home Squared. . . .
For you, Barack, we can call it "Home Cubed."
                                   —Barack Obama, *Dreams from My Father*[1]

Barack Obama's visits to his extended family at their rural homesteads in
Western Kenya during his first trip to Kenya in 1988 offer an important
avenue into the history of ethnicity and the related politics of belonging in
Kenya. Traveling via the railway line laid down by the British at the opening
of the colonial era that we learned about in the last chapter, Obama shared
this important overnight journey with Kenyans returning "home" from
Nairobi to their hereditary "homelands."[2] The sojourn from a "house" in an
urban, ethnically mixed milieu to a "home" in a more ethnically uniform
province, undertaken regularly by millions of Kenyans across the country,
speaks to the historical forces at work around the malleable categories of

"tribe" and "ethnicity."[3] A Luo at the end of such a journey exchanges the *nyumba*, or "house," in the lingua franca of Swahili, which he inhabits in the city, for the *dala*, or homestead, where he *belongs* in Western Kenya—"home squared." Such was the journey Obama's family understood him as taking, simply with a twice-removed point of origin in the United States.

Training a lens on the Obama family, this chapter examines how the idea of a Luo identity, of "Luoness," came to be and traces the social and political work that Luoness has done from the colonial era into the present day. We further challenge the notion that "tribe" was either an uncomplicated primordial artifact or a wholly colonial construction. Rather, we will show how Africans—whether recognized intellectuals like Barack Obama Sr. or more ordinary *wananchi* (citizens) like Hussein Onyanga Obama—have shaped the meanings and uses of Luoness over time in dialogue with a preserved past and contemporary politics. An array of historical sources shows that Luoness has been constituted through origin myths and oral traditions, through histories written by Luo members of the academy and amateur scholars of the "tin trunk history" guild, and through the political projects and partisan maneuverings of Luo political actors.[4] This chapter points to how ethnicity has become the narrative fulcrum on which representations of postcolonial Kenyan politics turn.

Luoland: Dala and Diaspora

Tera adhi aba Kisumu   Take me on a tour of Kisumu
Dala gi mama yooo   The home of my mother
Dala gi baba yooo   The home of my father.[5]

Having arrived in Kisumu, Obama made his way to the bus depot, "crowded with buses and *matatus* honking and jockeying for space in the dusty open-air lot," and crowded onto public transport for the next leg of the journey to his family's home in Kogelo.[6] Kisumu, which has grown from a sleepy market into Kenya's third-largest city, has been the center of Luo sociopolitical life from the colonial era forward.[7] Memorialized as the diasporic hometown of Luos worldwide by the popular Suzanna Owiyo song quoted above, the city has long been the locus of Luo political activity. Beginning in the colonial era, groups such as the Luo Union promoted cultural-political platforms built around the notion of a discrete Luo identity, and politicians such as Oginga Odinga launched themselves into the anticolonial movement in the 1950s.

The city's crumbling infrastructure and defunct lakeshore port point back to the 1960s, the decade that saw both a Luo, Oginga Odinga, as vice president in Kenya's first independent government, and the beginning of thirty years of Luo exile in the "political wilderness" as Jomo Kenyatta's Kikuyu cohort and Daniel arap Moi's Kalenjin contingent took center stage.[8] This experience of rapid ascent and steady marginalization over more than thirty years helps us to understand why by 2004 Luo people reached beyond the shores of Lake Victoria and into the diaspora in search of a powerful political patron whom they regarded as "belonging" to them—Barack Obama Jr. Analyses of how Luoness has been historically constituted through the experience of diaspora helps to illuminate how Obama, who first set foot in Kenya at the age of twenty-six, could be claimed by Luo as a "son of the soil" of Western Kenya.

Kisumu, while important from the late nineteenth century forward, was not the place where notions of "Luoness" first emerged. Present-day Luo speakers offer an array of responses about what constitutes "Luoness" and where Luo people originated. Their accounts, which weave together historical memory and myth, formal and local historical knowledge, contemporary political problems, and even biblical narratives, all emphasize migration and then subsequent material and emotional "belonging" to a particular landscape as key elements of what it means to be Luo. Over a decade of asking Luo people, from elders in Western Kenya to migrants in East Africa's major cities, what it means to be Luo, we were informed by nearly all our respondents that the Luo did not originate in Kenya, but rather that a founding ancestor, Ramogi, led a group of settlers from what is today South Sudan to an area on the present border of Kenya and Uganda sometime in the later fifteenth or early sixteenth century. Slowly and continuously until they were checked by the establishment of British and German colonial rule, waves of Luo-speaking migrants followed on Ramogi's heels.[9] Indeed, the British administrator and amateur ethnographer Charles W. Hobley recorded a version of the Ramogi story in the early 1900s, noting that "his [Ramogi's] offspring founded the Ja-luo race."[10]

Discussions of Ramogi's role retained their purchase in political discourse throughout the colonial period and into the present. For example, the Luo-language newspaper called *Ramogi*, founded in the 1940s, was a key site for debates about Luo politics and culture. During the 1950s Oginga Odinga, the foremost Luo politician, was also vested with the politico-cultural honorific Jaramogi, or "person of Ramogi." More recently, discussing the presidential campaigns and his preferred candidate in Nairobi in 2007, James Okoth, a Luo resident of Nairobi, quipped, "Just as Ramogi guided the Luo to Kenya, I know Raila (Odinga) can guide them to the statehouse."[11]

The Ramogi story does not just occupy a space in Luo historical imagination, but rather is a material (and commercial) site of memory as well. The popular radio station Ramogi FM promotes Luo vernacular music on the Kenyan airwaves, and "Ramogi Night" has become a regular Luo cultural event at the popular Nairobi nightclub Carnivore. Many of our informants even directed us to visit Ramogi Hill, where community-based tourism efforts are under way to commemorate the place believed to be the homestead of this mythical founding ancestor.

Weaving together linguistic, archaeological, oral, and documentary sources, most scholarship agrees that Kenya's Luo population, speakers of the Dholuo language who call themselves Jaluo, belongs to a wider, diasporic group of Nilotic-Lwo speakers across East Africa, which includes, for example, Acholi-, Lango-, and Padhola-speakers in Uganda and which is even related distantly to Dinka and Nuer populations in South Sudan.[12] The Luo of Kenya arrived in the latter of two waves of Lwo-speaking migrants, who had left South Sudan due to mounting environmental changes and competition over resources, beginning in the fifteenth century. Pastoralists and mixed farmers, the Luo found the verdant shores of Lake Victoria well suited to their needs and reminiscent of the lush Nile valley.[13] Overall, as migrating Lwo-speakers traversed East Africa, they blended with the various groups they encountered, taking on distinct practices that would distinguish Lwo-speaking groups from a cultural as well as a linguistic standpoint.[14]

Oral traditions do not reflect a conceptualization of a shared Luo identity across Lwo-speaking groups, nor do they evidence political organization beyond the local level in the precolonial era. Rather, populations were organized in terms of family or kin: *dala* (one's immediate homestead); *keyo* (one's extended patrilineage); *gweng'* (a collection of lineages bound by marriage or defensive alliances); and *piny* or *oganda* (multiclan, territorial conglomerates).[15] By the mid-nineteenth century, there were approximately thirteen *oganda* or *piny* representing localities that would become important population centers in the colonial and postcolonial eras: Kisumu, Siaya, and Homa Bay Counties. Luo people identified primarily with their home locations; for instance, a Luo from Alego, the Obamas' home location, would have likely called himself a Ja-Alego, or "Alego person," while a person from Gem would have called himself a Ja-Gem, and so on.[16] Nonetheless, as David William Cohen and E. S. Atieno Odhiambo explain, "These small ethnic units were eighteenth and nineteenth century rehearsals for the broadly inclusive ethnic unit of the Luo recognized in the colonial and post-colonial periods."[17]

Creating the Luo Community in Colonial Kenya

Our elders had good ethics and moral codes, which helped them to guide their communities. These were good customs that aided the Luo during their migrations, in the course of their daily work and discussion. No nation can prosper by adopting foreign cultures and ignoring its customs and practices.[18]

The implementation of indirect rule, as we learned in the previous chapter, was central to the colonial imagining of clearly defined "tribes" and the hardening of boundaries around preexisting ethnic affinities. At the same time, colonial land and economic policies both restricted black Kenyans to "tribal" reserves and drove them to work in the mixed-ethnic milieus of the colony's developing cities and settler plantations. From the early twentieth century, these developments steadily transformed the areas around Lake Victoria in Western Kenya to a labor reserve supplying both the colonial state and white settlers. A diaspora of Luo speakers from Western Kenya fanned out across the region and to the colonial cities throughout the first half of the twentieth century. Barack Obama's grandfather, Hussein Onyango Obama, who left Luoland to work as a domestic in a white household in Nairobi and served in the King's African Rifles (KAR) in both World Wars, was typical of Luo migrants who worked as domestic servants in settler households; agricultural laborers on Kenya's tea, coffee, and sisal plantations; as dockhands in Mombasa and Dar es Salaam; and in various capacities for the railway.[19]

For Luo people, steeped in oral traditions about a history born out of migration, relocation was not necessarily an utter rupture. Conditions of labor and life, particularly in urban areas, were particularly trying, however. For example, one Nairobi official noted with dismay in the 1940s that with explosive population growth in the city, "it was common" to see "Africans sleeping under the verandahs on River Road, in noisome shacks in the swamps, in buses parked by the road and fourteen to a room in Pumwani, two to a bed and the rest on the floor."[20] Labor migrants, particularly in urban areas, were also forced to endure the coercive tactics and generalized contempt of colonial authorities who regarded them as "delinquents" or "vagrants" operating dangerously outside the control of rural "tribal" discipline.[21]

Indeed, the problem posed by the "detribalized native" was a primary trope in colonial and anthropological discourse from the 1930s onward.[22] In much the same way that colonial authorities in the late 1950s focused on "tribal atavism" instead of valid economic and political concerns as the driving force behind Mau Mau, their predecessors and contemporaries argued that labor migrants engaged in "undesirable" activities like theft and prostitution because they were "detribalized." This ideology rendered ethnicity as a romanticized and rural variety of patriarchal control and argued that Africans who were separated "from family, clan and tribal authority as well as from social codes of behavior, discipline, custom and perhaps religion[,] which originally guided their thoughts and actions," were operating dangerously outside of customary and colonial legal systems.[23] Providing an easy alternative to dealing with the real structural problems of racial inequality, "detribalization" discourse helped squelch concerns about the squalid, precarious conditions of life and work that characterized urban African environments.

Luo people were deeply troubled not merely by the material hardships of migrant life, but also by the upending of sociocultural life and the absence of community. The twinned questions of how to survive in an urban setting and what it meant to be Luo outside of Western Kenya were answered through intellectual projects and politico-cultural organizations. These intellectual works and political labors built on shared linguistic capacities, cultural affinities, geographic origins, and economic needs that were much deeper and more complex than the blunt colonial category "tribe."

Intellectual projects undertaken by Luo from the mid-1930s onward were shaped by a confluence of internal forces and external influences. Luo identity—taking in concerns ranging from religious conversion to gendered social morality to civic virtue—was contested by a number of historical actors throughout East Africa's urban centers. In the cities, under the disciplinary gaze of colonial authorities and in the comparative view of black Kenyans from other ethnic groups, "Luo men knew themselves to be under examination," Derek Peterson writes. "They conceived of East Africa's urban environment as a competitive theatre in which men and women alike were obliged to behave with credible decorum."[24] Exclusive of these external influences, Luo struggled with how to reconcile notions of cultural comportment rooted in Nyanza with the demands of life in an environment that was constantly in flux. Luo intellectuals developed historical projects that addressed where the Luo had come from and where they were going; what had made "Luoness" over time.[25]

The text cited at the beginning of this section, Paul Mboya's *Luo: Kitgi gi tembegi* (Luo: Customs and traditions), effectively constituted a vernacular textbook for Luo identity and provided the foundation for future intellectual projects. Through a series of topical chapters—for example, "Law about War," "Matters on Marriage," "A Polygamous Man and His Home"—the text charts the cultural responsibilities and acceptable limits of "Luoness" with encyclopedic authority. Written at the apex of the colonial era, the book endeavors to answer many of the pressing sociocultural questions of the day through reflections on the preservation of the Luo past and to offer a set of principles by which every proper Luo speaker should abide.

Luo-language newspapers, most notably *Ramogi*, were another discursive space in which the intellectual project came to terms with urban life and its implicit demands to define and perform proper cultural comportment in circumstances that were very different from those of "home." The newspaper's editors, writers, and readers engaged in debates that aimed to define the responsibilities and limits attached to "Luoness." Some articles and letters called for Luo to invest in Western Kenya. Others debated the "immoral" lifestyle and habits of those living outside of Western Kenya. Articles often spoke of the need for greater social restraint and discipline in order to maintain Luo respectability in gendered ways. For example, a 1948 editorial labeled independent Luo women in towns as "prostitutes" and argued, "They should be watched by the Luo Union and any relative found allowing these girls to be prostitutes should be punished."[26]

While *Ramogi* often reinforced patriarchal notions of Luo identity, African women occasionally wrote forceful critiques of male attitudes. Connecting debates about the immorality of town life with the social responsibilities of rural familial ties, one woman admonished Luo migrant laborers, who, she explained, "cannot do without women and begin keeping prostitutes with the results that all the money they earn is spent on them and perpetual drinking, where as their wives and children are suffering in the reserves without any help or information through correspondence."[27] Overall, the newspaper provided a central arena in which migrant Luo connected and communicated with one another. As a Luo-speaking writer living in Ethiopia poignantly declared in a 1947 editorial, "*Ramogi* is the only connection I have with my people."[28] It served also to stimulate "belonging" to a shared Luo lineage. Indeed, authors frequently signed their articles with an emphatic phrase: "An Nyakwar Ramogi," or "I am a descendant of Ramogi."[29]

More materially, urban ethnic associations, in the Luo case the Luo Union, were formed in the 1930s to counter the alienating effects of urban life and to foster social and economic ties between the city and "home."[30] These associations, which would ultimately give rise to political organizations built around ethnic lines, were endorsed by the colonial authorities, who saw them as "the best answer to the detribalizing influences of town life," perhaps because they relieved colonial authorities of having to improve the conditions of urban life for their African subjects.[31]

The Luo Union had its roots in earlier clan societies that provided social welfare benefits for Luo-speaking migrants from particular locations in Western Kenya. As many Luo speakers believed that a person's soul could not rest until his or her body was buried at "home" (*dala*), that is, the place in Western Kenya where the person was born and where his or her placenta (*biero*) was subsequently buried, these early organizations functioned in part as burial cooperatives.[32] As one elderly Luo man recalled, clan associations often raised large amounts of money to ship the bodies of Luo-speaking workers from as far as Ethiopia, Uganda, and coastal Tanganyika to Western Kenya.[33] Further, these associations were instrumental in raising funds for development projects in the rural areas, especially in the realm of education.

Acting as a parent organization to the multiple clan societies, from the moment of its inception the Luo Union fostered educational opportunities for Luo-speaking youth, promoted economic and cultural investment in Western Kenya, and set about creating a new history written in the vernacular that codified the mythical shared past of the Luo-speaking community.[34] As colonial officials correctly understood, a central part of the Luo Union's work was "to examine and to choose the new customs which should be followed and bad ones which should be suppressed."[35] The organization's own 1945 constitution had the more expansive goals of promoting "mutual understanding and unity" among all Luo speakers while also shaping the cultural obligations of a growing ethnic constituency.[36] The promotion of "unity" was the principal aim of various constitutions, mission statements, and other documents produced by the Luo Union in the 1940s and 1950s, signifying both the organization's sociopolitical impetus and the fact that "Luo" was a contested and disparate identity. Under the banner "Riwruok e teko" (Unity is strength), Luo Union officials attempted to corral a diverse and increasingly diasporic linguistic community under a single ethnic banner.

The leadership of the Luo Union—mission-educated elites like Paul Mboya, Walter Odede, Oginga Odinga, and Achieng Oneko—also served in important intermediary positions. For instance, Mboya was a colonial chief in South Nyanza, Odinga taught at the illustrious Church Missionary Society (CMS) school at Maseno, and Oneko was a municipal councillor in Nairobi.[37] These positions imbued them with status, savvy, and experience in negotiating the colonial bureaucracy and earned them respect from colonial authorities and Africans alike. As the colonial era wore on, they were able to use their knowledge and influence to grow the scope and scale of the organization. For instance, in the mid-1940s, Odinga started

the Luo Thrift and Trading Company (LUTATCO), a highly successful sister organization that promoted migrants' reinvestment in Nyanza
and aimed to promote, in Odinga's words, "unity, common purpose and
achievement" among the Luo-speaking community throughout Eastern
Africa.[38] Ultimately, the union leadership mobilized its political capital to
become significant players in anticolonial politics and in the first independent government.

By the early 1950s, the Luo Union had thousands of paid members in
its sixty-plus branches throughout Kenya, Tanzania, and Uganda, and offered members of the Luo-speaking diaspora significant avenues for sociability and education organized along ethnolinguistic lines. The relational
opportunities that union meetings provided—to speak Luo, to swap news
of "home," to forge friendships in the dance hall or on the football pitch—
transcended clan ties as Dholuo-speaking labor migrants from across East
Africa developed a shared sense of "belonging" as fellow "Luos."[39] By the
early 1950s, the intertwined intellectual and politico-cultural projects of
negotiating labor environments far from Luoland and fostering Luoness
outside Western Kenya were well under way. By the end of the decade, Mau
Mau, the central event of Kenya's colonial history, demanded new answers
to the question of what it meant to be Luo and propelled Luo politico-
cultural leaders of political prominence onto the nationalist stage.

The Forest Conflict: Luo Loyalty and Subversive Politics

1. Generally speaking, within the Province itself, Mau Mau infiltra-
   tion into Nyanza tribes has been negligible since May 1954. There
   is however evidence to show that some Nyanza tribesmen have
   been contaminated through contact with Kikuyu, Embu, and
   Meru tribesmen while outside the Province.
2. During 1953 and 1954 at least 1,000 Nyanza tribesmen were believed to have taken a Mau Mau oath in Nairobi City.[40]

As we learned in chapter 2, Mau Mau was an overwhelmingly Kikuyu affair, and given the negligible nature of Luo involvement, it is far from plau-
sible that Hussein Onyango Obama was a Mau Mau adherent, let alone a

fighter.[41] When the rebellion commenced in the early 1950s, ordinary Luo readily denounced Mau Mau in the pages of *Ramogi*. For example, criticizing the character of Mau Mau and the disruptions it caused to potential social welfare projects, one Luo Union supporter wrote, "We remain unhappy because of the activities of Mau Mau and are shocked at the evil crimes committed. . . . People have asked for more pay, better trade, improved housing and better education, but everything is held up until Mau Mau is crushed. . . . We should seek means by which all can help stamp out Mau Mau and return to our former peaceful way of living."[42] Luo Union branches across Kenya consistently distanced themselves from the mounting violence and turmoil, insisting on numerous occasions, "The Union is purely social and has nothing to do with politics."[43] At the same time, Oginga Odinga was made *ker*, or cultural leader of the Luo, and took on the honorific title Jaramogi, reinforcing both the notion of a shared Luo identity that had been emerging since the 1930s and the cultural bent of the union.[44]

Anti–Mau Mau sentiments among the Luo community were particularly fueled by the murder of Nairobi city councillor and Luo Union official Ambrose Ofafa in November 1953. Ofafa had by the early 1950s grown to be a prominent figure in the African community in Nairobi and was also well liked by colonial officials. The African Affairs Department report of 1952 even referred to Ofafa as a "leading light of moderation in breaking Mau Mau tensions in Nairobi."[45] His tragic and brutal death in 1953 was pinned to Mau Mau fighters, and Dholuo speakers responded to this event: his funeral procession in Nyanza had several thousand attendees. Ogot has shown that Ofafa spoke strongly against Luo retribution from his deathbed, even as the colonial state tried to use the event to convince the Luo community to actively resist Mau Mau.[46]

Even with Ofafa's request, Luo Union members and officials used his death to increase their public denouncement of Mau Mau and gain favor with the state as 1954 rose to be a pivotal year in the organizations history. Odinga traveled throughout Kenya during the early months of 1954 to publicly denounce the movement at various Luo Union meetings, declaring, "The Luo as a tribe must be loyal to Government and any political advancement which the Luo sought must be done by constitutional means."[47] The year 1954 was also marked by widespread active repression of the

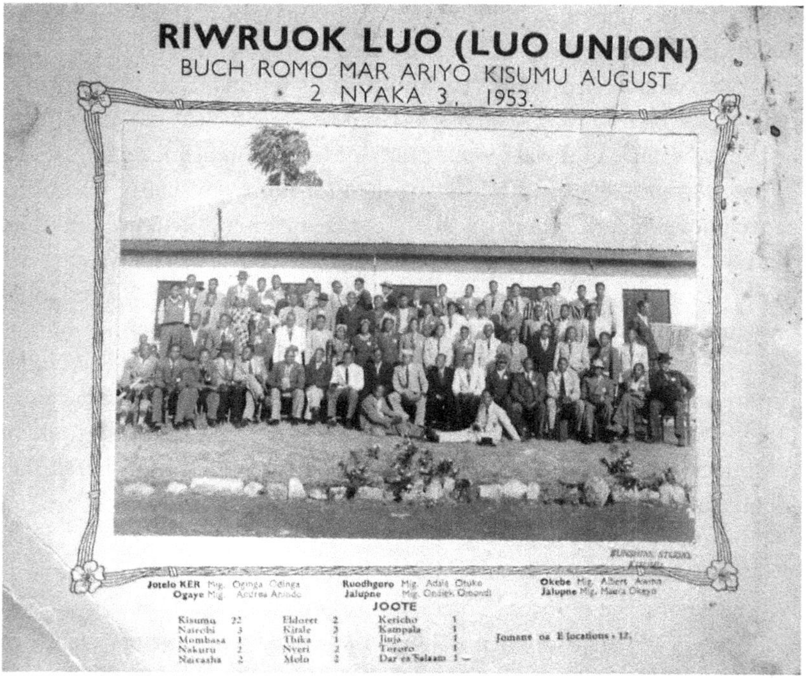

Figure 3.1. The first delegates conference of the new Luo Union (East Africa), 1953. Photo courtesy of the family of former Luo Union ker Adala Otuko.

Kikuyu community in Central Kenya. From April to May a raid by British forces, named "Operation Anvil," in Nairobi and other settler-dominated communities detained more than fifty thousand suspected Mau Mau supporters without trial. The roundup included an estimated 50 percent of the Kikuyu population of Nairobi, whose linguistic/ethnic identity made them guilty until proved innocent in the eyes of the state.[48] Although most were innocent migrant laborers, the sudden exodus of thousands of workers from Nairobi created a void in the workforce. Due to the colonial state's increasingly favorable view of the Luo community, many of the vacant jobs opened by Operation Anvil were filled by Luo workers. The district commissioner of Luo-dominated Central Nyanza noted that almost immediately, "Operation Anvil restored confidence, resulting in a heavy outflow of Luo families in search of ready employment and high wages in towns and plantations."[49] This trend continued throughout the 1950s as reports in Nairobi specifically noted that "it would appear that the Luo are taking the place of the bulk of the Kikuyu detained during the Emergency."[50]

Looking for African loyalty wherever they could find it, the colonial state and the settler community were willing to laud the Luo as a "loyal tribe." The file cited at the beginning of this section evidences a breathless relief about the lack of Mau Mau "contamination" among the Luo.[51] Luo attitudes and actions also drew praise from the settler paper, the *Sunday Post*. An editorial titled "The Strength of Luo Loyalty" noted that the settler community was "encouraged by the recent pronouncements of loyalty by the Luo Union. . . . Tribal discipline is still strong and elders and middle age Luo spend much of their time correcting and lecturing the young men of the tribe."[52] And settlers and officials were willing to regard the Luo Union as an apolitical, primarily cultural organization whose ethnicized membership squared nicely with colonial notions of "tribe" and whose promotion of Protestant-seeming values—thrift, education, gerontocracy, and patriarchy—soothed colonial fears about the dangers of "detribalization" and Mau Mau.

In 1954, as Kenya's struggle for independence began to crest, union officials also published a five-year plan, which sought to solidify the leadership's role as a leading voice among the Luo. The first order of business the association envisioned was to take a census of Dholuo speakers throughout East Africa as a way of defining the strength and limits of their community. They then planned to erect buildings in Nairobi, Kampala, and Dar es Salaam to function as an embassy in these cities by hosting social events as well as interacting with colonial governments. Finally, Luo Union members and officials even discussed building a Luo museum in Kisumu as a way of promoting a unified cultural heritage.[53] Clearly, union members and officials saw themselves as the leaders of the burgeoning Luo nation, which needed cultural and political symbols to construct the public image of Luo identity.

While many of the goals of the 1955 five-year plan were in actuality lofty aspirations that failed to materialize, the Luo Union's cultural-intellectual projects nonetheless positioned the organization as a central guardian of cultural heritage and as the political leaders of the broader Luo community. One tangible success of the association in the Mau Mau era was the fund-raising campaign for the erection of the Ofafa Memorial Hall in Kisumu. The hall represented an effort to honor Ambrose Ofafa, who was a colonial moderate and rising Luo political figure in Nairobi during the early 1950s and who became an early Luo martyr of Mau Mau–inspired political violence.

From 1954 to 1961, fund-raising for a social hall and new Luo Union headquarters was a staple of Luo Union meetings, dances, and sporting events.[54] Over these seven years the association managed to raise a large sum of money and complete the construction of the social hall in Kisumu. The Ofafa Memorial Hall was officially opened by Odinga and his then political ally Jomo Kenyatta in 1961, and the event marked an important moment of transition for the Luo Union from being a primarily cultur-ally oriented organization to serving as an important locus of Luo politi-cal power.[55] Beginning in the emergency period, as the political climate became increasingly fraught, the Luo Union moved from stressing its cultural role to engaging increasingly in political action. The imprison-ment of Jomo Kenyatta and other leaders of the Gikuyu, Embu, and Meru Association (GEMA) had created a political space that actors from other communities, including the Luo, were eager to seize. Also, despite their denunciations of Mau Mau and the generally favorable colonial attitude toward the Luo, the Luo Union had seen two of its key leaders imprisoned. Achieng Oneko was one of the "Kapenguria Six" arrested with Jomo Ken-yatta and accused of helping him to foment Mau Mau.[56] Walter Odede was an early leader of the Luo Union who took over as acting head of the prominent political organization KAU (Kenya African Union) after Kenyatta's arrest. Odede himself was arrested for being "in touch with the Mau Mau movement and attempt[ing] to spread their violent methods into Nyanza."[57]

In the mid-1950s, the bloody, complicated, and consuming nature of Mau Mau, together with intensifying demands for formal African politi-cal participation in Kenya but also on the other side of the continent in Britain's Gold Coast Colony, which became Ghana after independence, motivated Kenya's government to ease restrictions on African political organizations and to open a token number of seats for African represen-tatives on the colony's settler-dominated Legislative Council in 1957. With GEMA politicians largely barred from these elections, Luo leaders successfully contested available seats. Most notably, Odinga resigned as head of the Luo Union to represent Central Nyanza, and Tom Mboya, a popular trade unionist and child of the labor migrations who was born on a sisal plantation in Thika, carried Nairobi, defeating another Luo candidate, Arwings Kodhek.[58] The results of these elections also showed the growing political power of ethnicity in late colonial Kenya. Beyond the Luo community, elected leaders such as Ronald Ngala (Coast) and Masinde Muliro (North Nyanza) benefited from the political work done by ethnic associations in their home areas as well. Like the Luo Union, the Mijikenda Union of the coast and the Abaluhya Association in Western Kenya capitalized on shared interests in soccer, rural development initiatives, and cultural issues in order to help build ethnic political communities in the 1950s.[59]

By the late 1950s, it was clear that the end of British colonial rule was inevitable. With independence on the horizon, leaders like Mboya sought support and standing abroad.[60] Particularly urgent was the need to quickly grow the number of Africans who had access to higher education and would thus be prepared to work in the administration of independent Kenya. In 1959, Mboya undertook a high-profile American tour, speaking at universities across the country, appearing on *Meet the Press*, and developing relationships with Senator John F. Kennedy and African American celebrity activists such as baseball great Jackie Robinson, singer Harry Belafonte, and movie star Sidney Poitier.[61] With public and private funding raised through the African American Students Foundation, they secured scholarships that were billed as an investment in Africa's future for nearly eight hundred East Africans to attend colleges and universities in the United States from 1959 to 1963. Among the elite students of this era, who had to pledge to return to Kenya upon graduation, were future Nobel laureate Wangari Maathai, and the future father of an American president, Barack Hussein Obama.[62] Barack Obama Sr.'s early life would not necessarily have suggested that he would be part of this select group of young wananchi groomed to be leaders of the nation. Although he attended the prestigious CMS secondary school at Maseno like Odinga and Oneko before him, he was dismissed in 1953 before graduation for defying school rules. With his prospects dimmed, Obama Sr. followed in the footsteps of thousands of earlier Luo labor migrants, including his father, by finding employment in Mombasa and

Figure 3.2. Ofafa Memorial Hall, Kisumu. Photo by author.

Nairobi, and likely benefiting from the Mau Mau–driven repression of the GEMA community.Settling in Kaloleni, one of Nairobi's Luo-dominated middle-class neighborhoods, Obama Sr. had plenty of oc-casions to engage with fellow Luo migrants in between clerking at an Indian law firm and working on a literacy campaign run by an American woman.[63] The neighborhood's popular social hall was a space to seek out Luo sociability and a regular meeting place of the Luo Union and other ethnic associations. Built in the postwar era of colonial welfare and development, social halls were important sites of urban recreation, espe-cially during the tense year of Mau Mau. As the state sponsored sites to hold cultural events aimed at promoting "tribal discipline," Nairobi's Af-rican affairs officer noted that even during the State of Emergency, "every weekend all the available halls were booked for tribal society functions, dances and general meetings."[64] While state officials often lauded these disciplined cultural activities, social halls also provided a rare public space to gather and debate politics. As Mau Mau wore on, cultural de-bates about "Luoness" at the hall took on an increasingly political tone.[65]

Having established Tom Mboya as a mentor and having petitioned in *Ramogi* for additional support for his studies abroad, Obama Sr. was well placed when he left for university in Hawaii in 1959, the same year that the State of Emergency, which shaped Kenyan affairs from 1952 onward, was lifted.[66] In the five years that Obama Sr. spent at Hawaii and Harvard, Kenya was politically transformed. A series of constitutional conferences began in London in 1961, the year of Barack Obama Jr.'s birth in Hawaii. The political negotiations in Kenya resulted in Kenyatta's release that same year and in Kenya's independence in 1963. Kenyatta emerged from years in detention as a martyr to the Mau Mau cause and resumed his place at the apex of Kenya politics as leader of the new Kenya African National Union (KANU) party with widespread support, including that of Odinga and Mboya.[67] In 1963 Kenyatta was elected president; Odinga served as vice president, and Mboya served as a cabinet minister. By the time Obama Jr. visited his Kenyan family twenty-five years later, the optimism that was palpable in the early days of Kenya's independence had evaporated as authoritarianism, corruption, and often-violent politics held sway. In this environment Luo found themselves especially marginalized, and by 2004 Luo people were ready to reach into the diaspora that had spilled beyond East Africa and around the world to find a powerful patron.

The Rise and Fall of the Luo Community in Postcolonial Politics

What is even sadder is that each time a Luo, is about to achieve greater things, for a country, he is sabotaged by their own people in cahoots, with detractors. And in doing so, the whole nation is robbed of advancement, and great leaders.[68]

Political developments after Kenya's independence in 1963 added new layers to Luoness. During the 1960s and 1970s the relationship between the Luo community and the Kenyan state shifted. Throughout decolonization and the early days of the republic, Luo speakers had relatively cordial relationships with the colonial and national governments, and leaders like Odinga and Mboya rose to influential national positions. However, before

a decade of independence elapsed, Western Kenya became linked to political opposition due to Luo attempts to claim positions of power and the
efforts of the increasingly Kikuyu- and then Kalenjin-dominated state to
push them aside. The progressively more patrimonial and ethnicized landscape of the country's national politics and Luos' diminishment within it
simultaneously enhanced Luos' notion of their broadly constituted ethnic
identity—to be Luo was to be an outsider, an Other—and stimulated a
profound desire for a powerful Big Man who could promote their interests
and bring them back from the "political wilderness."[69]

By the time of independence, a shared sense of Luo identity—established
by history and in diaspora, and also confirmed through ongoing cultural
and material ties to Nyanza—had been cultivated through the intellectual
and political projects discussed above and through political participation
on the national stage as the colonial era ended. But as Kenya's political
landscape became more complex, so did the content of Luoness. The cases
of Oginga Odinga and Tom Mboya, the foremost Luo politicians of the
early1960s, point to the new layers of postcolonial Luoness as well as to the
Luo Union's unfinished and contested project of ethnic "unity." Odinga,
the elder of the pair, exemplified the more standard variety of Luoness;
he relied on his elevated cultural status as Jaramogi and on the support
of the Luo Union, and he drew his constituents from Dholuo speakers
across Nyanza. Mboya, in contrast, imbued Luoness with a cosmopolitan
character that was different from its diasporic one; Nairobi was his parliamentary constituency, and, as noted above, he had attained an impressive
international profile, even landing a *Time* magazine cover in 1960.[70] His
international profile made him competitive for high office. Starting out as
a trade unionist, he became the minister for Economic Planning and Development and had even been touted as a potential presidential challenger
to Kenyatta.

As part of the cosmopolitan "airlift" cohort, Barack Obama Sr. was
able to secure a highly sought after civil servant position as a planning
officer in the Ministry of Economic Planning upon returning to Kenya in
1964.[71] Working in Nairobi under his mentor Mboya, Obama Sr. would
have been immersed in the heated politics of the early independence era
as Kenya struggled to find its place in the global landscape of the Cold
War. Looking for the best "deal" between the two superpowers, leaders like

Odinga flirted with socialist ideologies and courted the Soviet Union and the United States, both of which were eager to move newly independent nations into their spheres of influence. Scant years earlier, the superpowers had jockeyed to bring newly independent Congo into their respective camps; the US and its allies referring to the left-leaning prime minister Patrice Lumumba, who was ultimately killed by secessionist Congolese and CIA operatives as a Communist.[72] British Intelligence reports that referred to Odinga as "an enigma . . . a contact man with the USSR and China," both recalled the language applied to Lumumba and foreshadowed the rhetoric that the American political Right applied to Barack Obama Jr. four decades later.[73]

Odinga's inclinations and the criticisms of them reflected not only Cold War geopolitics, but also an emerging ideological divide among Kenya's postcolonial leadership over the appropriate paths for development and in global affairs, and the ethnic tensions simmering below the surface of postcolonial politics.[74] As noted earlier, in the culmination of an apparent Kikuyu-Luo alliance, Odinga had become vice president in Kenyatta's administration, signaling to many that it was time for the Luo to take their share of the political cake. However, Odinga's political ambitions, socialist ideology, and connections to the Soviet Union did not mesh with the aims of Kenyatta, who was molding himself into a strong friend of the West and his administration into an ethnicized and patrimonial enterprise that failed to create a unified sense of Kenyan nationalism.[75] In a move that began the long period in which state development in Nyanza was largely abandoned and split the ruling party, Odinga broke away in 1966, forming an opposition party, the Kenya People's Union (KPU).[76]

The split between Odinga and the Kenyatta government also split Luo between supporters of Odinga and those of Mboya who had remained within the ruling party. Mboya's star rose even higher with Odinga's marginalization, so much so that he was even floated as a potential successor to the elderly Kenyatta. Yet, while the cosmopolitan Mboya had cultivated support across ethnic lines, the increasingly ethnicized political model reinforced the importance of "tribe." Mboya's Luo roots were regarded by many Kikuyu as a threat to the primacy of Kikuyu political power.

By the late 1960s, Obama Sr. was caught in the middle of the struggle between the Kenyatta administration and the Luo opposition. Perhaps seeking advice on negotiating this complex environment, Obama Sr. met with his mentor, Mboya, in Nairobi's central business district on a Saturday afternoon in July 1969. Shortly after the men exchanged greetings, Mboya was shot to death outside a pharmacy on Government Road. He died within minutes. Mboya's assassination, which was widely linked to the Kenyatta regime, both added another layer to Luo political marginalization and helped to renew the sense of shared Luo identity (and interests) that had been troubled by the split between Odinga and Mboya.[77] Indeed, when Kenyatta held a public rally in Kisumu to open a new Soviet-funded hospital a few months after Mboya's death, his entourage was pelted with stones while security forces opened fire. Eleven deaths resulted from the violence. The KPU was immediately banned by the state, and its leaders were imprisoned and stripped of their seats in Parliament.[78] In the tumult of postcolonial politics, the Luo Union had continued its intellectual projects to foster Luoness and to work on shaping what it meant to be Luo in the new era. On the eve of independence, the Luo Union held a four-day conference in Kisumu on Luo history that brought together many professional and amateur historians. As Derek Peterson writes, "Historical research was a consequential endeavor in Nyanza, a work for which dedicated people sacrificed time and money."[79] During this period, renowned Luo historian Bethwell Ogot was conducting fieldwork for his classic 1967 text, *History of the Southern Luo*, a definitive scholarly study of Luo oral traditions stretching back to the diaspora from Sudan and the advent of Ramogi. Using Luo Union elders as principal informants, Ogot gave the Luo community a codified written history based on scholarly research and continued the colonial tradition of oral and written historical narrative showing the Luo as a distinct social and political identity.[80] Ogot's pioneering role in the Kenyan academy is mirrored by that of other leading Luo academics such as Simeon Ominde and David Wasawo.[81] While the Luo community professed that Luo were banished to the *political* "wilderness," they were nevertheless able to exert their influence in academe.

Politically, the Luo Union had also aimed to play a conciliatory role after the rupture between Odinga and Kenyatta, and had worked to reunify the Luo after Mboya's death.[82] At a general meeting held in a Kaloleni social hall shortly after Mboya died and attended by thousands of Luo speakers, the sitting *ker* (president) of the Luo Union, Paul Mboya, began with a call for general unity. In turn, Achieng Oneko remarked that in death, Tom Mboya was returning "home" to the community he had abandoned to his cosmopolitanism. In a direct reference to the union's origins as a burial society, he called for the Luo community to raise funds to bury Mboya in triumphal style in Rusinga Island, noting, "Now he is back with us."[83] Luo efforts to reclaim their cosmopolitan kin prefigured Luo efforts forty years later to assert that a young politician from Illinois "belonged" to them.

A by-election in 1969 made Kenya a defacto one-party state and served as an indicator of the growing political factions that plagued the Luo Union throughout the rest of its official history.[84] More than a dozen new members of Parliament (MPs) were elected to replace Odinga and the other KPU exiles, which represented the rise of a new anti-Odinga KANU faction in Luo political circles. Even as the Luo Union's soccer club brought home international accolades, the association was embroiled in economic controversy during the waning years of the Kenyatta era. As it sponsored several *harambee* (fund-raisers) to develop the Ramogi Institute of Advanced Technology (RIAT) outside of Kisumu, allegations of misuse of funds further damaged the union's public image and hindered its activities.[85]

During the 1970s, Kenyatta ruled Kenya as a dictatorial patriarchal leader referred to simply with the honorific title *Mzee* (wise old man). Luo Union meetings during this time were sometimes denied government permission, as the political climate for Dholuo speakers allied to Odinga and the Luo Union worsened. For instance, when a group of students at the University of Nairobi attempted to form a Luo student league in 1970, the government denied them registration, stating: "It appears to the registrar that in the interests of peace, welfare, or good order in Kenya would be likely to suffer prejudice by reason of your registration as a society."[86]

Throughout the later years of Kenyatta's rule, union relations with the state grew increasingly distant and suspicious, and the association came into direct conflict with the KANU government. To attempt to control the Odinga opposition groups in Western Kenya, Kenyatta appointed Isaiah Cheluget as the new provincial commissioner (PC) of Nyanza in 1969. Originally from the Rift Valley borderlands of Nyanza, Cheluget was not a

Luo cultural insider, and he clashed with the union leaders. For instance, Cheluget campaigned that local Luo traditions of large public burials were too expensive and also a health threat if the individual had died from a highly communicable disease such as cholera.[87] Union members and officials vehemently opposed any cultural meddling by the Kenyatta appointee, arguing that it was their duty to regulate customary affairs free from government interference. A running battle ensued in the local press, with Cheluget and Luo Union officials accusing each other of neglecting the social welfare of the Luo community. Ker Paul Mboya summed up the view of union membership in 1978 by simply stating, "Just as I will not interfere in Mr. Cheluget's work, I like to ask him to keep his hands off of Luo Union affairs."[88]

Cultural interference by the state also spilled over into the political arena, as the KANU government aimed to draw Luo voters from Odinga through the same channels he used to build grassroots support. On many occasions following independence, union officials had adamantly tried to keep their nonpolitical image from the colonial period intact. However, by the mid-1970s, public opinion and political actions blurred the line between the social welfare and political activities of the Luo Union and other ethnic associations. Politicians became more publicly associated with the activities of state welfare associations such as the Luo Union, the New Akamba Union, and the Gikuyu, Embu, and Meru Association (GEMA) from Central Kenya. This active involvement by prominent politicians enshrouded the welfare activities of ethnic associations in political controversy.[89] By the late 1970s, union members were widely seen as staunch supporters of Oginga Odinga. While Odinga had been forced from government in 1969, he still garnered significant support from rural Nyanza, as union members had been his political supporters since the 1950s. The new KANU MPs, who had been elected to fill the void of exiled KPU leaders, had trouble garnering popular support for their positions even by the late 1970s. Some looked to the Luo Union as the answer to their political problems.

In January 1978, reports surfaced in the local press that the Luo Union was launching a campaign to raise nearly twenty million Kenyan shillings (KSH) to fund direct political campaigns. Their efforts were argued to be aimed at restoring ex-KPU officials such as Oginga Odinga and Achieng

Oneko in elected government positions during the 1979 general elections. Luo Union officials fervently protested any involvement and dismissed the reports. However, new Luo MPs still within the KANU government and opposed to Odinga, namely, Isaac Omolo Okero and William Odongo Omamo, called for a change in Luo Union leadership. From 1978 to 1980, Omamo took forceful control of union affairs and, backed by the KANU government, ran the organization through a caretaker committee. Paul Mboya's position as ker was then moot in the eyes of the state, and for the next two years political struggles within the Luo community ensued over the issue of controlling the Luo Union.[90] While 1978 symbolized the beginning of a chaotic period late in the organization's history, it also marked a time of political transition for Kenya itself that would result in the official end to ethnic welfare associations.

Kenyatta's death from natural causes in 1978 did not improve Luo political fortunes. Daniel arap Moi succeeded Kenyatta as president, and the political establishment expected that he would protect the interests of Kenya's close associates even though he came from the Kalenjin ethnic group, which had opposed the alliance between the Kikuyu and the Luo at independence. In keeping with the ever-increasing ethnicization of politics, Moi elevated many Kalenjin to key positions and continued Kenyatta's program of confining Luo to the "political wilderness."[91] For example, less than two years into his presidency, Moi called for the "winding up of all associations whose purposes and objectives are to serve as pressure groups in the interests of a single or multiple tribal, clan, race, conveniences or communities."[92] The result of this informal decree was that the Luo Union and other, similar ethnic associations were effectively banned, thus limiting their power to organize opposition at the grassroots level.[93]

By the 1980s, "tribalism" was widely used to explain divisive political policies, and as such this move initially had significant public support. However, voices in the Kenyan press asserted the social welfare benefits provided by ethnic organizations like the Luo Union and argued that banning them was not the way to remedy ethnic politics. For example, James Ger of Kisumu wrote in a 1980 editorial, "It was tribal consciousness which supplied the first weapon against colonialism. And KAU, the first national political party, was a union of ethnic organizations such as the Kavirondo societies and the Kikuyu Central Association [KCA]. Tribal consciousness can only be supplemented by a very strong national spirit which has been lacking in Kenya because of the predominance of 'the ruling class tribalism,' not by dissolving welfare associations formed to cater for the social cultural and economic needs of their members."[94]

While organizations like the Luo Union disappeared from public view during the 1980s, their social and cultural work continued.[95] For instance, the popular Luo Union and Abaluhya football clubs simply renamed themselves Reunion and AFC Leopards after the ban on ethnic associations in 1980. The more popular Luo Union football team Gor Mahia was apparently immune to this ban because it drew its name from a Luo folk hero and did not have an ethnic distinction. Among the most popular teams in the current Kenyan professional league, Gor Mahia and the AFC Leopards still draw the majority of their support from ethnic constituencies. For instance, when Gor fans march toward the Nairobi city stadium on game day, it is typical to hear chants and songs in Luo recalling the community's migratory origins in South Sudan, with fans proudly displaying tilapia from Lake Victoria as a symbol of ethnic cuisine.[96] As one lifelong supporter noted, the success of Gor Mahia has long been a "symbol of Luo strength."[97]

From the late 1960s onward, the political fate of the Luo overall was tied increasingly to the fate of the Odingas. In keeping with broader trends in Kenyan politics, Luo engagement in "Big Man Politics" reflects the belief held across ethnic groups that patrimonial patronage along ethnic lines is essential to getting a slice of the political cake, or, more simply, the notion that "if we can just get our man into office, it will be our time to eat."[98] The perilousness of being a popular Luo politician and the significance of the Odinga family were reinforced in 1990 with the assassination of Minister of Foreign Affairs Robert Ouko.[99] Like Mboya, Ouko was well respected abroad and regarded as a potential challenger to the sitting president. Speaking in the mid-2000s, informants drew parallels between the two assassinations and read both as specific attacks on the Luo body politic as a whole. In both instances, Luo rallied around the Odingas. One informant reflecting on the assassinations noted, "If it was not for Jaramogi [Oginga Odinga], the Luos would have been finished."[100]

Until his death in 1994, Oginga Odinga was a stalwart spokesman for the Luo community in Kenya and a key figure in the political opposition.

Upon his death, supporters in the Luo community still referred to Odinga through his former ceremonial title, Ker of the Luo Union, lamenting, "Ker Jaramogi is dead. Now who shall lead my people?"[101] Given Odinga's almost fifty-year career as a political leader, it is not surprising that the Odinga name and family remained powerful into the 1990s. The elder Odinga son, Oburu, took over his father's parliamentary seat in Bondo, Nyanza Province, while the younger Raila, who had been detained by the Moi regime in the 1980s, won a parliamentary seat in Nairobi in the first multiparty elections in 1992, took over the politico-cultural reins of the Luo community after his father's death, and ran for president in 1997, 2007, and 2013.[102] Many of his Luo supporters have regarded an investment in Raila's political success as an investment in the material success of Luo people overall, particularly those in underserved and underdeveloped Western Kenya. As one supporter speculated in 2007, "If only Raila can make it [as president], the problems of development in Nyanza will be solved."[103]

The investment in Raila Odinga's political success speaks not only to the history of the Odinga family, but also to Luo organizations' support for powerful political patrons. The Luo Council of Elders (LCE), formed in the 1990s and composed almost entirely of former Luo Union members and supporters, promotes investment in Western Kenyan and cultural solidarity across Luo-speaking communities in East Africa. Indeed, upon being installed as LCE chairman in 2004, Meshack Riaga Ogallo voiced his desire to visit with all the Luos across East Africa (and beyond) in order to promote "unity and investment at home."[104] These aims were echoed by other LCE members interviewed between 2004 and 2009 as they wove together conceptions of "Luoness" in terms of opposition politics and economic uplift while highlighting their cultural and political attachments to a far-ranging Luo diaspora. When talk turned to contemporary politics, LCE members were quick to introduce two figures whom they regarded as Luo Big Men—Raila Odinga *and* Barack Obama Jr.[105]

Finding a New Hero Abroad: Dala *(Home) or Diaspora?*

In 1988, nearly six years after the death of his father in an alcohol-fueled automobile accident in Nairobi, Barack Obama Jr. stepped into the complicated history of his paternal family and the fractured world of Kenyan politics for the first time. Obama Sr's life in Kenya had been characterized by personal and professional upheavals. On the personal level, Obama Sr's relationships with romantic partners and his children and extended family were unstable. Professionally, he experienced setbacks and challenges that were in part attributable to his habits, but which also reflected the profound loss of his mentor, Mboya, and the difficulties of being a Luo "in the wilderness."[106]

On trips from Nairobi to his family's "home" in rural Western Kenya, Barack Jr. would have experienced the material results of the long-standing conflict between Luo and the central government. The tooth-rattling journey along the potholed road from Nairobi to Kogelo was quite different from the smooth tarmac paving the way from the capital to President Moi's home district of Baringo. Moi's Kalenjin areas had experienced significant infusions of resources and infrastructure development, in part financed by funds deliberately diverted from languishing Western Kenya. In returning to "home [cubed]" in Siaya District, Barack Jr., like Luo migrants before him and like other young people of Luo heritage, was establishing a sense of "belonging" in Luoland. Such visits point to the realization of the priorities of the Luo Union and the LCE—cultivating a shared sense of "Luoness" throughout the diaspora and diasporic reinvestment in Western Kenya. Overall, returning "home," whether it is twenty times a year from Nairobi or every two years from Ohio or London or Dubai, has been a primary way in which contemporary Dholuo speakers have established emotional and symbolic stakes in their rural roots in Luoland and have helped to stimulate material investment in the region's development.

However, as the diaspora continues to expand and the mounting demands of maintaining a "house" away from Luoland trump the periodic visits "home," many young Luo have begun to ask if one's sense of "belonging" as a Luo can be renewed without treading the soils of rural Western Kenya. For example, David Otieno, a young Luo living in cosmopolitan Nairobi, commented ruefully, "I am one of those 'dot-com' Luos; the ones who go home once a year at best."[107] For the dot-com generation, many with ties to Kenya as loose as those of Obama Jr., "belonging" does not necessarily require a presence on the shores of Lake Victoria, but instead involves channeling increasingly globalized flows of capital to Western Kenya and using social media to debate what it means to be Luo in much the same way that their forebears hashed out the shape of Luoness in the pages of *Ramogi*.[108]

Even in cyberspace, popular political narratives about the Odingas and other prominent Luo politicians have shaped the ways Luo speakers at home and throughout the diaspora critique and comment upon the Kenyan state and Kenya's place in the world. By the era of Obama's ascendancy, the story of the Luo community's political rise and fall was firmly entrenched in political discourse in Kenya. The martyrdoms of Mboya and Ouko, and the political marginalization of Jaramogi and Raila Odinga, were mobilized in chat rooms and message boards like jalou.com and set the stage for Kenyans in general and Luo in particular to read political developments in the United States concerning a "Luo" politician through the lens of their own national and ethnic histories.

The experiences of the Luo community of Kenya show that ethnic identity is not a primordial artifact. Rather, "Luoness" emerged from determined efforts by formal associations like the Luo Union and the LCE and everyday Luo intellectuals to cultivate a shared way of being-in-the-world among Dholuo speakers in Kenya and across East Africa more generally. Yet, these endeavors did not occur in a vacuum. The migratory experiences of the colonial era, the political demands of the transition to independence, and the patrimonial politics of the late 1960s forward have all shaped ideas about what it means to be Luo, who gets to "belong" as a Luo, and what Luo people see as their obligations to their fellows and to Nyanza. This profound intellectual, cultural, and political history underpins the Luo embrace of Barack Obama Jr. in 2004 and again in 2008 and 2012. As the next chapters will show, it also became fodder for Obama's opponents abroad to contest the authenticity of his American "belonging" and to cast him as a "son of the soil" of Western Kenya.

Part II

Contested Histories and the Politics
of Belonging

4

The Politics of Condemnation

The American Right's Reactions to Obama's Roots in Kenya

> He was sired by a Kenyan father, born to a mother attracted to men
> of the Third World and reared by grandparents in Hawaii, a paradise
> far from the American mainstream.
> —Wesley Pruden, *Washington Times*[1]

With Barack Obama's victory in the US presidential election of 2008, Africans across the continent rejoiced that one of "their own" had ascended to the most powerful political office in the world. In Kenya, the *wananchi* (citizens) interpreted the Obama story through their experiences with colonialism and identity politics, embracing and celebrating Obama's African background. However, in the United States, and to a certain extent in Britain, from the 2008 presidential campaign through much of Obama's first term his political opponents took a very different approach to Obama's Kenyan heritage, using his African roots to cast him as foreign, and thus untrustworthy and perhaps even uncivilized. These critiques, emanating from the "Far Right"[2] of the American political spectrum and packaged neatly in political "best sellers" or messily disseminated throughout the blogosphere, offer the only substantive engagement that many Americans have had with Kenya's past and present. Subsequently, these critiques have had ongoing effects on the ways the wider American public has viewed the Kenyan heritage of the first African American president of the United States and Kenya's past and present more generally.

This chapter examines a variety of high-profile texts and media, generated by Obama's political opponents from 2008 forward, which aim to condemn Obama as a "son of the soil" of Western Kenya.[3] As many of these works exhibit pretenses to academic or journalistic authority, this chapter addresses a question central to historical practice: How does the historian assess the trustworthiness of a source? It draws the reader's attention to the importance of (1) identifying tropes, or familiar, stereotyped themes, in a source and among groups of sources; (2) discerning the agenda of the source's author and the perspective of its intended audience; (3) reading a source in context, that is, with a critical attention to the other sources surrounding it; and (4) considering a source in historical context, or as being situated within and produced by a particular social, political, economic, and cultural environment. Here we pay close attention to how online debates and "sources" can be easily divorced from the historical contexts in which they were produced. With Obama's political ascendancy occurring squarely in the digital age, professional pundits and amateur historians alike often turned primarily, if not exclusively, to Google for basic questions about Kenya's past and present, often tripping over and then uncritically embracing revisionist histories produced by the Right.

Overall, the chapter shows how written sources and media have drawn on familiar stereotypes about "tribalism" and "terrorism," renewed concerns about "Marxism," and introduced the "threat" posed by Islam to address contemporary politics and key moments in postcolonial Kenyan history. Deconstructing how members of the American Far Right have (mis)interpreted Kenya's past and present in their efforts to discredit Obama highlights how history can be rewritten to serve political ends, how the politics of "belonging" are figured in the United States, and how Africa is popularly imagined in the West.[4] The beginning of the American Right's revision of Kenyan history can be traced to Birthers, the group arguing that Obama's "actual location of birth is of great concern" and asserting the existence of a Kenyan birth certificate. This group has wielded notions of "belonging" most crudely, claiming that Obama was literally *not* "born from the soil" of the United States.[5]

Public condemnations of the Obama and Kenya connection in the U.S.

Figure 4.1. *Gun Rally Birthers Tell Fascist Communist Obama to Go Back to Africa.* (Fibonacci Blue, St. Cloud, Minnesota, February 23, 2013; https://www.flickr.com/photos/fibonacciblue/8502463974/.)

Figure 4.2. *Where's the Birth Certificate?* (Victor Victoria, South Gate, California, November 12, 2010; http://en.wikipedia.org/wiki/File:Billboard_Challenging_the_validity_of_Barack_Obama%27s_Birth_Certificate.JPG.)

The billboard pictured in the figure above was part of a campaign sponsored by media site WND.com, linked to Jerome Corsi, whose anti-Obama oeuvre is discussed in this chapter. CBS News reported in 2009 that WND.com had raised more than $75,000 for the billboards in a number of different US states.[6]

Often dismissed and disdained in mainstream discourse as a (crackpot) "theory in search of facts," the ideology of the Birther movement has influenced public opinion and helped package Obama's familial connection to East Africa as a political liability.[7] Resonating with conspiracy theorists and fraught with racial overtones, the Birther movement found traction in the United States during the 2008 campaign. Taking off from rumors spread initially by supporters of Obama's Democratic primary challenger, Hillary Clinton, the Birther movement resonated most intensely with Tea Party members and fringe elements of the Republican Party. Asserting that Obama had been born in Kenya and that it was immaterial to his electoral eligibility that his mother was undisputedly an American citizen at the time of his birth, Birthers commenced a spurious "debate" as to whether or not a child born abroad to an American citizen qualified as a "natural born citizen." For the purposes of presidential eligibility; the Birthers' position is no, and for constitutional scholars, the position is yes.[8]

Even more significantly, Birthers operationalized Obama's connection to East Africa to cast his politics and identity as dangerously outside of "mainstream" American values.[9] For instance, two writers quoted in a study of online comments made in reply to more than a hundred Birther-related articles in the *New York Times* and *Wall Street Journal* succinctly sum up Birtherist attitudes:

> If Obama didn't act like an alien, nobody would question his birth place. But he is so unAmerican in words and actions, people look for an explanation. The Birthers are just one group of questioners. . . .
>
> It is clear that Obama does not meet the "spirit" of the requirement that a president be a natural born citizen. Hawaii is pretty far from mainland US, Kenya is farther still and Indonesia still further.[10]

Such overt, racialized coding of Obama's cosmopolitan background could easily lead the critical reader to dismiss such comments as mere "fringe" discourse. However, coverage of the Birthers in the mainstream, national press tacitly lent the movement legitimacy and ultimately compelled Obama's campaign to release his Hawaiian birth certificate in 2008 and again in 2011. Even with this evidence made public and bona fide by the Republican governor of Hawaii, claims about Obama's Kenyan birth continued to be evoked by high-profile conservative politicians and celebrities, from Mike Huckabee to Donald Trump, and to occupy significant space in the blogosphere. As late as April 2011, a *CBS News/New York Times* poll found that 25 percent of Americans believed that Obama was born outside the United States, with 45 percent of Republicans asserting his foreign birth.[11] And in a simple Google search for the phrase "Obama and Kenya," the majority of search results are websites devoted to claims about Obama's Kenyan birth as a means to attack his political legitimacy.[12] With Google search rankings based more on popularity than credibility, the Internet is rife with amateur researchers promoting dubious evidence based more on political than objective scrutiny.

The proliferation of online rumors and revisionist histories related to Obama and Kenya fits into a deeper American history of conspiracy theories. From the famous Salem witch hunts of the seventeenth century to the 9/11 "Truthers" movement, conspiracy theorists often emerge in response to perceived threats to conservative notions of morality or in response to what scholars have sometimes called the "paranoid style in American politics."[13] In this way, Birthers belong to a strain of American political discourse and amateur patriotic histories that also claim President Kennedy's assassination, the 1969 Apollo 11 lunar landing, and even the 9/11 terrorist attacks are part of some grand government cover-up.[14] In the digital world of Obama's political ascendancy, online message boards, blogs, and fringe media outlets provided new platforms for dissemination and allowed amateur researchers and "conspiracy buffs" to hunt for "facts" to support sometimes outlandish ideas.

World Net Daily (*WND*), an epicenter of online Birther debates, often appropriates Kenyan discourse for political gain and dismisses the social and political context in which it was produced. For example, *WND* is among several web-based media outlets that, in an effort to advance their Birtherist assertions, have seized upon a 2004 Associated Press story that noted an article by the Kenyan daily the *Standard* had been erroneously titled "Kenyan-Born Obama All Set for US Senate."[15] Transforming typos and moments of misspeak into convenient "facts," pundits in search of "evidence" of Obama's Kenyan birth have even combed Kenyan parliamentary debates, recently made available via books.google.com. For instance, reports in 2010 cited an offhand remark recorded in the transcript of a parliamentary debate about ethnicity, exclusion, and the devolution of political power in Kenya. Debating the implications of instituting a federalized system of government similar to the US model, then minister for lands James Orengo suggested, "If America was living in a situation where they feared ethnicity . . . how could a young man born here in Kenya, who is not even a native American, become president of America?"[16] Taken in context, it is clear that in drawing a comparison between the freedom and fluidity of the American system and the political stagnation of Kenya, Orengo is arguing that the Kenyan governance is so hobbled by ethnic politics that a member of the "wrong" ethnicity, let alone a true outsider, could never become president. Reading deliberately out of context across the Atlantic, Obama's American opponents asserted that the member of Parliament's comment had confirmed Obama's Kenyan citizenship. Such assertions speak to the dangers of "research" in the digital age, where discourse is easily removed from the historical context in which it was produced and subsequently manipulated for political gain.

Beyond the overt claims questioning Obama's citizenship, members of the Far Right have drawn on more subtle emotional and philosophical aspects of "belonging" to contest Obama's legitimacy. Even if Obama is a "son of the soil" in the literal sense, so the argument goes, his identity and loyalties are too closely wrapped up in the Kenyan context, that is, with the culture, history, and politics of Kenya, for him to be authentically American.[17] Accordingly, the Far Right has employed a selective reading of the last six decades of Kenya's history in order to stake claims about Obama's "belonging," focusing on critical topics such as Mau Mau and the administration of Kenya's postindependence governments.[18] In this chapter, guided by our core question—How does a historian assess the trustworthiness of a source?—we apply critical attention to tropes, to authorial agenda and audience perspective, to context and to *historical* context in the two most commercially successful monographs to treat the Obama-Kenya connection from a Far Right perspective, and in the narratives of a minor event that the Far Right presented widely as irrefutable evidence of Obama's inherited, historical loyalties to Kenya. In doing so, we compare and contrast Far Right claims about Kenya's history with the established historical record and historiography.

Jerome Corsi's 2008 book, *The Obama Nation*, offers a prime example of the potent brew of emotional appeal and revisionist history produced by the Far Right.[19] Put forward as a combination of political rhetoric and African history, *The Obama Nation* reached #1 on the *New York Times* best-seller list in August 2008 and remained near the top throughout the campaign season.[20] Aimed at a US audience possessing limited familiarity with Kenya's complex history, Corsi's use of language and evidence, together with "Jerome R. Corsi, Ph.D." boldly emblazoned on the book's cover, serve to credential *The Obama Nation* as a scholarly work of "objective" truth. Such "knowledge" about Kenya's histories (among others) not only sells books, but also does *political* work, as evidenced by Corsi's 2004 political "biography" of presidential candidate John Kerry.

In *Unfit for Command: Swift Boat Veterans Speak Out against John Kerry*, Corsi attacks John Kerry's service in Vietnam to create a "rhetorically powerful indictment" of the presumptive Democratic challenger to George W. Bush.[21] Engaging in revisionist and decontextualized readings of Kerry's own words and statements about his military service, *Swift Boat Veterans* casts aspersions on Kerry's ability to be "commander and chief," even though his military service record far excelled that of his opponent. Part of a tradition of using biographies to both support and condemn aspirants for national office in the United States, Kenyan history is thus seamlessly adopted into an American genre of popular political biography and memoir.[22]

In *The Obama Nation*, Kenya looms large in Corsi's political takedown of the then Democratic nominee. In chapter 1, Corsi spends considerable time explaining Obama's Kenyan roots by exposing the "tall tales" of Obama's memoir *Dreams from My Father*. In doing so, Corsi repackages the biography of Obama Sr. by not simply describing him as a goat herder from rural Kenya but through inflammatory subtitles such as "Obama's Father, an Alcoholic Polygamist."[23] He then returns to Kenya in chapter 4, the title of which is replete with political buzzwords: "Kenya, Odinga, Communism, and Islam." In retelling Kenya's history, *The Obama Nation* draws on tropes about Africa common in American popular imagination: primordial tribalism, irrational violence, and postcolonial dystopia.[24] It also discusses Kenya's history within America's own contemporary idioms of crisis: Islam and terrorism.

In Corsi's analysis, the historical context and contemporary environment to which Obama truly belongs is soaked in tribalism. Corsi notes, "Tribal battles . . . have dominated Kenya's politics for centuries," and focuses on a primordial "tribalist" drama between the Kikuyu and the Luo.[25] Such an assertion, as we have shown in previous chapters, is not supported by the established, historical evidence. Yet, however inaccurate, Corsi's argument that "tribal battles" were a defining feature of Kenyan politics over hundreds of years helps him make important claims about Obama's "belonging" and Africa's place in the "modern" world. First, in linking Obama to a political environment that evokes violent primordial affinities, Corsi further distances Obama from an authentically American identity based on political rationality. This argument also helps to establish Obama as part of a politicized Luo ethnicity where "tribal" affiliation acts as the default explanation of political action and sets the stage to read political violence in Kenya as rooted in centuries-old "tribal" rivalries rather than in vote rigging or corruption driven by the deep dysfunction of Kenya's loosely veiled authoritarian politics and tremendous economic stratification, issues that we'll discuss in detail in chapter 6.

Corsi's main goal in analyzing contemporary politics is to bind Obama to Raila Odinga. In describing the relationship between the two men, Corsi repeatedly calls Raila "a fellow Luo tribesman" and asserts that at the time of Obama's 2006 official visit to Kenya, Raila "was running for president of Kenya as a Muslim sympathizer."[26] Corsi's characterization of Raila, well known to be a lifelong practicing Anglican, as a "Muslim sympathizer" occurs at the level of the personal and the political. The sincerity of the Obama family's Christian identity is frequently challenged by critics on the Far Right; Corsi casts doubt on the authenticity of Odinga's Christian identity as well. For example, writing on Raila's father, Oginga Odinga, (whom he erroneously refers to as Odinga Odinga), Corsi asserts, "It should be noted that Odinga Odinga was a Christian who saw that his son, Raila Odinga, was also baptized a Christian." Transforming his misspelling of the name of Kenya's first vice president into a historical argument, he asserts, "Odinga Odinga went by the double name to emphasize how completely he rejected his Christian name. Odinga Odinga also refused to allow his children to be baptized with European Christian names. Raila Odinga today professes to be an Anglican."[27]

Rhetorically, Corsi raises the subject of the Odingas' Christian faith in order to tacitly dismiss it. This analysis disregards the historical context of the Pan-Africanist movement with its assertive pride in African cultures and histories, from which nationalist leaders like Oginga Odinga and Jomo Kenyatta sprang. It depicts Oginga Odinga as somehow exceptional in using his Luo name and choosing Luo names for his children. It neglects to note, for example, that when launching his political career, Kenyatta refrained from using his baptismal name, Johnstone, in favor of Jomo (Kikuyu for "burning spear"), and later named his son and political heir Uhuru, the Swahili word for freedom/independence.[28]

On the political level, Corsi's characterization of Raila as a "Muslim sympathizer" is based on a false version of the memorandum of understanding (MOU) between Raila's Orange Democratic Movement (ODM) and the National Muslim Leaders Forum (NAMLEF) before the 2007 Kenya elections. Corsi cites an online version of this memorandum posted on the website of the Evangelical Alliance of Kenya. In doing so, he largely dismisses the document's historical and sociopolitical environment that shaped its production. While noting that "there is concern in Kenya that the document posted on the Internet by the Evangelical Alliance might not be the authentic MOU," Corsi nonetheless proceeds to engage in a detailed explanation of the posted memo.[29] In the same vein as his Birtherist colleagues at *WND* who consistently suggest that Obama is not merely foreign but also Muslim, he notes, for example, its claim that as president Raila would revise the constitution to make sharia, Islamic law, the law of the land in Kenya's Muslim majority regions.[30] Corsi does *not* acknowledge that NAMLEF responded to the posted memorandum. The organization's deputy chairman commented drily (and evidenced a clear understanding of historical context) in the widely read Kenya daily newspaper the *Standard*, "We are not such fools to draft such an MoU demanding the introduction of Sharia law and other unthinkable demands."[31]

Corsi's treatment of the MOU episode, framed by his goal of tying both Raila and Obama to radical Islam, overlooks two central elements of historical context. First, Islamic law has existed constitutionally in Kenya since colonial times, with *kadhi* courts having jurisdiction over a limited number of civil matters and applying only to Muslims who volunteer to have their cases heard by these courts.[32] Second, Mwai Kibaki, elected president in 2002 and 2007, whom Corsi casts as a stalwart Christian in stark opposition to Raila's suspicious religious status, actively sought Muslim support; Muslims constitute a significant minority, especially along the Kenyan coast.[33] Ultimately, Corsi acknowledges that a "much less inflammatory" version of the memorandum, "different in form and content from the document posted by the Evangelical Alliance," had been shown up close on Kenyan television and discussed point by point by the chairman of NAMLEF, whose signature, together with Raila's, appeared on this second, moderate memorandum.[34]

Corsi opens his chapter on Kenya with a discussion of the meanings behind an AP photo of Obama donning Somali dress in Northern Kenya during his 2006 official visit to Africa. In the photo, the senator from Illinois wears a white turban and a *futa*, or cloth wrap, as he is anointed as a Somali elder during his visit to Wajir. This ceremony is a common means through which visiting dignitaries are honored and welcomed by the community, and is recognized as such in both Kenyan and diplomatic circles. Indeed, commenting on the photo, the US ambassador to Kenya noted, "Wherever I travel I get dressed up in same way, out of consideration for the hosts."[35]

Though the photo was shot in August 2006, it went viral during the early months of 2008 (it was rumored to have been supplied to the *Drudge Report* by one of Hillary Clinton's staffers) and was widely reprinted during the primary season.[36] Recognizing that the photo would be interpreted by Obama's opponents through the lens of post-9/11 fears about radical Islam and terrorism in order to appeal to a base deeply concerned about "Muslim terrorists," Obama's campaign manager described the photo's dissemination as "the most shameful, offensive fear-mongering we've seen from either party in this election."[37]

Writing in *WND* in the same vein as many other right-wing pundits, Corsi took up the photo in a piece titled "'Muslim' Photo Raises Obama Connection," reading Obama's donning of Somali garb and his recognition as an "elder" not as an expression of diplomatically suitable cultural sensitivity on the senator's part or as a standard gesture of respectful welcome by the Wajir community, but rather as evidence of *candidate* Obama's Muslim sympathies and affinities.[38] Interestingly, in none of his writing does Corsi note, for instance, that President Kibaki sported a *kofia* (cap) and a *kanzu* (robe)—traditional clothing worn by Muslims on the Swahili Coast—when attending celebrations in Mombasa to mark the end of Ramadan in 2007.[39] Overall, strategically stripped from its historical and cultural context, the Wajir photo operated as a powerful vehicle for politicized innuendo about Obama's alleged "Muslim" sensibilities and affiliations.

The historical inaccuracies, deliberate misreadings of evidence, and purposeful omissions of central context in Corsi's writings could easily lead scholars of Kenyan history and politics to dismiss his brand of political commentary as the mere ravings of a disaffected right-winger. However, *The Obama Nation* and similar texts, such as Dinesh D'Souza's discussed below, are best sellers, and websites such as wnd.com have a vast readership. As such, they have political valence and do political work. In many instances, these sources are the only space in which millions of Americans encounter narratives of Kenya's past and present, some even focusing the country's history in the decade *before* Barack Obama Jr. was born. The next section turns to how Far Right misreadings of Kenyan colonial history aim to link Obama to an earlier group of "terrorists"—Mau Mau rebels.

Mau Maus of the (American Far Right) Mind

> A great part of America now understands that this president's sense of identification lies elsewhere, and is in profound ways unlike theirs.
> —Dorothy Rabinowitz, *Wall Street Journal*[40]

A further array of Far Right blogs, broadcasts, and books have worked to insert Obama into the narrative of Kenyan history in places and at depths where he does not belong. Most significantly, Far Right discourses have interpreted the character of the Obama administration's relationship with Britain and the administration's economic approaches as functions of Obama's historical relation to the Mau Mau rebellion.[41] More generally, Far Right readings of Mau Mau and the Obama family's relation to it hint that the president maintains an affinity for "terrorists."

Mau Mau persists as a central concern in the history and historiography of Kenya and in the nation's popular imagination and political discourse. As noted historian of Kenya John Lonsdale has argued, different images of Mau Mau have developed among groups with varying proximities and attachments to it. He writes of Mau Mau, "It has lived in British imagination as a symbol of African savagery, and modern Kenyans are divided by its images, militant nationalism or tribal thuggery."[42] To the mind-sets identified by Lonsdale, we can add the Mau Maus of the American Far Right, which read Obama as the symbolic and *literal* inheritor of an anticolonial, anti-British, and even antiwhite and anticapitalist legacy rooted in the bitterness of Mau Mau.

While Obama's autobiography, *Dreams from My Father*, states that his paternal grandfather, Hussein Onyango Obama, had been interned by the British during Mau Mau, the earliest press reports to link the Obama family to Mau Mau emanated from the Right-leaning media in Britain and were quickly co-opted by their counterparts in the United States.[43] In late 2008, the *Daily Mail* published a lengthy exposé detailing how Onyango Obama had been interned and tortured by the British for his alleged participation in Mau Mau.[44] While we have shown that this assertion does not rest easily with the substantiated history of Luo participation in Mau Mau, subsequently, bloggers and broadcasters alike have seized upon this point to reinforce Barack Obama's purported loyalties as a son of the *Kenyan* soil and to interpret the administration's engagement with Britain.

The Mau Maus of the Right offer messily overlapping views of the rebellion. They suggest that British atrocities against known and suspected Mau Mau adherents were so extreme as to stimulate among black Kenyans—at home and in the diaspora—a literally inheritable hatred of Britain capable of crossing both international borders and generational boundaries. At the same moment, Far Right readings of Mau Mau highlight the racialized brutality of Mau Mau "terrorists." Such readings wield a trope potent in the context of post-9/11 American politics to tacitly deny any legitimacy to the Mau Mau cause. They willfully combine "anticolonial" with "antiwhite" and "anticapitalist" through language suggesting that a rejection of *colonial* rule like Mau Mau is equivalent to rejecting "the West" and its capitalist values. Both suggest that Obama inherited the malignant genes of Mau Mau through his father's family, in turn mutating his relationship to Britain and to the capitalist "values" of the (white) West.

Mau Mau was first introduced into the American Far Right's discursive toolbox in the course of a kerfuffle initiated by the Right-leaning press and members of the diplomatic community in Britain over the Obama administration's return of a bust of Winston Churchill, which had been loaned to George W. Bush by Tony Blair, and its replacement with a bust of Abraham Lincoln. In early 2009, the *Daily Telegraph* published a story placing the return of the Churchill bronze within the context of Obama's connections to Mau Mau, asserting that "Churchill has less happy connotations for Mr. Obama than those American politicians who celebrate his wartime leadership. It was during Churchill's second premiership that Britain suppressed Kenya's Mau Mau rebellion. Among Kenyans allegedly tortured by the colonial regime included one Hussein Onyango Obama, the President's grandfather."[45] The article further noted that British diplomats were "nervously reading the runes" in an effort to determine whether the "special relationship" between the United States and Britain would be damaged by Obama's supposed special relationship with Mau Mau. Ultimately, the article acknowledged the British embassy's official statement that the bust had been "uniquely loaned" to George W. Bush and that as president, Obama had "decided not to continue the loan." The bust was to instead be displayed at the British ambassador's residence in Washington, DC.[46]

The controversy, however, was not completely extinguished. In spring 2010, a House of Commons select committee called for a "reassessment" of Britain's "special relationship" with the United States in light of Obama's Kenyan roots, which, according to comments that former ambassador to the United States Sir David Manning made before the committee, rendered the president "less sentimental" about long-standing ties between Britain and the US. Manning, who had served as ambassador for four years, spanning both of George W. Bush's terms in office, added, "We now have a Democrat who is not familiar with us."[47]

As early as the spring of 2009, members of the American Far Right quickly seized upon the spiraling diplomatic row over the bust's return and its replacement with a bronze of Lincoln, asserting that the two actions were mutually reinforcing and demonstrated both Obama's favoring of his black, African identity and his detestation of the former colonial masters of Kenya. They willfully misread the content and character of the Mau Mau rebellion, often echoing British propaganda of the 1950s that established the "myth of Mau Mau" discussed in chapter 2.[48] To refresh, British propaganda, taken up as fact by major media outlets in the United States, deliberately ignored the historical context of the rebellion—long-standing political and economic grievances of the Kikuyu throughout the colonial era. Instead, it cast Mau Mau as a form of contagious, collective madness; a return to pagan primitiveness expressed through brutality and brought about by the inability of the Kikuyu to cope psychologically, emotionally, and intellectually with "modernity." For example, a 1952 article in the *New York Times* contended that Mau Mau violence resulted from "the frustrations of a savage people neither mentally nor economically able to adjust itself to the swift pace of civilisation."[49] This story was part of a larger series that the *New York Times* and other US-based news sources ran throughout the mid-1950s, which read Mau Mau through the lens of terrorism.[50]

In recent US political discourse, members of the Far Right in the United States have eagerly grabbed the "myth of Mau Mau" and used its themes in a variety of ways. Most egregiously, a *Newsmax* article treating the Churchill bust's return asserted, "Perhaps Obama, the son of a Kenyan, took umbrage at Prime Minister Churchill's actions in 1953 of wiping out the Mau-Mau, the Kenyan terrorists who made a specialty of slitting throats of sleeping white and Black Kenyans."[51] In addition to clearly echoing the theme of "terrorism," this reading inaccurately compresses the historical time line of Mau Mau. In 1953, the rebellion was far from being "wiped out," but rather its perceived threat was such that the colonial state launched a wide-scale, anti–Mau Mau crackdown dubbed "Operation Anvil" across Nairobi in the spring of 1954. The State of Emergency was not lifted until 1959, during the tenure of Harold Macmillan, British prime minister for the bulk of the Mau Mau era.[52] And, importantly, as Mau Mau narratives of the Obama presidency continued to be reproduced in 2011, David Anderson, renowned historian of Kenya, spelled out,

> To portray the Obama family as being part of Mau Mau is stir-fry crazy. Let me explain why: The Obama family come from western Kenya, which is about as different from Nairobi and the Kikuyu area as Utah is from New York City. And it's almost as far away. They come from an area where there was no rebellion, there was no Mau Mau. So while his father and his grandmother may well have been nationalists—I'm sure they were—they weren't directly involved in the Mau Mau rebellion.[53]

Overall, in order to do the political work of demonstrating that the malignant, anti-British gene of Mau Mau has found expression in Barack Obama Jr., sources like those discussed here rely equally on their audiences' ignorance of Kenyan political history and their facility with the theme of terrorism, which is an intensely popular trope in American political speech in the post-9/11 era.

Dreaming of Marx and Morel—in Luo

> Barack Obama, Sr., became an important figure in the Kenyan independence movement, but his greatest influence was not in Kenya. Rather, through incredible osmosis he was able to transmit his legacy to his son living in America.
> —Dinesh D'Souza, *The Roots of Obama's Rage*[54]

The Far Right's imperative to merge indictments of Obama's politics, parentage, *and* patrimony was inaugurated during the first year of Obama's presidency by popular media personalities Glenn Beck and Rush Limbaugh, who planted seeds in the minds of their millions of Tea Party–supporting listeners that indictments centered on Obama's imagined engagements with British colonialism—and anticolonial movements—mattered to the present-day politics of the United States.[55] Dinesh D'Souza built most extensively on this foundation, first in a *Forbes* article lavishly praised by Newt Gingrich as offering a "stunning insight" into President Obama's "Kenyan anti-colonial behavior" and for its value as "the most accurate, predictive model for his behavior."[56] With the publication of this article and with the backing of former Speaker of the House Newt Gingrich, who ironically has a PhD in African history (his armchair dissertation lauds the benefits of Belgian colonial rule in the Congo), D'Souza, then president of the King's College in New York, found credibility and fame as a political pundit in 2010.[57]

Given D'Souza's propensity for politically inflected cherry-picking, it is tempting for scholars to dismiss him as a propagandist. However, like that of Corsi, his work has had tremendous popular success—*The Roots of Obama's Rage* spent nearly two months on the *New York Times* best-seller list, and the film *2016: Obama's America* grossed over $33 million at the box office.[58] Here again in D'Souza's work, a vast swath of the American public encounters erroneous depictions of Kenya's past and present, which likely form the entirety of their knowledge of the country. As such, D'Souza's work demands deconstruction.

In his book *The Roots of Obama's Rage*, D'Souza further develops his thesis that Barack Obama Jr. "took to heart" his father's "anti-colonial ideology," and that as a result, "the U.S. is being ruled according to the dreams of a Luo tribesman of the 1950s."[59] His 2012 film, *2016: Obama's America,* expands his revisionist approach by plunking ideologies from 1950s Kenya down on the Obama administration's policy platform. As the trailer for this popular conservative documentary notes, "Obama has a dream. A dream from his father, that the sins of colonialism be set right."[60] Both in print and on film, D'Souza aims to train a revealing lens on the "anticolonial" worldview of Barack Obama Sr. and treats his 1965 journal article, "Problems Facing Our Socialism,"[61] as a strident example of this mentality. Yet, a critical examination of D'Souza's analyses illustrates that his readings of anticolonialism, of Kenya's political and economic history, and of the journal article falter dangerously on both theoretical and historical grounds. These misapprehensions are in turn supported by an underlying neocolonial narrative.

Though it constitutes the bedrock of his arguments about Obama's worldview, D'Souza misunderstands and misplaces anticolonialism. He writes, "Anticolonialsim was the rallying cry of Third World politics for much of the second half of the 20th century. Anticolonialism is the doctrine that rich countries of the West got rich by invading, occupying and looting poor countries of Asia, Africa and South America."[62] In reality, anticolonialism refers not to a "doctrine" predominant in the "second half of the 20th century," but to globalized, sociopolitical *movements*, which peaked in the 1950s and 1960s and took in colonized people's social, economic, and political struggles against the ravages of colonial rule like those noted by D'Souza.[63] Indeed, at the 1945 Pan-African Congress in Manchester, together with twenty-four other delegates from Africa, Kwame Nkrumah, the first president of Ghana, whom D'Souza derides as the avatar of socialism in Africa, and Jomo Kenyatta, the first president of Kenya, whom D'Souza cheers as the vanguard of the free market on the continent, rubbed shoulders in support of the common causes of freeing African colonies from colonial oppression and of improving basic conditions on the continent and among people of African descent worldwide.[64]

Economic restructuring was a key issue that postcolonial African governments struggled with throughout the 1960s. Upon independence in 1963, Kenya found itself wrestling with economic policies, practices, and structures that, as we learned in chapters 2 and 3, had been imposed by the colonial government in order to develop an extractive, export-driven economy that concentrated land and wealth in the hands of white settlers while commerce was controlled largely by the small Asian community. William Ochieng' neatly summarizes the economic situation in early postcolonial Kenya, writing how the nation displayed characteristics typical of an underdeveloped economy at the periphery: the preponderance of foreign capital, the dominance of agriculture, the limited development of industry and the imports of capital and manufactured consumer goods. This underdeveloped state of the economy meant that independent Kenya would have to formulate policies that would not only arrest Kenya's mounting urban and rural poverty and decay, but would also put the economy into the hands of indigenous people.[65]

Given this situation, a primary question confronting President Jomo Kenyatta's government was how to indigenize the economy. In order to spell out its aims and strategies for the economy, in 1965 the government produced Sessional Paper No. 10, titled "African Socialism and Its Application to Planning." Tom Mboya, minister of Planning and Economic Development, wrote the paper with the input of Mwai Kibaki, then an assistant minister. Kenyatta contributed the preface to this paper, whereas, Ochieng' notes, the new president underscored how "the economic approach of the government would be 'dominated' by the desire to ensure the Africanization of the economy and public service."[66]

This paper was produced, as David William Cohen describes, within a particular historical context of "roiling debates in Kenya during the first half of 1965, especially from mid-April to early June, regarding the path that the Kenya government should pursue in regard to economic development and the path that it should pursue amidst east-west tensions and alignment pressures affecting newly independent African governments."[67] It was subject to various critiques, including the article "Problems Facing

Our Socialism," by Barack Obama Sr., which ran in the July 1965 issue of the influential *East Africa Journal*.[68] Obama Sr.'s stated goal regarding Sessional Paper No. 10 was to "follow step by step what has been included in the paper and analyze each point sequentially."[69]

To the limited extent that D'Souza engages these two complementary texts contextually and reads them within the complex historical environment that produced them, his analyses waver on a variety of grounds and lead to significant historical inaccuracies. D'Souza presents Obama's article as a freestanding document, not as a response to Sessional Paper No. 10, thereby tacitly suggesting that African socialism is Obama Sr.'s personal invention.[70] For example, he takes one of Obama Sr.'s statements, "We need to eliminate power structures that have been built through excessive accumulation so that not only a few individuals shall control a vast magnitude of the resources as is the case now," as evidence of a radical "anticolonial" mentality. In fact, this statement both describes the socioeconomic situation of early 1960s Kenya and reflects the Kenyatta government's priority, stated in Sessional Paper No. 10, of economic indigenization in order to rectify the colonial situation in which the "people of Kenya had no voice in government; the nation's resources were organized and developed primarily for the benefit of non-Africans."[71]

Further, by omitting these various levels of documentary and historical context, D'Souza is able to present Obama Sr.'s responsive critiques as independent policy prescriptions. For example, D'Souza writes, "The senior Obama proposed that the state confiscate private land."[72] The established historical record, however, clearly shows that African land tenure had been of particular concern throughout the late colonial period in Kenya, and through a series of laws and the Swynnerton Plan, the colonial government aimed to consolidate and institutionalize individual African landholding and reward those loyal to the colonial state.[73] Decolonization, particularly the deracialization of the White Highlands and the lifting of restrictions on the crops that African farmers could produce, rendered land tenure an even more urgent issue in the 1960s.

Unsurprisingly, Sessional Paper No. 10 offers proposals for dealing with land distribution and ownership. Rather than prescribing blanket confiscation of private land as D'Souza suggests, Obama's article responds to Sessional Paper No.10, asking if the government could achieve consolidation more rapidly through "clan co-operatives" rather than through individual holdings. He added, "If the government should, however, feel that individual ownership is the best policy to take in order to bring development, then it should restrict the size of the farms that can be owned by one individual throughout the country and this should apply to everybody from the President to the ordinary man."[74] In light of the extent to which land ultimately became consolidated in holdings belonging to members of the Kenyatta regime and their families and friends, Obama Sr's suggestion today reads as prescient.[75]

D'Souza also writes that the senior Obama "proposed" that the government "raise taxes with no upper limit" and that he had "insisted that 'theoretically there is nothing that can stop the government from taxing 100% of income so long as the people get benefits from the government commensurate with their income which is taxed.'"[76] Rather than offering a prescription, Obama Sr. was writing both within the historical context of Kenya's deep economic inequality and in the documentary context of Sessional Paper No. 10, a text that highlights "progressive taxation to narrow the gap between rich and poor" as a key tenet of African socialism, but also favors individual savings as a means to accumulate domestic capital.[77] Noting that the vast majority of Kenyans had "such a low per capita income that it is almost impossible for them to save," Obama Sr. highlights taxation as a means of domestic capital accumulation, and in turn as a means to cut reliance on foreign aid.[78] In writing that "theoretically there is nothing that can stop the government from taxing 100% of income," Obama Sr. plays devil's advocate to the sessional paper's tentativeness about taxation, highlighting the need for accountability and for local tax benefits, both of which were absent in the colonial era.[79]

Finally, in ripping Obama Sr's article away from its socioeconomic, political, and historical and documentary contexts, D'Souza fails to acknowledge how the article, and indeed also the sessional paper to which it replied, were part of broad, continent-wide debates about African socialism.[80] These debates were particularly relevant in Kenya as Oginga Odinga, the country's vice president, had avowed socialist leanings. For example, at a moment when the White Highlands were being expropriated to the black Kenyan elite, Odinga mused the value of precolonial Luo land tenure systems based on communalism.[81] Further, the economy of Kenya's close neighbor Tanzania was being reoriented to a model of African socialism called *ujamaa* (familyhood/community) that was developed by Julius Nyerere, Tanzania's first president.[82]

In *The Roots of Obama's Rage*, D'Souza again turns to Obama Sr.'s article, revisiting the topics and themes addressed above, this time reading them through a tribalist lens. Acknowledging in the book that Obama Sr.'s article was "examining the premises of Mboya's paper," D'Souza depicts Sessional Paper No. 10 as Mboya's personal production rather than as an official statement by Kenyatta's administration. D'Souza locates the production of the sessional paper and Obama Sr.'s article within a "tribalist" history in which Luo socialism is placed next to "the free-market capitalism" of the Kikuyu, and Mboya's benign "African" socialism is offered as the lesser of the two Luo evils, a counterpoint to Oginga Odinga's "Soviet-style socialism."

The bluntness with which D'Souza handles African socialism and the ahistorical way he treats anticolonialism come together in his musings on colonialism. He writes, "Colonialism today is a dead issue. No one cares about it except the man in the White House."[83] However, it is clear that D'Souza himself cares very much about colonialism, as his book offers a loosely veiled apologia for it. The development of a story in which "anticolonialism" is the driving force behind the "dreams" and actions of Obama is supported by an underlying narrative suggesting that colonialism is the natural, normal order of things and, ergo, that *anti*colonialism is the pathological condition. He writes, "Empire is nothing new in world history."[84] Borrowing (without crediting) the title of early twentieth-century activist Edmund Morel's exposé of the atrocities in King Leopold's Belgian Congo, D'Souza titles one of his chapters "The Black Man's Burden."[85] Yet, his analysis of empire is more in the tradition of Rudyard Kipling's famous poem "The White Man's Burden," complete with heroic, outnumbered British soldiers protecting (white) settlers from "new caught sullen peoples, half devil, half child."[86]

This attitude emerges especially strongly in D'Souza's analysis of a key moment of Kenyan history—Mau Mau. Offering his own riff on the return of the Churchill bust, D'Souza does not gloss over the atrocities of Mau Mau. Rather, he offers a justification for British brutality, noting that the reason for the scope and scale of British violence is "obvious." He writes, "By the end of the nineteenth century, the small island of England controlled a worldwide empire. It had to maintain this empire through a very small distribution of soldiers and settlers living abroad, in every case outnumbered by the natives."[87] Continuing to normalize colonial violence, D'Souza adds that the British response to Mau Mau was not unusual "because colonial powers have used their powers to crush such revolts," and offers as an example the 1857 Sepoy rebellion in his native India, during which the British put down a revolt by their crack Indian troops.[88] The British colonial state's use of internment camps during the Anglo-Boer War in early twentieth-century South Africa and during the anticolonial insurgency in Malaya that preceded Mau Mau by a few years provides much more apt historical parallels.

Finally, D'Souza dismisses the rebellion from Kenyan popular consciousness, noting that "though Kenya became independent in 1963, few people remember the Mau Mau rebellion today."[89] This statement is not only historically inaccurate but deeply ironic, given that in building a history of Mau Mau he relies heavily on recent books by David Anderson and Caroline Elkins, works whose interview data demonstrate that many Kenyans remember Mau Mau all too well and that the Mau Mau reparations case we addressed in chapter 2 was already under way at the time D'Souza was writing.

This interpretation reinforces the pathological nature of Obama's proposed second-generation obsession with Mau Mau and the supposed "anticolonial" mind-set that this fixation has allegedly stimulated. It locates the historical significance of Kenya's experience with colonialism not in the ravages of colonial rule or in the achievement of independence, but in the benefits brought by colonial rule. D'Souza explains, "Even using the colonial model, one could say that former colonies that have democratic governments have them because of the example impressed on them by the former colonial powers; there is no other reason why Kenya should have a parliamentary system of government and judges who wear white wigs."[90] In D'Souza's estimation, rather than lending support to Obama's contention that "when we seek to impose democracy with the barrel of a gun" we are "setting ourselves up for failure," the Kenyan experience of colonialism—Mau Mau and all—contradicts it.[91]

For their part, Kenyans at home and in the diaspora have evidenced little patience either with Far Right narratives of their history or with the politics of such revisionist interpretations of Kenya's past. In fact, when Corsi descended upon Nairobi in October 2008 to launch the *Obama Nation* book tour, he was quickly arrested and subsequently deported for attempting to publicize his book without a work permit.[92] Articulating the sentiment underpinning the wananchi's broad support for the deportation, one Kenyan commentator explained, "If you must insult black people, do not try to do it in the black people's own homestead."[93] More lightly, but still pointedly, shortly after a spring 2010 Tea Party rally at the Capitol during which protesters challenging Obama's American "belonging" carried signs emblazoned with slogans like "Somewhere in Kenya a Village is Missing its Idiot!" and "Go Back to Kenya!" the Embassy of Kenya threw its own "Tea Party," hosted by then deputy prime minister Uhuru Kenyatta, with the dual purposes of promoting the country's status as the world's largest tea exporter and of giving Washingtonians an opportunity to "experience a proper Kenyan tea party on Capitol Hill."[94]

In sum, books like *The Obama Nation* and *The Roots of Obama's Rage*, and media like those examined here, offer not simply examples of the American Far Right's approaches to Obama and Kenya in particular and Africa more generally, but also of how history can be manipulated for political ends when the sources used to write it are severed from context and when it is framed according to "hot-button" tropes that resonate with an audience largely ignorant of the historical topics and trajectories under consideration. Despite the inaccuracy and extremism of their claims—they actually fall in the middle of a conservative spectrum that has conspiracy theory sites like wnd.com and InfoWars.com at the farthest right end. However, as noted above, Corsi's and D'Souza's productions and similar media have evidenced too much commercial success to be dismissed out of hand as the mistaken rantings of ultimately marginal figures. In dialogue with one another, these books and films help to shape an Internet echo chamber in which rumors and misreadings take on the appearance of "fact." For example, *WND*'s review of D'Souza's film ran under the headline "Does Obama Really Hate America?" and suggested that "if D'Souza is right that Obama has concealed a raging anti-colonialist worldview in a false cloak of Ivy-league liberalism, then many of the Internet's wildest rumors could prove legitimate."[95] Overall, however problematic these texts may be for scholars, they signal the broader trend toward the commodification of history and identity.[96]

The Far Right's colonial visions of Kenyan history and Obama's place in it invite the questions of what long-term effects politically interested revisionism will have on popular understandings of Kenya's past and present and what work such understandings will do ultimately. In the next chapter we turn away from the US politics of condemnation and back to the Kenyan politics of celebration to capture another brand of historical entrepreneurship, albeit with a very different political tone and substance. These Kenyan histories—which also situate the Obama family in places and spaces to which they do not belong to serve local and national political ends—likewise demand scrutiny.

5

The Politics of Celebration

Ethnic Grandeur and Obama's Heroic Embrace

In April 2004, Walter Gor looked up from his cup of tea in the small Western Kenya village of Lela and asked, "Who is this American boy we are hearing about whose father is from Siaya?"[1] At the end of a two-hour-long discussion about Kenya's colonial history and the origins of the Luo Union, this seemed like an odd and misplaced question. Sensing the confusion, Gor, a member of the Luo Council of Elders (LCE), elaborated, "Yes, you know, the one from Chicago who is contesting a seat in Parliament?"[2] Faithful students of Kenyan politics, we were nonetheless stumped by his queries. We thought to ourselves, *An American from Chicago running for the Kenyan Parliament? But it is not even an election year in Kenya!* Exhausted at the end of a long day of intensive interviews about colonial Kenya and slightly embarrassed by our lack of knowledge about US links to the region, we simply replied that we did not know.

We realized a few months later that we had missed a prime opportunity to engage with the early Kenyan roots of what grew into full-fledged "Obamamania." Having spent the first several months of 2004 alternately buried in colonial documents at the Kenya National Archives (KNA) and traversing the country to do oral histories on various topics in Kenya's past, we had not been following the American media's tracking of

Obama's meteoric rise from representing Chicago as a state senator, to nominee for an open US Senate seat in Illinois, to emerging political star of the Democratic Party. Our April interview with Gor came a few months before Obama's keynote address at the 2004 Democratic National Convention, which introduced the young senatorial candidate onto the national political scene in the United States and drew global attention to his paternal roots in Kenya.[3] In the wake of Obama's overwhelming victory in the Democratic primary in Illinois, Kenyans embraced him as a "son of the soil" in ways very different from how the candidate himself positioned his relationship to his Kenyan heritage. Remarking in a March 18, 2004, *New York Times* article, Obama presented himself as American first and African American second: "I have an unusual name and an exotic background, but my values are essentially American. . . . I'm rooted in the African-American community, but I'm not limited by it. I think this election shows that."[4]

Obama's message in the *New York Times* was a clear attempt to highlight his mainstream American "belonging," and to thus legitimize him politically as a serious contender for national office in the United States. Africa figured only in the hyphenated, secondary identity of "African-American," and Kenya not at all. However, in Lela, some fifty kilometers away from the Obama family homestead in Kogelo, Walter Gor and others did not need the American media or US political pundits to place Barack Jr. into popular narratives of Kenyan history. Since early 2004, the Kenyan state and the *wananchi* (citizens), particularly Luo from Western Kenya, had been actively engaged in fitting Obama into local history long before US media began describing him as a "son of a Kenyan goat herder."[5] From popular narratives in the Kenyan press to local interpretations used to market Luoland to the global tourist market, histories emanating from Western Kenya have had political and socioeconomic applications. Their tone and goals, however, have been radically different from the Far Right forays into Kenyan history discussed in the last chapter.

"Obamamania"

In Kenya, culture brokers—state officials and Luo elders and amateur historians alike—have employed selective narratives in order to claim Obama as a "son of the soil." Mobilizing print and digital media, oral histories, and cultural monuments, state officials have aimed to weave Obama into the contested narrative of Kenyan nationhood, while Luo elders have focused on Obama in order to stake claims to political power and market Luo identity to a mass audience.[6] Here the tone is not one of condemnation, but widely celebratory, explaining Obama's political ascendancy in the United States through local ethnopolitical histories. Reading Obama's connections to Kenya through the local politics of "belonging," by 2008, Kenyans were asking if it was indeed possible that "a Luo may be president of the United States before a Luo becomes president of Kenya."[7]

In 2004, expectations of how the election of a "Luo" to the United States Senate might change the socioeconomic landscape of Nyanza began to be articulated months in advance of Obama's senatorial election. By the fall of 2004, enthusiasm for Obama's election reached fever pitch among Luo populations across Kenya as people plied the busy Westlands *matatu* (minibus) route in a vehicle christened "Obama" and swapped their home-brewed *chang'aa* for East African Breweries Limited's new "Senator" brand beer that was aptly and instantly redubbed "Obama."[8]

Given the importance of patronage in contemporary Kenyan politics, it is not surprising that speculation about what Obama's senatorial election might mean to the remote reaches of Luoland had accompanied the excitement surrounding Obama's rise.[9] Commenting to a *USA Today* reporter on the indirect benefits expected with an Obama victory, candidate Obama's uncle argued, "In order to develop, we need aid from the International Monetary Fund and the World Bank. The U.S. Senate carries a huge amount of weight, so it is important that one of our own will be there."[10] Outside the Obama family, the connections were even less subtle and more directly interpreted through the local politics of patronage. For example, Kisumu resident Frederick Otieno noted succinctly, "We will get support from America, as Africans, as Kenyans and particularly as Luo."[11]

Upon Obama's election to the US Senate, jubilation swept Western Kenya, and Luos expressed their hopes that his election would render Western Kenyan communities "Illinois, Kenya Chapter."[12] Rural residents across the region continued to articulate their demands of the newly famous member of the Luo diaspora through calls for public works projects and jobs, the sorts of goods that could typically be expected to accompany the election of a "kinsman" to a Kenyan political office. One man stated simply, "If Obama will be giving funding to his State, we request that he sends a small percentage."[13] Another man stipulated, "Now that our son has won, we can look forward to better roads, improved health and educational facilities since we know he can provide us all that."[14]

As many Luo people articulated their material expectations after Obama's election, they drew on images of power and ethnic responsibilities first cultivated by the Luo Union in colonial Kenya and further realized by the postcolonial politics of regional-ethnic favoritism. Predicting a future visit to the region involving all the pomp and circumstance appropriate to that of a visiting dignitary of note, one young man explained, "We expect him [Obama] to fly into Nyangoma-Kogelo by helicopter soon. In fact we have identified a spot where it will land."[15] These statements demonstrate the belief that infrastructure in rural Western Kenya would be upgraded, and also reflect the common knowledge that the Kenyan political elite frequently travel in opulence unimaginable to the average Kenyan. People brought up "flight" in a more abstract sense as well, expressing their hopes that Obama could facilitate local people's flight from the poverty of Western Kenya to a better life in America. One man asserted, "Obama should now start planning on how some of our people from this village and all over Kenya can go to America and work."[16] And perhaps, reimagining the Mboya "airlifts" that we learned about in chapters 3 and 4, a self-professed friend of Barack Obama Sr. insisted, "I don't see why his son cannot airlift my children to America."[17]

In sum, the wild excitement in Kenya surrounding Obama's senatorial election showed the wide definition of Luoness forged in the colonial period and the patrimonial character of postcolonial politics to be mutually reinforcing in contemporary Kenya. Due to the history of political marginalization, in particular the detentions of political leaders like Oginga and Raila Odinga and the assassinations of Tom Mboya and Robert Ouko that chapter 3 explores, Luos across Kenya believed that they needed a patron to develop and protect their interests, and they were willing to cast a wide net, even into the diaspora, to find such a Big Man. As one reporter for the *Daily Nation* neatly summarized, many Luo "had vested in Senator Obama the attributes expected from a local MP."[18]

Even before his first official visit to Kenya in 2006, Obama sought to dispel expectations that his election in the United States had necessarily rendered him a Luo patron. As the *Daily Nation* reported in late 2004, "US Senator-elect Barack Obama says he cannot bring development to Kenya. He told a delegation of Kenyan community leaders in Detroit and Chicago that no favours should be expected from him."[19] He sought to reinforce this message during his official trip two years later. He criticized patrimonial politics generally, speaking out against rampant governmental corruption in Kenya in a highly publicized speech at the University of Nairobi that earned him the anger of the Kibaki regime, particularly that of its ambassador to the United States. Casting accusations that put him at odds with local interpretations, he argued to a packed Taifa Hall at the downtown University of Nairobi campus:

> Finally, ethnic-based tribal politics has to stop. It is rooted in the bankrupt idea that the goal of politics or business is to funnel as much of the pie as possible to one's family, tribe, or circle with little regard for the public good. It stifles innovation and fractures the fabric of the society. Instead of opening businesses and engaging in commerce, people come to rely on patronage and payback as a means of advancing. Instead of unifying the country to move forward on solving problems, it divides neighbor from neighbor.[20]

Obama also forcefully addressed expectations about his own capacities. During an interview with the *Daily Nation*, he was asked how he had handled the "high expectations of what [he] could do for Kenya now that [he is] a senator." In reply, he dismissed his singularity, noting, "In terms of expectations, I've to explain very early on that I am just one senator out of a hundred senators. Ultimately decisions about programs, projects, are made in collaboration, by persons other than myself. I don't have a chequebook where I can write a cheque directly for the US Treasury."[21] He reiterated these sentiments in the documentary *Senator Obama Goes to Africa*. Continuing to advance his anticorruption platform, he explained how he had aimed both to make it clear during his 2006 visit to Kenya that his role as a senator was to facilitate relations between the United States and Kenya and to disabuse people of the notion that he might have arrived with "bunches of money" to hand around.[22] A letter to the editor of the *Daily Nation* suggests that Obama's message did not go unheeded. The author wrote, "The idea of goodies flowing from the US to our country is ridiculous. Kenyans must work at improving their own lives. Leaders have an even bigger challenge to emulate the Obama vision."[23]

As much as Obama's political rise fueled the hopes of Luo politics at home, his ascendancy also highlighted the familiar history of political and social marginalization. In the colonial and early postcolonial past, high-achieving Luo, as Lesa Morrison points out, "were not only notable, but they stood out—quite literally physically—in the society."[24] This singularity emerged hand in hand with a certain degree of sociopolitical exclusion. In an interesting twist across time and space, critiques of Obama in the international arena, and especially in the United States, have been cast in much the same terms as the exclusion of Luos in Kenya. As James Howard Smith explains, "Non-Luo have justified Luos' marginalization from politics by arguing that they are somehow foreign: their language is exotic, they eat mainly fish (a major aspect of Luo ethnic identity) and their men are uncircumcised. Many have asserted that because Luo men are uncircumcised, they are not fully adult, and their immaturity makes them ill-suited to participate in national politics."[25]

By the winter of 2008, when it was clear that Obama was now vying for the Democratic nomination for the presidency, Kenyan interpretations at home and abroad were both celebratory and divisive due to the increasingly volatile politics of ethnicity. In the wake of the contested Kenyan election, which had seen a Luo and a Kikuyu wrangling for the presidency in December 2007 and the dramatic violence that followed, Kenyan political discourse began to reflect both local histories of Luo exclusion and contemporary realities of ethnic politics. Commentary in digital fora discussing the heated Democratic primary races in the United States noted that many Luo in Kenya voiced their support for Obama, while non-Luo, especially Kikuyu, enthusiastically supported Hillary Clinton.[26] A discussion thread on the popular diaspora blog site Mashada.com even posed the question "Will Kikuyu Americans vote for Obama?"[27] A few posters construed their responses along ethnic lines. For example, one poster expounded, "Majority of kikuyu are campaigning for sen hillary clinton and praying day and night for sen barak obama to loose because they cant rig election in usa the way they did in kenya. Kikuyus are known thieves and their no. 1 thief is emilio mwai kibaki."[28]

However, the overall tone of the thread was reflected in the reply to the above remark in an attempt to downplay the role of ethnicity in the Kenyan diaspora: "WHAT? Such sentiments shock me at times! Am kyuk and Obama is my guy!!!"[29] Another poster rounded out the discussion, reading "Folks, there's no kyuk or luo voter here (nor should there be anywhere!). It's either Obama or the other guys. And if Obama loses, then much love to the winner. I'll act grown up and live with it!!"[30] And again such sentiments were expressed in the Kenyan press. As one letter writer argued, "Kenyans are not happy with Sen. Barack Obama just because he was fathered by a Kenyan. If our support for Obama was merely ethnic-based, only a section of Kenyans would be rooting for the Senator because the rest don't share his ethnic background."[31]

In early November 2008 the question "Will there be a Luo in the White House before there is a Luo in the State House?" was answered. Obama's victory was not a surprise to anyone in Kisumu, where a mock election preceding the official one gave Obama a landslide victory.[32] It was not just Luos, but Kenyans as a nation, who toasted Obama's victory with even more zeal than did his supporters in the United States as "Senator" beer sold out across the country.[33] More soberly, Kenyans lauded the peaceful transfer of power. Celebrations were official, as the Kenyan government declared a national day off, "Obama Day," and East African Breweries launched a special release of their popular Senator beer, under the elevated title of "President Lager."[34] Beyond these political and commercial attempts to market Kenya's connection to the newly elected American president, efforts to "cash in" on Obama's ascendancy spread throughout the country. From T-shirts and other Obama memorabilia widely available across local markets to an increasing number of babies christened with names like Barack, Michelle, Sasha, and Malia—the symbolism of these real and imagined connections sparked new narratives of Kenya's contested past produced to market the importance of local and regional histories.[35]

Figure 5.1. "Congratulations Barack Obama: Love and Peace has been granted to us by God." This *leso* (wrap) has been sold across East Africa since the 2008 US election. Photo by Emma Burr.

Luo Incorporated: Monuments, Tourism, and Diaspora

> Intangible cultural heritage . . . transmitted from generation to generation, is constantly recreated by communities and groups in response to their environment, their interaction with nature and their history, and provides them with a sense of identity and continuity.[36]

Across Kenya, Obama's status as a "son of the soil" has been unquestioned. Under the National Museums and Heritage Act, which provides for the "protection, conservation, and transmission of the cultural and natural heritage of Kenya," the national government gazetted the village of Kogelo, location of the Obama family homestead, as a protected national heritage site.[37] The following sections of this chapter engage the diverse "heritage work" concerning the Obama family that has been undertaken by culture brokers, ranging from government officials to local ethnic entrepreneurs, in Western Kenya since 2009. Tracing the development of the array of heritage-based enterprises that have grown up around the Obama family and their Kenyan roots shows how, to borrow from Derek Peterson, Kodzo Gavua, and Ciraj Rassool, "heritage work" constitutes a key space in which "ideas about tradition, patrimony, and authenticity are debated and defined."[38] In Luoland, with the history of the Obama family at the center, such work has transformed local narratives of Luo diasporic affinity and belonging into a basis for international ties and into a brand to be marketed to a global audience. On a popular level, by the summer of 2009, Kisumu, Western Kenya's principal city, was solidly gripped by "Obamamania," awash with both paraphernalia and discussions of the benefits the Obama presidency might bring to the region and the country. From government efforts to improve rural infrastructure in the Obama family's village of Kogelo to hotel expansions in Kisumu, local interpretations of these projects were often filtered through a bold government prediction that the region would witness a 10–15 percent jump in international tourism.[39] However, while many local residents were eager to transform Western Kenya into an international tourist destination, others interpreted government efforts within a more personal connection with the US president and his family roots in the region. For instance, in response to a state project to lengthen the runway at the Kisumu airport, a number of informants casually quipped that "Air Force One will now have a place to land."[40]

Yet, despite this clear desire to claim Obama for Kenyan development, his particular function within ethnic and national histories has been more complicated. The Kisumu branch of the National Museums of Kenya provided a ripe terrain for examining state and local concerns of how to represent the Obama story within local histories. Situated in the urban heart of Luoland, the Kisumu branch museum exhibits the flora and fauna of Western Kenya, with the museum's cultural displays focusing on the Luo community and the "mythical descendants of Ramogi."[41] Representing the local histories of identity and belonging common across regional affiliates of the National Museums of Kenya, the Kisumu branch has also attracted increasing numbers of international tourists newly drawn to Western Kenyan by an interest in the history of the Obama family.[42] As of the summer of 2016, an exhibit devoted to President Obama and his Kenyan family had yet to be developed. The potential for such an exhibit in Kisumu and Kogelo and the associated issue of how to best situate the president's familial history within wider regional and national narratives were, however, the subject of much discussion among museum curators and staff.

Though enthusiastic about rising interest in the museum and in Luo culture and history more generally, curators and staff expressed concerns about implicit and explicit pressures to "distill local knowledge into a brand" and sell it to an expanding and diversifying audience.[43] First was the issue that the expectations brought by local visitors to an Obama exhibit might be colored by styles of local history strong on ethnic patriotism and hagiography like those discussed in chapter 3; they could demand a celebratory portrayal of Luos overall and the Obama family in particular. Second was the direct pressure—emanating from influential political circles—to officially represent the Obama family's history with a reverential respect that glossed over the more checkered elements of the life history of Barack Obama Sr., such as his problems with alcohol and his tumultuous career in the Kenyan civil service that we learned about in chapter 3. Museum employees revealed that they were coaxed after the 2008 US election to be sure the Obama family history was told according to local conventions of patriotism, particularly emphasizing the connection to the historic and broader migratory origins of the Luo diaspora in South Sudan while ignoring any focus on election violence, or Mau Mau–inspired colonial histories that the American Far Right has so eagerly repackaged.[44]

Yet, the problems of how Obama histories should be pitched and packaged are not confined to the Kisumu branch museum. Since late 2008, government directives like that officially making Kogelo a national heritage site have evidenced a clear goal of marketing the cultural history of Western Kenya to an international audience.[45] In early 2009 the position of "Cultural Development Manager" for Kogelo was created, a position that at the time did not exist for any other community in Kenya.[46] This post, sponsored directly by the Office of the Vice President, was part of a larger initiative of the Ministry of State for National Heritage and Culture to develop Kogelo in support of Kenya Visions 2030, the country's new development blueprint, which aims to make "Kenya among the top ten long haul tourist destinations."[47] The symbolism of using heritage to attract international investment and remittances was not confined to the discourse of tourism and even reached the floor of Parliament. In 2010, during a debate about repatriating Kenyan cultural artifacts from US museums, Boni Khalwale, member of Parliament (MP) for Ikolomani, clearly evoked the connection between cultural heritage and political patronage, noting, "The biggest artefact in the USA today that belongs to this country is one Barack Obama. How does he intend to repatriate himself or part of the money that is realized from all the royalties that he is attracting all over the world."[48]

In a related vein, in November 2008, a delegation led by then minister of tourism Najib Balala and including other high-profile politicians descended on Kogelo and announced that the Kenyan state planned to build a multimillion-shilling museum and cultural center in Kogelo.[49] Loosely reminiscent of presidential libraries in the United States, the Kogelo center is intended to house documents pertaining not merely to the history of the Obama family, but to the Kogelo subclan more generally, as well as "artifacts and works" belonging to Barack Obama Sr.[50] Mobilizing UNESCO (United Nations Educational, Scientific, and Cultural Organization) rhetoric, the minister of state for national heritage and culture, William Ole Ntimama, noted that his ministry planned to develop the Kogelo Community Cultural Center "not only to serve as a cultural centre but also to promote and safeguard intangible cultural heritage."[51] In turn, Luo patrimony was performed at the Obama Kogelo Cultural Festival, held at the Senator Obama Kogelo Primary School in mid-January 2010, to mark the first year in office of "the 44th President of America who traces his cultural roots in Nyang'oma Kogelo village Kenya."[52] While these grand visions of diaspora remittances and tourists flocking to Kogelo on Obama "heritage" tours did not immediately materialize, by 2011 the new Kogelo Cultural and Tourism Information Office housed a number of local businesses selling souvenirs to the estimated 150 local and international visitors that Kogelo village receives on a weekly basis.[53]

Overall, the inhabitants of Western Kenya heartily embraced Obama. As journalist Philip Ochieng pithily put it on the eve of the presidential inauguration and at the height of Obamamania, "As far as the Luo are concerned, Barack Obama is 200 per cent Luo."[54] However, in many instances Luos have greeted development initiatives dependent on the commodification of history with some reluctance and suspicion since government projects were all but absent from Kogelo before 2008. For example, res-

Figure 5.2. Senator Obama Kogelo Secondary School, a short walk from the Obama homestead in Kogelo. Photo by author.

idents of Kogelo were shocked that a cultural development manager had been appointed with no prior consultation with the Kogelo community and were suspicious when the manager starting making her rounds.[55]

The commodification of history has also been keenly experienced at the Senator Obama Kogelo Secondary School, renamed in 2006 to celebrate Obama's visit to Kenya and site of the Obama Kogelo Cultural Festival.[56] Despite the state's grand plans for the material memorialization of Luo history, curious tourists arriving in Western Kenya since 2009 have had very little to see by way of the Obama family's history. As a result, they have decamped unannounced to Obama Secondary. As English teacher Samuel Opondo commented, everyone from foreign dignitaries to international tourists and local politicians "arrive without an appointment. . . . We have to receive them as they have traveled a long distance, but it makes teaching very difficult."[57]

Read within the interpenetrated contexts of Obama's ascendancy and Tom Mboya's illustrious "airlifts," the preponderance of visitors to Senator Obama Kogelo Secondary School also serves to create untenable expectations among many students and their families about the advantages of attending a school named after the foremost "son of the soil." As Opondo noted, the consistent presence of visitors "falsely raises the students' hopes of scholarship opportunities."[58] A group interview with twenty students further confirmed their teacher's view, as many expressed that they felt pressure from family and friends to attend and that they were expected to be awarded university scholarships to the United States upon graduation. Others complained that they had to spend long hours trying to convince family and friends as to why the school charged tuition at all. One student recounted her uncle's insistent query: "I'm sure the president himself will pay the school fees of students from his namesake?"[59] While the Obama links to Kogelo and Kenya have been championed by the national government, local political actors with roots in the colonial past have also situated Obama's "belonging" within their own local and diasporic claims to political power.

With Obama's 2004 senatorial victory and the fresh touristic interest in Western Kenya, the LCE mobilized narratives of both distant precolonial migration and more contemporary political histories in a broader project of ethnic "branding." As we saw in chapter 3, the contemporary work of LCE is rooted in the colonial activities of the Luo Union and reflects long-standing attempts by cultural brokers and amateur historians to package Luo history in grand reverence. At the same moment, the organization has endeavored to retain control over the modes and meanings of Luoness in an environment in which "ethnicity is also becoming more corporate, more commodified, more implicated in the economics of everyday life."[60] The contentious nature of these aims emerged in high relief at a July 2009 meeting of the LCE's Maseno West branch at Kit Mikayi, a religious and cultural site marked by a picturesque boulder formation towering just off the busy Kisumu-Bondo highway.[61]

As residents from farms near Kit Mikayi came forward to collect from the day's visitors a set entry fee to the site, LCE members (a contingent composed primarily of former local government officials) swooped forward, intercepted them, and commenced a heated argument over who had

Figure 5.3. Members of the Luo Council of Elders, with Kit Mikayi in the background, 2009. Photo by author.

rights to profit from this particular piece of the Luo past. The LCE members pushed their way onto the grounds, asserting that "Kit Mikayi belongs to the whole community and thus only the whole community should benefit from it."[62]

Having asserted themselves as broad custodians of Luo cultural heritage, LCE members reclaimed Kit Mikayi in the name of moral ethnic development. Commencing first with a prayer that marked the site's spiritual significance, the LCE then proceeded with a detailed work of historical theater, which paid homage to local notions of Obama's "belonging." In an oral narrative titled "A Brief History of the Rock," ex-chief and local teacher James Gwada repackaged the common story of the fifteenth- and sixteenth-century Luo migrations to Kenya from as far as South Sudan. However, while the mythical journeys of Luo ancestors are often locally retold, Gwada made a specific point to emphasize a certain stream of this migration. In retelling the origin stories of Luo communities in Western Kenya, Gwada deliberately highlighted the centrality of Alego—Obama's ancestral home area—to Luo migratory histories, thus rendering him a

The Politics of Celebration | 109

legitimate "son of the soil." Gwada went further, emphasizing the relationship between Kit Mikayi, Kogelo, and journeys of Ramogi (the mythic original ancestor of Kenyan Luo). He declaimed that Ramogi's direct descendants had been told to "settle on the land with many hills and rocks" and emphasized that the elders were the ones entrusted with their protection.[63] To wide assent offered by the nearly fifty LCE members present, Gwada asserted that LCE was the logical caretaker of the site and outlined a larger plan to build a museum and guesthouse so that "key artifacts are displayed for [future] studies."[64]

The incident at Kit Mikayi was not isolated, but rather part of a longer conflict in which LCE members were pressuring neighboring landowners and lobbying government officials to declare Kit Mikayi officially a national monument and to prevent locals from collecting entrance fees.[65] Throughout the Kit Mikayi conflict and beyond, the LCE has set itself up as both the official arbiter of Luo culture and the marketer of Luoness, harkening to its 2001 constitution, which stipulates that the LCE represents the "apex for guidance of the entire Luo Community," whose work is to "restore, regularize, update, consolidate, propagate, disseminate, defend and protect the time tested Luo culture."[66] The view was rearticulated by LCE secretary general Gilbert Ogutu that the organization's head (ker) should be regarded as royalty, similar to the kabaka (king) of Buganda, and serve as the ultimate "defender of norms and values" for the whole Luo community.[67]

The LCE's narrative of the Luo past has not been confined to merely staking out culture and politics at the local level. Rather, "homegrown" Luo histories have offered a vehicle by which to critique national politics and have served to link the Luo past to urgent issues of geopolitical import, from the ascendancy of Obama to the emergence of South Sudan. For example, when parsing popular historical discourse about Obama, journalist David Kazia noted, "Public descriptions of Obama sound like a recycling of phrases used of men like the Odingas, Tom Mboya, Apollo Milton Obote, Kabalega and Labongo before him."[68] This list of names operates both as a recitation of the patriotic and patriarchal Luo diasporic past and as a cautionary tale about how Luo speakers have been eliminated from the upper echelons of political power through military coups, assassinations, and political marginalization. In a similar vein, discussing the Mau Mau era, LCE chairman Riaga noted, "If you look into history, without Odinga (Sr.), Kenyatta could have died in jail. But he insisted that without him, there would be no Kenya. He made Kenyatta a gift of Kenya. But when Kenyatta became president, his first plan was to eliminate the Luo from power."[69]

The LCE's recent narratives of the Luo past have also worked to extend the scope and significance of the Kenyan Luo community in particular and of Luo "male stars" more broadly.[70] For example, in a 2004 interview, Riaga reiterated the opinion common among LCE leadership that claims the Kenyan Luo under a broad umbrella of the bulk of Nilotic speakers from Uganda to Egypt.[71] Indeed, in a 2001 keynote address to the LCE, the organization's secretary general went so far as to link the origins to the biblical exodus of the Israelites from Egypt.[72]

While these glorified and patriotic accounts linking Obama loosely to the distant Luo past might not stand up to close archaeological or linguistic scrutiny, the grand vision of the broader Luo community of East Africa has linked Nilotic Lwo–speaking communities in more tangible ways. As early as 1927, the newly formed Luo Language Committee (LLC), which was based in Kenya and led by emerging ethnic patriots such as B. A. Ohanga, Paul Mboya, and Achieng Oneko, was concerned not only with the standardization of Dholuo but also with creating connections among the greater Nilotic Luo–speaking diaspora of Eastern and Central Africa.[73] Two decades later, Ohanga traveled to Uganda, Congo, and the Sudan in an effort to make cultural-linguistic connections with other Lwo-speaking groups. Leaders of these societies expressed a strong sense of shared history and common identity, which was echoed by Ohanga and Luo Union members. For instance, when Ohanga visited leaders of the Acholi Association in Uganda, its chairman stated in clear diasporic terms that he "wished the Luo to be informed that in fact their neighbors in Uganda had not forgotten them. . . . If any Luo cared to go back to their land of origin, they would be well received."[74] A closer connection between Nilotic Luo speakers was subsequently championed by the LLC and promoted in the Luo Union publication *Ramogi*.[75]

When, six decades later, LCE informants recounted the popular narrative of Luo origins in the southern Sudan in 2004, it was often accompanied by more contemporary political statements such as "You know,

Figure 5.4. Luo Council of Elders chairman Riaga Ogallo, center, with LCE members, June 18, 2009. Photo by author.

Garang is our friend."[76] Referring specifically to the now deceased leader of the South Sudanese secessionist movement, John Garang, recent efforts by LCE reveal the ways a shared Luo historical narrative is employed to bolster the political community at "home" by claiming historic links to political luminaries "abroad." In May 2009, the LCE consummated these implied ties by officially installing Garang's successor and first president of South Sudan, Salva Kiir, as a Luo elder. The event coincided with a ceremony that awarded the South Sudanese president an honorary degree at the Great Lakes University of Kisumu after he reportedly donated some $100,000 to the university to construct a hall in honor of Garang. According to local press reports of the event, LCE chairman Riaga Ogallo remarked to Kiir, "We are bestowing you with these honours because you are one of our most respected sons. You are a Luo like us, it is only that you remained in Sudan as we trekked south to Kenya."[77]

In the wake of this vibrant reaffirmation of diasporic political ties, Riaga Ogallo and LCE members were asked again in 2009 about their recent activities. Meeting LCE officials outside the Luo Union–built Ofafa Memorial Hall in Kisumu, Ogallo was literally crowned with evidence of his new political ties. Sporting a hat adorned with the South Sudanese flag and the political slogan "New Sudan," Ogallo and other LCE officials had recently returned from a weeklong visit to Juba, where they reportedly held extended talks with Kiir and other political leaders.[78] Thus, clearly emboldened by both the continued excitement of a "Luo in the White House" and the renewed friendship with their linguistic neighbors in South Sudan, it is no surprise that LCE officials have been keen to assert their cultural legitimacy throughout Western Kenya in the wake of an Obama presidency.

This "Nilotic embrace" has served to shore up Obama's "belonging" even further and has inspired others not only to link Obama's ascendancy to the contemporary political fortunes of South Sudan but to assign him a broader place with the royal lineages of East Africa's distant past.[79] Indeed, after interviews with the LCE leadership, Kazia was prompted to write of the Ugandan Bunyoro-Kitara kingdom, "Some 628 years ago, a time barely thought of now, the seeds of Obama's ascendancy to the world stage were sown here."[80] Whether or not these accounts of the Luo past would withstand close scrutiny, they offer prime exemplars of local attempts to brand Luo identity within ancient royal reverence. As Cohen and Odhiambo have explained, "Historical accounts within Western Kenya" should be read as "intensely negotiated and arbitrated."[81] It is through such histories that "the past is brought to bear on the untangling and resolution of a variety of conflicts."[82]

Toward a Popular History of Obama and Kenya

From museum exhibits and cultural monuments to memorabilia and heritage tours, efforts to claim Obama have reshaped the popular oral and written histories of Kenya in a variety of ways. Since 2008, the commodification of Kenyan history and Luo identity has transcended the discourse of tourism and identity in Western Kenya and even moved beyond the pages of the popular press. Scanning the bookshelves of bookshops and libraries in Nairobi or Kisumu, one can even encounter an increasing body of children's literature that reinforces many of the notions of Obama as both "Kenyan" and "Luo." These texts market the US president with a patriotic reverence usually reserved for his most ardent political supporters at home. Using both the language of ethnicity and Kenyan nationalism, these texts make Obama into an uncritical hero and role model for Kenyan youth in ways similar to the portrayals of Kenyan political luminaries like Odinga, Mboya, and Kenyatta found in popular histories produced for young audiences.[83] Lila Luce's *Barack Obama: Yes, We Can!* describes the ways in which Obama was both welcomed and worshipped in Kenya. Communicating to her "young adult" audience, she describes a roadside portrait during his 2006 visit where, "in the picture, Barack had a glow around his head, almost like a halo. . . . On the painting were the words '*Waruaki, Dala*,' Dholuo for 'We welcome you home.'"[84]

Even though the influence of the Obama presidency on the wider historiography of Kenya is still fairly new, it is evident already that the Kenyan/Luo past has been used alternately to reinforce and combat political aspirations at home and abroad and to market Western Kenya on a global scale. As shown above, the majority of Kenyan efforts since 2004 have worked to claim Obama in grand diasporic splendor, and these diverse local narratives have reinforced the celebratory, popular ethnic notion that in January 2009 a "Luo" was inaugurated to the highest political office in the United States. Yet, in the American context, celebratory popular accounts of the Obama-Kenya connection are beginning to emerge, and they share a similar glorified narrative akin to the patriotic histories emanating from Western Kenya. For example, Peter Firstbrook's popular genealogical tale *The Obamas: The Untold Story of an African Family* even includes a family tree linking Barack Obama Jr. directly with the mythical Luo founding ancestor, Ramogi.[85] In contrast, recent media commentary in Kenya has begun to take a more critical view of the Obama-Kenya connection, in particular by looking more openly at the contentious history of Barack Obama Sr. and providing an increasingly balanced, nuanced analysis more critical than the historic reverence exhibited by members of the diaspora.[86]

As historians, we again ask what effect these histories have on popular understandings of Kenya. The histories and discourses examined here stake strict claims to the politics of belonging, ultimately demonstrating the contentious yet malleable nature of identity politics within a specific sociopolitical framework; a malleability that makes the growing popular historiography of Obama and Kenya ripe for historical analysis. As a symbol of cultural and political identity, the distant past has loomed large in local celebrations of Obama in East Africa and in condemnations of him in the United States. Yet, the question of what can be made of Obama's actual political influence in Kenya and throughout the African continent remains. How, if at all, would the election of the first African American president of the United States change the trajectory of US-Africa relations? The next chapters turn to this question.

6

Political Violence and History at the Ballot Box

Our social and political environment has been susceptible to manipulation and practices that have made it difficult to reduce inequality in a meaningful manner. This, in turn, led to disenchantment, insecurity and suffering. In addition, our competing ethnic and political interests connived to override the national interest, with serious repercussions. This, tragically, has on occasion led to violence and loss of life and property.

—Uhuru Kenyatta, 2013[1]

Much like their colonial counterparts, Kenya's political elite have long practiced the politics of divide and rule to monopolize power and divert attention from pressing national issues. In the first five decades of independence, Kenyans have grappled with bouts of violent political conflict that stems from unresolved issues of the colonial past. From the politics of land tenure to the manipulation of ethnicity, the colonial legacy still looms large over contemporary Kenyan concerns at the ballot box. Unpacking this history reveals a complex story that tends to be hidden in simplistic, popular narratives of endemic government corruption and primordial "tribal" violence. However, the political violence in Kenya's recent past has had as much to do with the legacies of land policy and regional favoritism dating from the colonial period as with the failures of postcolonial political leadership.

As we have seen, much of Kenya's postcolonial political history has been dominated by a highly centralized government composed of long-lived "Big Men" and imperial presidents. By 2002, the country had been independent for nearly forty years, but had been ruled by only two presidents and one political party. In five out of the first seven presidential elections held since independence, Jomo Kenyatta and Daniel arap Moi stood unopposed. And after an attempted coup to overthrow Moi in 1982, Kenya was officially declared a one-party state. Nearly a decade later, growing domestic activism and international pressure forced the reintroduction of a multiparty political system. This reform did not immediately lead to greater freedom, cooperation, diversity, equality, or transparency in Kenya's political, social, or economic life. Rather, it provided the country's political elites with both the impetus and the means to use Kenya's complex politics of belonging as a tool with which to grab and consolidate political power. Fifty years removed from independence, Kenyans ushered in a new constitution in an attempt to decentralize power and address the legacy of "Big Man" politics. However as the son of Kenya's first president faced off against the son of the nation's first vice president in 2013, the nation was still grappling with the social, economic, and political legacy of colonial inequality and postcolonial governance.[2]

Since 1991, bouts of election-related violence have plagued the political system in Kenya and resulted in thousands of deaths and hundreds of thousands of internally displaced persons (IDPs). This chapter analyzes the violence surrounding the ballot box and the historical issues at its root. It addresses the sociopolitical circumstances surrounding recent presidential elections, paying close attention to the ways in which the stakes of ethnicity hardened over two decades. Focusing again on representation, this chapter addresses international press coverage of the 2007–2008 Kenya elections, which alternately suggested that the postelection violence was an anomaly in a country known as the "island of peace in a sea of conflict" or the result of primordial "tribalism," tropes repeated during the 2013 election campaigns. Drawing on Kenyan commissions of inquiry and observers' reports about electoral violence, the chapter challenges both notions, setting the 2007–2008 violence and the 2013 campaigns within the broader history of the politics of "belonging." In doing so, it also attends to how the *wananchi* (citizens) "wrote back," mobilizing social media to critique outsiders' depictions of Kenya and to develop and disseminate their own analyses of the sociopolitical scene. As the 2007 and 2013 period spanned Obama's rise from senator to president, this chapter also examines the ways US political rhetoric impacted the representation and reality of Kenya's electoral politics in both countries and beyond.

Land, Ethnicity, and Elections, 1991–2002

To simply summarize a complex history, beginning in 1991, multipartyism wound ethnicity and politics even more tightly together as the ruling Kenya African National Union (KANU) party now had to actually contest elections and do so across areas inhabited by multiethnic populations with variable interests, loyalties, and histories. Multipartyism also exposed the unfinished struggles of the independence era, when the promise of greater access to land and resources motivated thousands to risk their lives in the struggle against colonial rule.

To comprehend Kenya's history of electoral violence, it is necessary to understand the intertwined problems of land tenure, land transfer, and the uses of access to land and to land ownership as political tools. In 1963, faced with the overwhelming tasks of trying to recover from and get past the depredations of the colonial era, the Kenyatta government came to adopt a policy of "forgive and forget."[3] Addressing the settler community on the eve of independence, Jomo Kenyatta noted that he wanted to focus on the future and not dwell on "the bad old days."[4]

Under Kenyatta, the general policy was not to forcibly restore land seized by white settlers to black Kenyans, but to work with the settler community to repatriate land on a willing- buyer/willing-seller basis, thereby limiting land ownership to black Kenyans with sufficient means to purchase property. As a result, throughout the 1960s and 1970s, settler land was not transferred to the wananchi, but to the emerging African elite. Black Kenyans who had prospered under colonialism pooled their resources to purchase thousands of hectares, particularly in the Rift Valley, and politically connected families like the Kenyattas acquired huge tracts all over the country.[5] Claims by more humble black Kenyans dispossessed of their lands during the colonial era were virtually ignored by postcolonial governments.

In the Rift Valley in particular, postcolonial land policy exacerbated tensions between the pastoralist Maasai and Kalenjin communities, who had lost significant grazing and farmland due to colonial appropriation schemes, and the "newcomers," who had arrived as part of colonial-era labor migrations or who had migrated in response to land policies implemented by the postcolonial state.[6] Further, throughout the 1980s, as the Moi government seized land to redistribute in exchange for the loyalty of its clients, these tensions emerged in high relief while at the same time land tenure became even more tied up with ethnic exclusivity and regional favoritism.

In this context of conflicts over land, "belonging," and political favor, the reemergence of multiparty politics in the 1990s rekindled debates about regional versus national governance dating from the independence era. *Majimboism*, the strategy of dividing Kenya into provinces with equal political power that would handle their domestic matters while the central government controlled defense and foreign relations, had first been entertained in the 1950s. During the struggle for independence, majimboism was championed by political leaders who represented smaller regional communities in an attempt to diversify a political system dominated by one political party, KANU, and controlled by a tenuous Kikuyu-Luo alliance.[7] As David Anderson writes, majimboism reemerged in the 1990s, "first from within KANU by Moi's Kalenjin and Maasai supporters seeking to defend themselves against the rising tide of the opposition,"[8] and was eagerly reimagined as a political tool with which to grab more land and gain more political capital. As the chairman of the Law Society of Kenya explained, majimboism also "means the displacement of non-indigenous communities from their region to wherever they came from."[9] More pointedly, in 1991 the member of Parliament (MP) for Baringo, Moi's home area, stated of government critics, "Let them keep quiet or else we are ready for the reintroduction of *Majimbosim* whereby every person will be required to go back to his motherland. Once we introduce Majimbo in the Rift Valley, all outsiders who acquired our land will have to move and then leave the same land to our children."[10] The incitement, exacerbating, and sponsoring of violence directed at ethnic "Others" was the approach taken by Moi, his associates, and supporters in dealing with the electoral challenges posed by multipartyism and ethnically mixed constituencies.

By 1991, with its already ethnicized political landscape and a governing culture dominated by the "Big Man" model critiqued in chapters 3 and 4, Kenya remained ripe for further electoral manipulation carried out through violent means. At its most mild, violence was intended to cow potential opponents in Kalenjin-dominated and -allied areas into voting for KANU or refraining from voting at all. At worst, violence was directed at literally eradicating those who were not regarded as "sons of the soil." Testifying to Kenya's political context in the International Criminal Court (ICC) proceedings against Deputy Vice President William Ruto, who had been charged with crimes against humanity carried out during the 2007–2008 election period, political scientist Hervé Maupeu explained, "During the 90s . . . then President Moi progressively moved on to the policy of ethnic cleansing in order to keep tight control of his region, which has many constituencies. . . . This strategy was targeted at the migrant population who had settled in the Rift Valley."[11] This testimony echoes the findings of the Akiwumi Commission, which investigated the waves of violence from 1991 forward, concluding that "ethnic cleansing" was one objective of the clashes.[12]

Violence erupted in the fall of 1991 as Kalenjin youth in the Rift, equipped with *rungu* (clubs), *panga* (machetes), and spears, attacked local Luo, burning thirty homes and displacing thousands. According to *Daily Nation* reports, such violence was preceded by inciting statements made by KANU MPs at political rallies in the Rift, such as "The Kalenjin, Maasai, Samburu and West Pokot . . . were ready to protect the Government 'using any weapon at their disposal,'" and urging "the people of the province to arm themselves with bows and arrows and 'destroy any FORD [opposition] member on sight.'"[13] As violence persisted through the autumn and expanded to the western Luo areas of the country, the conflict between the Luo and the Kalenjin spread to include Luhya and Kikuyu people. This violence preceding the December 1992 elections (in which Moi again secured the presidency in the face of a fatally divided opposition) helped produce a hardening of ethnic identities and a heightening of politico-economic stakes around ethnicity. Accordingly, after a lull during the elections, conflict reignited across another swath of the Rift to include new groups—the Maasai and the Pokot—with Kikuyu again as targets. After a respite, violence between Kalenjin and Kikuyu again plagued the Rift in the mid-1990s. In total, Human Rights Watch estimated that by 1993, up to 1,500 people had been killed, with over 300,000 internally displaced.[14]

The second round of multiparty elections in 1997, which again enabled Moi to retain the presidency, was accompanied by violence that flared intensely on the coast. Like the "sons of the soil" of the Rift, the ethnic groups of the coast who claimed to be the original inhabitants—the Mijikenda and Digo—were profoundly discontented with the "newcomers" who had settled on the coast during the colonial era and with the array of up-country migrants drawn by work opportunities that the tourism industry provided in the postcolonial era.[15] Digo and Mijikenda looked to KANU's promises about majimboism to cure their ethnic ills, carrying out violence against "newcomers" to generate support for the party. Echoing Mau Mau, this violence included an attack on a police station in which guns were stolen for use in later attacks and an oathing campaign to recruit and bind fighters. The net results of the clashes of the 1990s were massive destruction of property, largely through arson, the deaths of several thousand people, the internal displacement of hundreds of thousands more, many of them violently exiled "newcomers,"[16] and the overall intensification of the politics of "belonging." As Daniel Branch emphasizes,

> The bitter violence of the multiparty era led to a new emphasis on notions of identity that emphasized autochthony, the notion of belonging to a particular place or, in everyday parlance, of being a son of the soil. Older notions of what it meant to be Kikuyu or Luo, for example, were formed during long histories of migration. By the early 1990s, these identities were more commonly anchored in a particular place. . . . But these newer notions of ethnicity conflicted with the realities of people's lives and made no allowance for those living outside their supposed home provinces and districts.[17]

While well-documented and well-known in Kenya, these ethnic clashes that form the backdrop to 2007–2008 and 2013 were neither widely reported nor, would it seem from the coverage of the 2000s, remotely remembered in the international press. Rather, the peaceful transfer of power in 2002–2003, in which Moi was (finally) outmaneuvered by Mwai Kibaki and Raila Odinga's National Rainbow Coalition (NARC) in elections deemed free and fair by international observers, provided one lens through which subsequent elections would be read, while tribal atavism provided another.

Luo Marginalization and the Longevity of the Odingas

The story of power in the middle decades of the postcolonial period was largely that of the Mount Kenya peoples, Kenyatta's Gikuyu, Embu, and Meru Association (GEMA), and then of the Kalenjin, an amalgamation of Moi's Tugen, Nandi, Kipsigis, Marakwet, Sabaot, and Pokot peoples. At independence this collection of colonial "tribes" was transformed into a broad supraethnic group based on their geographic and cultural proximities and the mutual intelligibility of their languages. "Kalenjin," Gabrielle Lynch points out, refers to a Nandi word meaning "I say to you," which began to be used as an ethnic identifier during radio broadcasts in the 1940s.[18] As Charles Hornsby explains of the "Kalenjin veneer" overlying Kenyan governance and business by the early 1990s, "Kalenjin were parachuted at every level into parastatals, universities, and the civil service, and held many of the top jobs in the police, the provisional administration, finance, telecommunications and agricultural parastatals. Even private businesses saw it was in their interest to ensure that the president's community were represented in their management teams."[19] Concretely, Kalenjin predominance in essential positions and sectors facilitated the ethnic violence discussed above, while, more abstractly, it helped heighten the stakes of ethnic patrimonialism.

This period was the low ebb of Luo power on a national stage, when Luo were marginalized generally and political figures, including Raila Odinga and his wife, Ida, and intellectuals, such as Professor E. S. Atieno Odhiambo, were detained and subjected to tortuous persecution and imprisonment. In maximum security prisons built on the sites of former Mau Mau interrogation centers and camps and in the basement cells of Nyayo

House, the stuccoed, mustard yellow high-rise in downtown Nairobi intended as a monument to Moi's signature development program, political opponents of the ruling regime were routinely tortured and sometimes even murdered.[20] For the Luo community, the 1990 murder of Robert Ouko, discussed in chapters 3 and 4, is the most sober memory of this time.

In the summer of 1991, on the eve of the restoration of multiparty politics, Oginga Odinga and five of his allies announced the formation of a new lobby group (political parties other than Moi's KANU were outlawed) called the Forum for the Restoration of Democracy (FORD). When FORD was registered as a party in late 1991, it won the support of nearly every Luo, including Ramogi Achieng Oneko, whom you will recall from earlier chapters was a leading light of the Luo Union and among the famous alleged Mau Mau imprisoned with Kenyatta known as the Kapenguria Six. The group also came to count numerous Kikuyu among its ranks who perhaps recalled the Kikuyu-Luo alliance of the early colonial period. By the time of the election, however, FORD had split into two parties—FORD-Kenya and FORD-Asili. The question of who should be its presidential candidate, Jaramogi Odinga or the young Kikuyu businessman and dissident Kenneth Matiba, and contention over Odinga's vision of a social justice approach to the country's rampant inequality versus Matiba's market-based plans for development, drove the split.[21] With the opposition thus split, and having employed the strategies of manipulation and intimidation discussed earlier, Moi and KANU sailed to victory in the 1992 elections, with Kalenjin-dominated areas voting 93 percent for Moi.[22] Odinga came in fourth with slightly over 17 percent of the vote, two-thirds of which came from Nyanza, reflecting the ongoing marginalization of the Luo and the continuing importance of ethnicity in voting. Odinga's death in early 1994 set off a period of profound personal and political mourning among Luo in Nyanza and in the diaspora. One Luo Council of Elders (LCE) supporter summed up Luo despair with the collective cry, "Ker Jaramogi is dead! Who shall lead my people?"[23]

With Oginga Odinga's death, the torch of Luo leadership passed to his son Raila Amolo Odinga. As noted in chapters 4 and 5, Raila, the second of Jaramogi Odinga's sons, was a successful businessman educated as an engineer in East Germany who had been detained on multiple occasions by the Moi regime and who had won the parliamentary seat for Nairobi's Langata constituency in 1992. The political vacuum in the opposition created by the senior Odinga's death was not filled without controversy. Raila, deputy chairman of FORD-Kenya, tangled with another "son of the soil" of Western Kenya, Michael Kijana Wamalwa, a Luhya chairman of FORD-Kenya, over leadership of the opposition and ultimately split off to create his own party, the National Development Party (NDP).

By the time of the second round of multiparty elections in 1997, Raila had built a formidable political machine that included the majority of the Luo political establishment and that evidenced an "enduring commitment to the Odinga dynasty."[24] The fracturing of the opposition, accompanied by significant voting irregularities and the violent clashes described above, again paved the way to victory for Moi and KANU. Raila finished a distant third, again gathering up nearly all the Luo vote and solidifying himself as the scion of Ramogi.[25] With the established Luo elite largely out of government and watching a schism develop in KANU over who would be Moi's successor in 2002, Raila threw NDP support behind KANU, the party of the man who'd had him detained and tortured scant years earlier and whom he had plotted to overthrow in a failed 1982 coup that constituted the primary challenge to Moi's power before the introduction of multipartyism.[26] Raila went on to serve as minister of energy in the Moi administration.

Raila's move, to borrow a phrase from another bold "Luo" politician, pointed to the "audacity of hope"; hope that through collaboration he would emerge as the KANU flag-bearer in 2002. This hope was upended, however, by Moi's effort to designate the young Uhuru Kenyatta, Jomo Kenyatta's son, who had been appointed by Moi as chairman of the Kenya Tourist Board and who was also the party chairman in Thika outside Nairobi, as his successor. *Africa Confidential* reported, "When Moi anointed Uhuru Kenyatta as KANU's presidential candidate, Odinga stormed out, taking an improbable gang of KANU stalwarts with him. . . . This broke KANU in two."[27] Raila began talks targeted at uniting the opposition and negotiated a secret deal with Mwai Kibaki, a venerable Kikuyu politician who, as we learned in chapter 4, had worked in the Kenyatta government with Mboya and Obama Sr. The two men made an agreement reminiscent of the collaboration between Jaramogi Odinga and Kenyatta at independence: Kibaki would stand unopposed as the opposition presidential candidate, constitutional reform would be completed in three months to create the office of prime minister for Raila to occupy, and half the cabinet seats would go to Raila's supporters.[28] With this agreement, the NARC was formed and organized a rally in Nairobi's Uhuru Park scheduled to coincide with the announcement of Kenyatta's candidacy. Flanked by the opposition leadership, Raila expounded in Swahili to the cheering crowds "Harambee!!! Tunataka serikali ambaye inaweza kubadilika na wananchi wa Kenya. . . . Kibaki tosha!" (Pull together! We want a government that can be changed by the people of Kenya. . . . Kibaki is enough!).[29]

Campaigning around the country, NARC politicians of all ethnic groups took "Unbwogable," a song by the Luo hip-hop group Gidi Gidi Maji Maji, as their unofficial theme song. The lyrics in English, Dholuo, and Sheng invoke the names of Luo luminaries and martyrs—Oginga Odinga, Tom Mboya, Robert Ouko, and Raila Amolo—in between demanding "Am a Luo but who are you?" and declaring, "You can't bwoga me! I am unbwogable!" that is, "You can't scare me! I am undefeatable!"[30] The song proved quite prescient, as the opposition, united for the first time in the multiparty era, defeated KANU in the elections of December 27, 2002, ending forty years of the party's domination. Three days later, Mwai Kibaki was sworn in as Kenya's third president before jubilant crowds in Uhuru Park.[31] In his inaugural address, Kibaki challenged the political naysayers. "Some prophets of doom have predicted a vicious in-fighting following this victory," he explained. "I want to assure you that they will be disappointed. When a group of people come together over an idea or because of a shared vision, such a group can never fail or disintegrate. NARC will never die as long as the original vision endures. It will grow stronger and coalesce into a single party that will become a beacon of hope not only to Kenyans but to the rest of Africa."[32] The next five years showed the predictive powers of the new president to be unreliable.

The 2007–2008 Elections: Contest and Context

A year after the 2002 elections, palpable optimism could still be felt across the country. The new government had taken important steps, such as providing free primary education and overhauling the public transport sector to enhance safety. Yet, despite the new government's vaunted anticorruption initiatives—which involved sacking Kalenjin from their Moi-era appointments in the civil service and public sectors—the 2004 Transparency International Corruption Perceptions Index, which defines corruption as the "abuse of public office for private gain" and measures "the degree to which corruption is perceived to exist among public officials and politicians," ranked Kenya among the most corrupt countries in the world.[33] Indeed, by 2005, John Githongo, who had been appointed to lead the government's anticorruption campaign, was forced into exile in the United Kingdom after he unearthed a major public procurements scandal dating from the Moi era.[34] Involving a company called Anglo-Leasing, the affair was quickly dubbed "Anglo-Fleecing" in popular discourse. Insecurity ranging from petty theft to carjackings continued to be rampant in Nairobi, and the tensions that had driven the clashes of the 1990s had never been resolved. Daniel Branch explains, "The failure to enact change was partly a result of the simple fact that the government included many of those responsible for earlier misrule."[35] Indeed, responding to the administration's plan to reshuffle ministers suspected in the Anglo-Leasing affair, Raila noted that reshuffling "is like saying to them: You have eaten enough from this side, now go and eat from the other side."[36]

The agreement between Raila and Kibaki disintegrated as the constitutional review process that was meant to establish the office of prime minister to be occupied by Raila stalled, only to be concluded with a draft for public referendum from which had been purged earlier sections laying out fresh limits on presidential power. Together with other NARC ministers, Raila formed the Orange Democratic Movement (ODM) to oppose the draft. ODM took its name from the orange symbol indicating "no" on the constitutional ballot ("yes" was indicated with a banana) and from the Orange Movement in Ukraine.[37] In the referendum, oranges topped bananas in every province except Kibaki's home area, Central Province.[38] The grand coalition party of 2002 was destroyed as ODM, now a political party, joined the opposition, while Kibaki huddled with his "Mount Kenya Mafia" and GEMA supporters. Kalonzo Musyoka, a Kamba, split off and founded his own party, ODM-Kenya.

As the 2007 presidential elections grew near, Kibaki headed a new party, the Party of National Unity (PNU), which campaigned on economic growth—its Swahili slogan was "Kazi endelea," or "Work should continue." Raila headed ODM, which, recalling the socialist principles of Jaramogi Odinga and Raila's own background, campaigned on a platform of socio-economic justice, constitutional reform, and a decentralized majimbo model of federal governance. As Hornsby neatly sums up, Raila "personified a popular movement for radical change, while Kibaki was positioned as leader of a reactionary, tribalist, old guard that had mismanaged Kenya in the past."[39] With leaders from every major ethnic group, ODM spoke to ethnoregional grievances across the country, and Raila built a wide web of alliances that even reached into the international Luo diaspora for financial and political capital. Polling in late autumn of 2007 showed that Raila and ODM had a comfortable lead everywhere except ethnically mixed Nairobi, Kikuyu-dominated Central Province, and Kamba-dominated Eastern Province.

Two months later, on election day, Friday, December 27, 2007, Kenyans turned out in droves to vote for the president, MPs, and local representatives. Daniel Branch, who served as an election observer in Nairobi's Kibera slum, described voters' certainties: "First, that if a free and fair election were held, Raila Odinga and his Orange Democratic Movement (ODM) had sufficient support to win Kenya's presidential and parliamentary elections. Second, that the polls would be fixed in order to ensure a second term of office for President Mwai Kibaki of the Party of National Unity (PNU)."[40] Kibera's voters turned out to be astute political analysts. Parliamentary returns showed a resounding victory for ODM, which won ninety-nine parliamentary seats to PNU's forty-three.[41] Early tallies showed Raila ahead by close to a million votes, and, as Branch notes, the morning editions of Kenya's major dailies "had effectively called the election for him" on December 29.[42] But by early afternoon Raila's lead had dwindled to a mere one hundred thousand votes, and on the third day after the election, the Electoral Commission of Kenya (ECK) declared victory for Kibaki before teatime.[43] In a telling contrast to his jubilant inauguration before thousands of wananchi and foreign dignitaries a few years earlier, Kibaki's 2007 swearing-in occurred in private at State House before a small group of close associates, with Moi the chief dignitary present.[44]

The vote tabulation was regarded by observers, by NGOs, and by many of the wananchi as a deliberate shambles of epic proportion, carried out by PNU with the collusion of a number of operatives in the ECK. Even before the tallies were complete, ODM levied allegations of vote rigging as Raila's lead dropped off suspiciously and precipitously. After Kibaki was declared the winner, Raila reinforced the message that the election was rigged, noting at an international press conference, "Kenyans are deeply disturbed and angered by the attempt of this Government to steal this election through a process that was fraudulent at every step of the way," and adding, "I cannot and would not accept a Kibaki win; the results are there, if I had lost I would have accepted, this is fait accompli (over)."[45] The ODM leadership called for a campaign of civil disobedience, and as Human Rights Watch reported, "Police in Nairobi shot demonstrators under circumstances that remain largely unexplained on every day that significant opposition protests attempted to convene in the capital."[46]

Similar crackdowns on ODM protesters occurred in other major urban centers. And when ODM supporters in Kisumu and other urban centers targeted Kikuyu property, turning to vandalism and looting to the chant of "No Raila, No Peace!" the police used live ammunition to subdue them, injuring many bystanders as well. As the official government inquiry, the Waki Commission, later explained, "Luo Nyanza rose up to protest what was seen as a rigged election. . . . Unlike other parts of the country that were ravaged by violence in the postelection period, the majority of deaths recorded in Luo Nyanza were as a result of shootings attributed to the police."[47] In Nairobi, running battles took place across Kibera and the city's other poor neighborhoods as youthful gangs of ODM and PNU supporters attacked each other and the police used live ammunition against them.

The violence that broke out with the announcement of a Kibaki victory was not merely a response to the election results, but deeply rooted in the politics of "belonging," postcolonial land policy, and the personalization of political power. Tensions around these issues had only increased since the violence of the 1990s, with many state actors working to actively exploit rather than to curb them, some going so far as to develop ethnic militias and co-opt criminal gangs. Disaffected urbanites regarded their material existence as inextricably linked to having "their" Big Men at the pinnacle of power. "There appeared to be a strong perception among voters," the report of the Commonwealth Observer Group noted, "that having a kinsman in State House would substantially increase their access to the national cake."[48]

In a brutal redux of the violence of the previous decade, Kalenjin in the Rift turned on "outsiders," primarily Kikuyu who were perceived as supporters of Kibaki, while the local Kalenjin supported Raila.[49] It is worth noting the similarities between the discussion of electoral violence in the Akiwumi Commission of 1998 and the Waki Commission of 2008. The earlier commission reported, "In each clash area, non-Kalenjin or non-Maasai, as the case may be, were suddenly attacked, their houses set on fire their properties looted and in certain instances, some of them were either killed or severely injured with traditional weapons like bows, arrows, spears, panga, swords and clubs. . . . The attacks were barbaric, callous and calculated to drive out the targeted groups from their farms, to cripple them economically and to psychologically traumatize them."[50] The Akiwumi Commission arrived at the conclusion that the clashes were "carefully planned" to "recover ancestral land" for the Kalenjin and "to drive away the '*madoadoa*' (spots/foreigners) in order to achieve the main political purpose" of renewing the Rift into a Kalenjin zone.[51] The 2008 commission reported that around Eldoret, a major town in the Rift, "gangs with crude weapons also barricaded access to various sites, including farming communities in the largely Kikuyu inhabited settlement schemes. Here, mostly unsuspecting and terrified victims were suddenly overwhelmed by large numbers of Kalenjin youth who set fire to their compounds, burned and stole their possessions, as well as maiming, gang raping, and hacking to death large numbers of defenseless families, most of whom were Kikuyu."[52]

In areas of the country where Luo and Kalenjin were "strangers," Kikuyu militias began a violent reprisal campaign using the same tools of terror and intimidation mobilized in the Rift Valley to reclaim territory for the "sons of the soil." For instance, criminal gangs, such as the infamous Mungiki, carried out attacks against supporters of Raila Odinga in the Rift Valley towns of Nakuru and Naivasha, targeting mainly Luo and Kalenjin residents, and forcing thousands to flee their homes.[53] By mid-January 2008, the cycle of violence had spread west from Nairobi and engulfed much of the Rift Valley and reached as far as Kisumu.

In early February peace talks organized by the UN and led by former UN secretary general Kofi Annan were under way, and Kibaki and Odinga came to the negotiating table to avoid greater civil unrest. When a power-sharing deal, the National Accord and Reconciliation Act, was signed on February 28, Kenya was pulled back from the brink of disaster.[54] The agreement provided for the creation of the post of prime minister to be held by Odinga, but there was no talk of overturning the election results and starting campaigns anew.[55] With the agreement, Kenya's most violent electoral season, which had seen rigging on both sides and continuation of the "tradition" that no sitting Kenyan president be voted out of office, was finally concluded. The Kibaki-Odinga government and the wananchi had to come to terms with the aftermath of the violence, which had claimed upward of fifteen hundred dead and added nearly six hundred thousand to Kenya's already significant number of internally displaced persons (IDPs). By mid-2008, with basic security restored, questions of justice, reconciliation, and the development of a new constitutional framework had emerged in high relief.

Representations and International Relations: From "Tribal Atavism" to Obama

International press coverage of the postelection violence was structured by common tropes about violence and conflict in Africa and overwhelmingly ignored the long-standing patterns of electoral manipulation and related violence detailed above as well as the deeper issues of colonial land policy and postcolonial regionalism. Even the most respected news agencies could not resist tantalizing readers with reductive descriptions of the "tribal" violence and "primitive" conflict exploding from beneath Kenya's veneer of civilization and modernity. Most pointedly, Jeffrey Gettleman, East Africa Bureau chief for the *New York Times*, wrote within scant days of the outbreak of violence, "The election seems to have tapped into an atavistic vein of tribal tension that always lay beneath the surface in Kenya but until now had not provoked widespread mayhem."[56]

Failing to situate the violence within Kenya's particular history and contemporary politics, coverage also lumped the country's specific struggles together with the cataclysmic ethnic cleansing and genocide that had engulfed the nearby Great Lakes region in the 1990s. Within a few weeks of the election, the BBC dared to ask, "Could Kenya Become Rwanda?"[57] Writing on the church burning in Eldoret discussed earlier, the correspondent for *Der Spiegel*, Germany's major daily, observed, "The scenes are grim reminders of the genocide of Rwanda, where hundreds of thousands of people were massacred in just a few weeks in 1994. Many of the deaths in Nairobi too seem to have resulted from tribal clashes."[58] Such comparisons to the Rwandan genocide were dangerously unfounded, with the violence and rhetoric more about electoral politics and land rights than a function of an orchestrated campaign to eradicate entire ethnic communities. Overall, such broad comparisons and bald stereotyping failed to inform audiences abroad about the political complexity of the conflict, the organized and diversified character of the perpetrators, and the historical issues at stake. Calling to mind the coverage of Mau Mau analyzed in chapters 2 and 4, the 2008 images of young men wielding spears, machetes, and bows and arrows, together with simplistic discourse about the tools of violence, did little to explain the historic realities and marketed the mistaken, simplistic notions that the election had "re-awakened ancient ethnic rivalries" and that Kenyans were "settling scores the old fashioned way."[59]

Kenyans, in contrast, understood how the complicated history and contemporary stakes of the violence were rooted in ethnic patrimonialism and attendant inequality, regionalism, and political corruption. As one perpetrator in Eldoret stated, "We got incited. . . . They would tell us, 'Now you see the government has gone to Central Province. We should fight to ensure that all the resources come back in accordance to our wish.' The businessmen said that roads would be built in Central Province only. They said that if the ODM had won we could have received favors and develop more economically than the other regions."[60] For others the motivation to pick up arms was to simply put money in their pockets, as perpetrators were widely reported to have been paid, with the violence carried out overwhelmingly within poor communities. Many also cited the contested land question in opportunistic and historical context. As another perpetrator lamented, "Maybe in the next 10 years we will have such a generation when all the outdated leaders who plant colonial thoughts in us will be no more. Maybe one acquired two acres of land illegally during the colonial times and so he wants to protect it. Those who stole public property earlier are the ones who are sponsoring such activities to safeguard their corrupt gains."[61]

The violence surrounding the election coincided with the middle of the US presidential campaign season. Kenya's troubles provided a fresh space for Obama's supporters and detractors to insert him into narratives of Kenyan history and contemporary politics where he did not belong and to characterize him again as a "son of the soil" of Western Kenya. In general, discourse on Obama's connection to Kenya's election crisis cast Kenyan politics in boldly "tribalist" terms; more specifically, it attached him directly to the Odinga dynasty. For instance, in a BBC interview shortly following the election, Odinga claimed that Obama's father was his maternal uncle, making the two "Luo" politicians blood relations.[62] Even though the Obama campaign denied such a relationship, Raila's claiming of Obama was eagerly taken up by Obama's political opponents in the United States, who wove together narratives asserting that Obama actively supported his "cousin" Odinga and was structuring a foreign policy platform accordingly.

Unsurprisingly, Jerome Corsi, who, as we learned in chapter 4, developed a cottage industry of publishing revisionist narratives of Kenyan history meant to discredit Obama, was among the most active in endeavoring to connect Obama and Odinga personally and politically. *Obama Nation* presented Raila as "the most extreme Luo in Kenyan politics," and as a closeted Muslim, invoking the lexicon mobilized by the American Far Right to rebuke Obama and reinforcing claims about the association and affinity of the two "Luo tribesmen."[63] At the same moment, such characterizations laid the foundation for dangerous misreadings of the sources and nature of the 2007 election, and the involvement of Raila and Obama in the postelection strife.

Corsi ascribed responsibility for the violence directly to the actions of Raila and ODM. Noting Raila's claim that he lost the presidency due to electoral fraud, Corsi stated, "Odinga's claim led to widespread fighting that killed more than 1,000 people." He also asserted that "while proving involvement is difficult, many in Kenya assumed the postelection violence was supported, if not organized, behind the scenes by Odinga and his Orange Democratic Movement."[64] Corsi thereby situated the blame for the violence explicitly in Raila's declaration and tacitly in an ODM plot rather than in the complex material reasons detailed above.[65]

Corsi also addressed Obama's phone call to Odinga, made from the campaign trail a week after the announcement of the election results, and points out that Obama had reiterated to reporters that Raila believed "the votes were not tallied properly."[66] "Odinga's charge against Kibaki, namely that there had been irregularities in the vote tabulation," Corsi contended, "was certain to play well with liberal Democrats who still believe that George W. Bush stole the 2000 presidential election from Al Gore."[67] Such a contention elided the statements of various international election observers discussed above, tightened the ties between Obama and Odinga, and underscored similarities in the electoral fortunes of Obama's Democratic Party and Raila's Orange Democratic Movement.

Characterizing Raila as a "Muslim sympathizer," Corsi offers an egregious and dangerous misreading of the postelection violence as religiously based. Privileging the voices of evangelical "Christian missionaries," Corsi noted that they had "reported that more than three hundred Christian churches were severely damaged or destroyed in the wave of violence that swept the country, but mosques were left undisturbed."[68] Corsi extrapolated, "The violence was not only Luo against Kikuyu, it was also Muslims against Christians, reflecting the divisions that opposed Kibaki and supported Odinga."[69] A demographically grounded analysis of the church burnings indicates that the overwhelming majority of violence occurred in Nyanza Province, Central Province, and the Rift Valley, all heavily Christian areas, and among Kikuyu, Luo, and to some extent Kalenjin, all of whom are predominantly Christian, with pockets of adherents to traditional religions and scant Muslims. Corsi's figuring of the postelection violence along clear binary religious lines also draws from the stream of American popular idioms of the "clash of civilizations." This religiously driven reading pointed tacitly to the dangers and risks of having a "Muslim sympathizer" in a position to contest the presidency in Kenya—or in America. Overall, *The Obama Nation*'s narrative of Kenya's political history maps onto Raila and ODM the same kind of threatening "Otherness" that the American Far Right has applied to Obama, and in drawing tight, even familial connections between the two men reinforces the perception of Obama as a "stranger" to America and a "son of the soil" of Kenya. In reality, Obama himself remained way outside the fray of Kenya's electoral conflict. When he did address the violence from the campaign trail in an interview with Capital FM Kenya, he did so in decidedly neutral terms:

> I have personally been touched by your generous, democratic spirit through my ties to my own family, and during my travels to Kenya— most recently as a United States Senator in 2006. This Kenyan spirit rises above ethnic groups or political parties, and was on display in Kenya's recent election, when you turned out to vote in record numbers, and in a peaceful and orderly way. But recent troubling events in Kenya bear no resemblance to the Kenya I know and carry with me. . . . We must not look back years from now and wonder how and why things were permitted to go so horribly wrong. Kenya, its African friends, and the United States must now be determined pursuers of   peace—and this determined pursuit must start today with individual Kenyans refusing to resort to violence, and Kenyan leaders accepting their responsibility to turn away from confrontation by coming together.[70]

Celebrating his Kenyan heritage in a general way, and putting the primary onus on the wananchi and the Kenyan political leadership to achieve unity and restore peace, Obama disappointed observers on both sides of the political spectrum in the United States and many in Kenya who expected him to come out strongly in support of a more intensive US role in mediating or even intervening in Kenya's troubles. This broad-based, neutral statement prefigured the Obama administration's approach to Kenya and to the president's heritage during the first term. Five years later, the president's own response to Kenya's 2013 contested election and the ICC indictments of Kenya's top two politicians for their alleged roles in the violence of 2008 proved much the same, although members of the administration took a more critical line. The next section turns to Kenya's tenuous efforts to cope with the aftermath of the electoral violence and forge a fresh political path.

Building the Coalition of the Accused

As a tense peace was restored in Kenya over the winter of 2008, justice and reconciliation emerged at the forefront of public discourse. The country's future was debated on the street and in the press, and memories of the violence of 1992 and 1997 discussed above and of the political assassinations of Mboya and Ouko examined in chapter 3 rose to the surface. The most pressing question was whether or not Kenya's historic culture of impunity would be allowed to continue. The hope was that this time would be different as evidence from investigations and observations by international agencies like Human Rights Watch and the new government's own official inquiry, the Waki Commission, clearly demonstrated that the violence had been orchestrated by Kenya's politically connected class: elected politicians, employees of the civil service and security forces, and members of the media.[71] Yet, the Waki Commission report, published in October 2008, failed to specifically finger perpetrators from among the highest echelons of the political elite—the commissioners were unwilling or unable to name their own bosses. The commission's most significant contribution was its specific recommendations to establish a local tribunal to "seek accountability against persons bearing the greatest responsibility for crimes, particularly crimes against humanity, relating to the 2007 General Elections in Kenya."[72]

As the next year elapsed and international pressure mounted on the Kenyan government to prosecute those responsible for the violence, no action was taken to establish the judicial framework recommended by the commission. Despite their initial hopes, the wananchi were unsurprised; numerous Moi-era commissions had failed to go anywhere.[73] In this context, Kofi Annan sent the names of the alleged orchestrators of the violence to the ICC in the Hague during the summer of 2009. The Kenyan public was initially supportive, with "Don't be vague, let's go to the Hague," becoming a catchphrase around the country.[74]

By December 2010, ICC chief prosecutor Luis Moreno Ocampo had identified six individuals deemed most responsible for the violence. While Kibaki and Odinga were not named, MP and Deputy Prime Minister Uhuru Kenyatta, son of Jomo Kenyatta, MP William Ruto, as well as the commissioner of police, the director of a Kalenjin-language radio station, and four key political operatives were eventually indicted to wide international praise.[75] Almost a year into his first term, Obama commented, "Kenya is turning a page in its history, moving away from impunity and divisionism toward an era of accountability and equal opportunity."[76] In early 2012, charges were confirmed for four of the six indictees, including Kenyatta and Ruto. At the same time, Kenya was engaged in crafting a new constitution, a key stipulation of the 2008 power-sharing agreement, and in August 2010 Kenyans voted on a new constitution aimed at establishing a federalized system of government with clear checks on presidential power. Accepted with 68 percent of the vote, the constitution fundamentally changed Kenya's political landscape, breaking up colonial-era provinces and devolving power into forty-seven counties, each with its own governor and county legislature.[77]

Questions of devolution, justice, and Kenya's relations with the West dominated the political scene in the buildup to the March 2013 presidential elections as establishment politicians jockeyed for position and formed new coalitions.[78] Prime Minister Odinga emerged as the standard-bearer for the new Coalition for Reform and Democracy (CORD).[79] Ruto, who had held two ministerial posts in the second Kibaki government as well as being an MP, made his ICC indictment work for him, teaming up with fellow indictee Kenyatta; this "alliance of the accused" campaigned on the idea that the court was a neocolonial institution that the West was using to again determine Kenya's fate.[80] The pair's political allies even went so far as to argue on the floor of the Parliament that Kenya should withdraw as a signatory to the Rome Statute, which had established the ICC. Summing up the attitude of Kenyatta-Ruto supporters, Kiriatu Murungi, who was then minister of energy, argued, "If you look at the signatories of the statute you will see only African and former colonies appeared to be tried at the ICC. . . . There will be no American who will ever be tried by the ICC. No Briton will be tried at the ICC. No French will be tried at the ICC. Why should we allow ourselves, as independent countries, to willingly go back to colonial or neo-colonial situations?"[81] This notion began to resonate with Kenyans, evidenced by opinion polls showing a decline in earlier support for the ICC, especially in Kenyatta and Ruto strongholds. Despite the slaughter in the Rift not even five years earlier, ordinary Kikuyu and

Kalenjin lined up behind their Big Men, believing that Kenyatta and Ruto had been unfairly targeted.[82]

Representations, International Relations, and the "O Factor": The Wananchi Write Back

Unsurprisingly, Kenyatta's and Ruto's unprecedented situations—simultaneously occupying top spots on the Jubilee Alliance ticket and on the docket of the ICC—attracted international attention. Foreign leaders and dignitaries hinted that a Kenyatta-Ruto administration would render Kenya a pariah state in the eyes of the international community. Obama made very few direct statements about the ICC or Kenya's upcoming elections, and when the "Ocampo Six" were named, Obama urged "all of Kenya's leaders, and the people whom they serve, to cooperate fully with the ICC investigation," but he also cautioned, "No community should be singled out for shame or held collectively responsible. Let the accused carry their own burdens—and let us keep in mind that under the ICC process they are innocent until proven guilty."[83]

A month before the 2013 elections, Obama again spoke in general terms, reiterating the call for peace: "The choice of who will lead Kenya is up to the Kenyan people. The United States does not endorse any candidate for office, but we do support an election that is peaceful and reflects the will of the people."[84] Overall, Obama's statements reflected neutral support for the institution of the ICC and for Kenyan electoral sovereignty.

While the president's words were measured, members of his administration made more direct statements, suggesting that the ICC case would be significant to US relations with Kenya in the future. Responding to the president's statement about the Kenya election, George Harris, special assistant to the president and senior director for African affairs, stressed that the election was "a moment to put strife and impunity firmly in the past."[85] More pointedly, Johnnie Carson, the assistant secretary of state for African Affairs and former ambassador to Kenya, repeatedly responded at a press conference to questions about Kenyatta with the remark "Choices have consequences."[86] This language was widely quoted in the Kenyan media.

Many Kenyans read the administration's rhetoric as evidence of the neocolonial character of the ICC and of the West's attitude toward Kenya's domestic affairs. Opponents of Raila Odinga took statements by Obama and members of his administration as opportunities to bind Odinga with Obama, characterizing the Kenyan prime minister as a lackey of his fellow Luo and "cousin" in the White House. For instance, the *Huffington Post* reported in a widely reposted article that there was widespread belief in Kenya in the "O Factor." The article explained, "Obama, Ocampo, Odinga—they all share the distinctive first letter of members of the Luo tribe in Kenya, and some in this East African nation believe that the three are brothers in a conspiracy to see six suspects convicted at Ocampo's Hague-based court so that Odinga can become president in the land where Obama's father was born."[87]

By the time the ICC case was launched, Odinga's opponents had already been borrowing tactics and remaking rhetoric from the American Right to portray Raila as a dangerous extremist with disturbing politico-religious ties to Kenya's Muslim community and worrying ethnic and familial ties to the neocolonial West. For example, outlandish claims linking Obama and Odinga published on *WND*—that Raila was an "Obama funded foreign thug who promised an Islamic state" and that the "communist" Raila's career was being manipulated by a "Democrat firm"—gained traction among anti-Odinga circles in Kenya.[88] Indeed, when Miguna Miguna, formerly a chief aide to Odinga, wrote a "tell-all" book about the prime minister after a bitter falling-out with him, Miguna forwarded his manuscript to Corsi, who promoted it on his website for months before copies hit the shelves in Kenya.[89] Articles containing broad, unsubstantiated claims about Raila's purported political ineptitude appeared in a flurry in the more mainstream Kenyan media as well during the summer before Kenya's election, providing fodder for Odinga's and Obama's respective political opponents.[90]

As the campaigns heated up and the ICC cases developed, the international press covered events in Kenya and the Hague through the lens of "tribalism," figuring another outbreak of "tribal violence" to be inevitable during the 2013 elections. For example, *New York Times* Nairobi Bureau chief Jeffrey Gettleman invoked the same sort of simplistic, ahistorical analysis he had used to characterize the "tribal clashes" of 2008, writing,

"Every five years or so, this stable and typically peaceful country, an oasis of development in a very poor and turbulent region, suffers a frightening transformation in which age-old grievances get stirred up, ethnically based militias are mobilized and neighbors start killing neighbors."[91] One CNN segment went so far as to showcase a costumed "local Kikuyu tribal militia" preparing for "war" by theatrically engaging in simulated fighting with bows and arrows for the camera.[92]

In the intervening years between the elections of 2007 and 2013, Kenyans had acquired new tools and technologies with which to "write back" against the simplistic depictions of their country's history and politics as being driven solely by "tribal atavism." The tremendous growth in Internet and mobile phone availability in Kenya gave the wananchi access to global content and global audiences and reinforced connections between Kenya and its politically interested, wealthy diaspora. Now able to respond in real time to Kenya's critics, Kenyans at home and abroad did so with satire and seriousness. For example, an article in the *Daily Nation* quipped that foreign journalists were "armed and ready to attack Kenya."[93] Noting that foreign "demand for Kenyan clichés is outstripping supply," the article proposed an itinerary and lexicon to aid foreign journalists:

> Outings for journalists will include a guided tour of Kibera, a Nairobi slum. It should be described as Africa's largest, teeming with residents who are resilient, cheerful and enterprising. Trips to Mombasa will include word-packs with steamy, Moslem, tinderbox, golden sand and azure sea, designed to fit into any intro. Colour intros should include a reference to Happy Valley, Kenya cowboys, leafy suburbs and dusty streets. Finally foreign correspondents are urged to put their name for "Meet the Mungiki," who have kindly agreed to perform a traditional oathing ceremony, which can be described as "bloodthirsty." No goats will be harmed.[94]

More serious critiques were forthcoming as well. For example, Mukoma wa Ngugi, an English professor at Cornell and son of Kenya's most famous novelist, explained in one of Britain's major dailies, "Journalists have been left behind by an Africa moving forward: not in a straight line, but in fits and starts, elliptically, and still full of contradictions of extreme wealth and extreme poverty, but forward nevertheless."[95] Such pieces were complemented by the voices of numerous members of the Kenyan media calling for peace and denouncing ethnic rhetoric as a political tool.[96]

The elections of March 4, 2013, proved that ethnic violence was *not* an inevitable accompaniment to Kenya's electoral process. By all reports, voting was carried out peacefully, with the wananchi turning out in high numbers at polling stations across the country. When tallies began to suggest that the Kenyatta-Ruto ticket had defeated Odinga and his running mate, Kalonzo Musyoka, by the slimmest of majorities (50.07 percent of the vote), allegations of vote irregularities were voiced alongside calls for peace and unity. In this contested election, Kenyans took their challenges to the courts instead of to the streets. On March 30, 2013, the Kenya Supreme Court confirmed Kenyatta's win, and Raila conceded his claim to the presidency.[97]

Since the beginning of the multiparty era, electoral violence rooted in a deep history of inequality and ethnically based patrimonialism has shaped the Kenyan political landscape. This violence went largely unacknowledged by the international press, which chose to recognize the unhampered elections of 2002 as confirmation of the West's image of Kenya as "an island of peace in a sea of conflict." When violence in 2008 shattered these illusions, Western observers read the situation through the uncomplicated lens of "tribal atavism."

Occurring in the same year as the violence, the election of the first African American president of the United States, and one of Kenyan descent to boot, did not transform life in Kenya or US-Kenya relations, contrary to the expectations of many wananchi. Kenyans' patrimonial expectations of their "son" did not accord with American political realities. At the same time, political pressure on Obama applied through the American Far Right's continued efforts to paint Obama as a "son of the soil" of Western Kenya and thus a dangerous outsider were reinforced by images of "ethnic clashes" and "tribal war" in his alleged home country and by depictions of his purportedly close relationship with "his fellow Luo tribesman," the "radical" Raila Odinga. For their part, by 2010 the wananchi consumed and reacted to these representations of Kenyan history, politics, and culture through mobilizing digital media to "write back" against them or to rework them to forward their own political ends on the local and global levels. The upcoming final chapter delves deeper into American foreign policy toward Africa in the Obama era, inquiring into the ways in which the president's Kenyan heritage has or has not interacted with American and Kenyan politics to shape his administration's approach to Africa.[98]

7

Obama for Africa or Africa for Obama?

Mr. Deputy Speaker, Sir, indeed, history is in the making. I knew that we can all try to relate to President Obama in various ways. This morning I was listening to the BBC and I heard the Southern Sudanese claim that President Obama is Sudanese. Just sitting here next to my learned friend, Mr. James Orengo, he is saying that even the Irish are claiming parentage of President elect Barack Obama. Everybody is claiming a piece of Barack Obama. Be that as it may, what does it actually mean for the world today?

—Kalonzo Musyoka, 2009[1]

Across the continent, the initial years of the Obama administration were marked by a flurry of excitement about the potentially positive implications the election of the first African American president of the United States held for Africa. While the Kenyan press dubbed Obama "Kenya's Gift to America," efforts to claim the US president were certainly not confined to East Africa.[2] Discourses flowing from myriad African nations broadly embraced Obama as a symbol of diasporic leadership and simultaneously read his political ascendancy through conspicuously local politics of belonging.

This chapter examines how Obama's ascendancy has affected Africa, tracing the broad brushstrokes of American foreign policy to the micropolitics of uneven development in the village of Kogelo. It explores whether the Obama administration's Africa policy has reflected a nuanced, second-generation "immigrant insider" view of the continent's place in the world or a more blunt Western perspective, that of a world leader interested primarily in the primacy of American political power. It asks to what degree the efforts to paint Obama as a "son of the soil" of Kenya discussed throughout this book have or have not influenced the administration's Africa policy. In so doing, the chapter addresses how since Obama's election in 2008, Africans generally and Kenyans in particular have mobilized digital media to compare and contrast American politics with those across the continent, to articulate their expectations, desires, and disappointments vis-à-vis Obama, to hash out ethnic politics, and to write back against the inaccurate representations of Kenya's past and present that have proliferated with Obama's ascendancy.

Obama's Kenyan heritage opened a space for lively debates about the nature of African versus American politics.[3] From the 2008 campaign to the 2009 inauguration, African writers across the continent and throughout the diaspora addressed the *Americanness* of Obama's rise, drawing upon it to express African desires and African discontents. Kenyan commentary was particularly pointed, suggesting that the politics of patronage would have made Obama's ascendancy impossible in Kenya itself. Marking out a sharp contrast between Obama and the archetypal Big Man, one editorialist explained, "You are in business if you are a son of a past president or party leader, a political opportunist as opposed to a crusader for people's rights, have vast wealth, have been on the political scene for awhile and can bring the advantage of your tribal numbers."[4] Likely with the histories of the entrenched Kikuyu and Luo political dynasties discussed in this book in mind, one writer even suggested that as a "Luo" in Kenya, Obama would have met the same fate as Odinga, Mboya, Ouko, and other past political luminaries.

In a similar vein, during the US campaign season, a writer from Cameroon described Obama's success as a most extraordinary feat that could "only be achieved in America, the land of opportunities, even if these opportunities are not always equal," and further speculated that if Obama had been born Cameroonian, local authorities "would have banned his political rallies, brutalised his followers and sympathisers,

Figures 7.1 and 7.2. "Obama Inc." African merchants selling Obama wares in Djenné, Mali (*left*), and Accra, Ghana (*right*). Photographs courtesy of Doris Wright and Don Wright.

and ordered [him] to toe the line."[5] And, while a writer from Namibia called Obama's rise stuff of "a fairytale nature" possible only in the United States, another author from Abuja noted that Nigerians had to embrace a message of "change" emanating not from their own government but from America.[6]

Celebrations of Obama's rise were also made to speak to particular political contests and to Pan-Africanist attitudes more generally. For one, taking a cue from Obama's own campaign rhetoric, the Zimbabwean opposition party Movement for Democratic Change (MDC) noted that the Obama election was "a victory of hope, faith, change, a restart, values and dreams which have underpinned our fight . . . against dictatorship and the neo-fascism of (President) Robert Mugabe."[7] Other writers from around the continent used the 2008 election to affirm broad, Afrocentric readings of world history, claiming, for instance, that Obama was simply the latest in a long line of "Great Black Men Who Dominated the World."[8] The 2008 US election provided an important space for Africans to debate "the politics of victimhood" versus "the politics of hope" in ways that both shined significant light on African governance generally and promoted local politics with an entrepreneurial spirit.[9]

While the press and other media outlets across the continent approached Obama's rise with largely unfettered optimism about the benefits that the election of an American president of Kenyan descent could potentially hold both for the continent as a whole and for their own localities, African scholars and intellectuals were more circumspect about what an Obama presidency would mean for Africa. For example, renowned Cameroonian philosopher and political theorist Achille Mbembe remarked with caution during the campaign that even with all the praise erupting from across Africa, Obama himself had not yet "indicated a willingness to significantly depart from the outdated view of the continent that has underpinned US policy since the end of the Cold War."[10] Indeed, Africa seemed to feature only minimally in Obama's larger foreign policy visions.[11] According to a former assistant secretary of state for Africa who served as an adviser to the campaign, while Obama's strategy for the continent was focused on economic integration, security, and democratization, this strategy was rarely addressed by the campaign.[12] Further, analyses of the transcripts of the three presidential debates and the one vice presidential debate of 2008 show that "Africa" was uttered only three times and "Kenya" was mentioned just once.[13]

After the excitement of the campaign and election died down, more sobering scholarly critiques of Obama's foreign policy vis-à-vis Africa emerged—his Kenyan heritage provided no free passes. During the first years of the Obama presidency, scholars pointed out that despite an increase in foreign aid during the Bush administration, the post-9/11 focus on the "war on terrorism" had actually eroded American diplomatic influence on the continent. Taking note of the mounting pressure in domestic politics, the ongoing wars in Iraq and Afghanistan, and the global economic recession, intellectuals were quick to remark that Africans should not expect much more than "symbolic support" from the first African American president of the United States.[14]

During the summer of 2009, Obama made his first presidential visits to the African continent, traveling to Egypt and then to Ghana—but not to Kenya. Delivering a speech in Cairo popularly dubbed as "an address to the Muslim world," he emphasized his own familial connections to Africa and Islam with the aims of highlighting shared cultural affinities and diffusing popular notions that American foreign policy was shaped by religion.[15] Perhaps as a reward for Ghana's successful 2008 democratic election, or their emerging role as a new oil-producing state, or as a nod to the long affinity African American civil rights leaders have had for the country, Ghana's coastal city of Accra was selected as the location for Obama's first official statement in sub-Saharan Africa.[16] Reflecting on Ghana's history as the first country south of the Sahara to win freedom from colonial rule and emphasizing his African heritage, Obama's remarks in Accra reinforced his policy agenda for the continent. His focus on the role Africans should play in fighting corruption and promoting development in a later speech before the Ghanaian Parliament echoed remarks he had made as a senator in regard to Kenya discussed in chapter 3. Obama argued, "We must start from the simple premise that Africa's future is up to Africans. I say this knowing full well the tragic past that has sometimes haunted this part of the world. After all, I have the blood of Africa within me, and my family's own story encompasses both the tragedies and triumphs of the larger African story."[17]

Media and scholarly responses to the statement and speeches and to the Obama administration's Africa policy followed trajectories like those of reactions to the 2008 campaign and election. Both the Cairo and the Ghana speeches were met with great celebration and fanfare in the domestic and international press, signaling perhaps hopes for a new and more personalized engagement with Africa by the administration. Scholars in turn were quick to point out the disconnects between hopeful expectations and policy. Early assessments of the Obama administration's track record regarding Africa pointed to more continuities than changes. For example, while at first glance portions of the Accra statement seem to suggest a departure from neocolonial modes of political engagement with the continent, Obama's repeated stressing that African issues should be left "up to Africans" was reminiscent of a 1970s call by Jimmy Carter for "African solutions to African problems."[18]

In many respects, however, Obama's approach to Africa was hamstrung by global forces. The advent of the world economic recession and the ongoing "global war on terror" left little political and practical capital for fresh initiatives on the continent. Consequently the administration's African agenda mirrored long-established paradigms of engagement through humanitarian aid, security issues, and the politics of oil. Of these, security initiatives have been the most visible element of the administration's approach to Africa and reflect the legacy of the Bush administration's "global war on terrorism."

From active military involvement in Libya to US support for antiterrorism operations in Somali, security interventions even inspired a feeling among some African politicians that Obama's foreign policy agenda was detrimental to Africa. For instance, some critics of the US military intervention to overthrow Mu'ammar Gadhafi of Libya in 2011 argued that Obama's actions were contrary to historic Pan-Africanist goals of African unity. Dictator of Libya for decades and chairperson of the African Union (AU) from 2009 to 2010, Gadhafi lent significant financial support to the AU. He had also been a major supporter of the antiapartheid movement, so much so that one of Nelson Mandela's grandsons was called "Gaddafi."[19] The patronage of the "King of Kings" (Gadhafi had been styled as such by a conclave of one hundred Kenyan elders for whom he sponsored a lavish junket to Libya in 2010) on the continent extended even to the humble shores of Lake Victoria, as members of the Luo Council of Elders (LCE) made several trips to Libya between 2009 and 2011, returning each time with monetary donations.[20] This sort of patronage, carried out on a microscale but across far-flung locales, together with a nostalgia for Kwame Nkrumah's vision of a "United States of Africa" that Gadhafi had cleverly co-opted, prompted strong critiques of the Obama administration's activities in Libya in particular and across the continent more generally. Most boldly, Namibian prime minister Nahas Angula asserted, "Obama did not show any respect for the African continent during his first term."[21] Generally less influenced by notions of "respect" and "diasporic responsibility" than members of the media, numerous scholars have posited that the administration's modes of engagement on the continent gave lie to Obama's rhetoric voiced in Accra that "Africa's future is up to Africans."[22]

By the beginning of Obama's second term in office, the formerly glowing estimates of African media outlets had taken on more critical tones as well. While people across the continent widely celebrated Obama's reelection, the level of excitement, even in Kenya, was nowhere near that of 2008.[23] African supporters in 2012 often framed their praise less with presumptions of diasporic loyalty and more with inducements to the American president to work harder for the continent. For one, a Kenyan editorial in the wake of Obama's 2012 electoral victory expressed both resounding praise and an overt call for more action:

Africanists who believe Obama has not helped the continent out of its vicious cycle of violent conflict, poor governance and wanton poverty will be looking for hope in the sober and humane face of Obama to light their lives. He cannot shy away from the conflicts in Congo, the Maghreb or Horn of Africa any more. Obama should look beyond the Arab-Israel conflict and take his eyes off Iran, which has become the pet obsession of the West. There is more to world peace than Iran's exaggerated nuclear program.[24]

Writing after Obama's reelection, many African journalists offered explanations of why the president had demonstrated no special commitment to the continent during his first term, a number positing that pressures on Obama to show clearly that he was a "son of the soil" of the United States had played a role. For example, Boniface Mwangi, a Kenyan photographer and political activist who admitted Obamamania drove him to take out a loan to finance his US trip to the 2009 inauguration, read the administration's lack of special concern with Africa through the lenses of political patronage in Kenya and the complex politics of "belonging" in the United States. While he noted Obama's links to Kenya and Africa with pride and expressed hopes that Obama's second term would lead to more tangible engagement, his optimism was tempered by the recognition that the president's approach to Africa was circumscribed by domestic politics. He explained, "Obama is afraid of how he'll be judged, how he'll come out. So he's not truly himself."[25]

More pointedly, in a *New York Times* op-ed, Kenyan journalist Murithi Mutiga noted simply, "Obama has not been perfect," but also included a lengthy rebuttal of the American Far Right's efforts to paint Obama as a Kenyan socialist that this book details in chapter 4.[26] Responding directly to attempts to situate Obama in an inaccurate, revisionist narrative of Kenyan history, Mutiga worked to reframe Kenya's relation to the United States, underscoring, "Kenya is anything but a socialist haven. Since independence in 1963, Kenya has been America's staunchest ally in East Africa."[27] Such reflections point to the keen awareness among Kenyans of how Obama's personal history, and by extension the history of Kenya, was being distorted, politicized, and exploited abroad.

Four years after his visits to Accra and Cairo, a five-day, three-country African tour marked Obama's first substantial engagement with the con-

Figures 7.3 and 7.4. President Obama (*left*) looking out from the infamous slave quarters on Gorée Island in Senegal. Michelle Obama (*right*) places a wreath with Tanzanian first lady Salma Kikwete at the Dar es Salaam memorial to the victims of the 1998 Al-Qaeda bombing of the United States Embassy Building. Official White House photos, https://www.whitehouse.gov/africa-trip-2013.

tinent during his second term, undertaken at a time when his popularity on the continent and foreign policy approval numbers had dropped significantly since the euphoria expressed in 2008.[28] The itinerary—Senegal, South Africa, and Tanzania—was targeted to speak to America's contemporary interests in and historical ties to the continent. The bulk of the tour was devoted to South Africa, which receives more than one-third of all US exports to Africa.[29] There the Obamas visited Nelson Mandela's cell at the Robben Island Prison, which offered a space to reflect on the United States and South Africa's common historical experiences of profound racial discrimination and heroic civil rights struggles. An official stop at the infamous and controversial "door of no return," through which slaves departed from Senegal's Gorée Island, emphasized the United States' historic connections with West Africa. And a wreath-laying ceremony paying tribute to victims of the 1998 Al-Qaeda bombing of the US embassy in Dar es Salaam, Tanzania, served to reinforce ties forged between the two countries in fighting the "global war on terror."[30] Official rhetoric throughout the trip remained little changed from that of 2009. Kenya was not a part of this second and more extensive African tour.

Questions of when Obama would next visit Kenya persisted after the 2009 visit. For example, in a brief interview on the eve of Vice President Joe Biden's trip to Kenya in 2010, Rachael Nakitare, a senior producer and journalist with the Kenya Broadcasting Corporation (KBC), queried

Obama about plans to visit the country. Obama made the widely cited comment, "Well, I'm positive that before my service as President is completed I will visit Kenya again."[31] Thus, when plans were being discussed for the 2013 African tour, Kenyans were hopeful that their country would receive the special recognition accorded to South Africa, Senegal, Ghana, and Tanzania, and were optimistic that they might get an opportunity to relive the Obamamania of 2008 through pageantry and an official visit.[32]

However, the highly contentious results of Kenya's March 2013 elections and the International Criminal Court (ICC) indictments of Uhuru Kenyatta and William Ruto, the newly elected president and vice president, disqualified Kenya from potential itineraries. Indeed, during a televised "town hall" meeting in South Africa in 2013, Obama spoke to what members of the Kenyan press had deemed a "snub" of his ancestral homeland.[33] Alluding to the indictments, he explained, "I was very proud to see the restraint in which the election was held. We did not see a repeat of the violence that we saw in the last election. But with a new administration that's also having to manage some of the international issues around the ICC, I did not think it was the optimal time for me to visit. But as I said, I'm going to— I've got three and a half years. So if in three years and seven months I'm not in Kenya, then you can fault me for not following through on my promise."[34]

Kenyans offered a variety of responses to Obama's decision to not visit the country. Most dramatically, Vice President William Ruto's comments hinted that the "snub" potentially threatened bilateral relations, arguing, "Obama's failure to visit the country does not stop us running the government. We have other friendly nations we will partner with."[35] Kenyans easily grasped the politics of a presidential visit and the shape of the tacit dialogue between the American president and the Kenyan vice president being carried out in public remarks. As one Kisumu resident remarked, "I understand Obama's decision. His relatives in Kogelo, and in fact all of Nyanza will be sad, but our politicians are corrupt, so what can we expect?"[36] Nonetheless, disappointment was palpable in Kenya as Obama again stayed away. For example, in responding to the selection of Tanzania over Kenya, one Luo noted, "It is like hearing that your son came so close to home, but just visited your neighbours and not you his father or mother."[37]

We next turn to developments in Obama's "home cubed" since his election in 2008.

Back in Kenya: A Tale of Two Kogelos

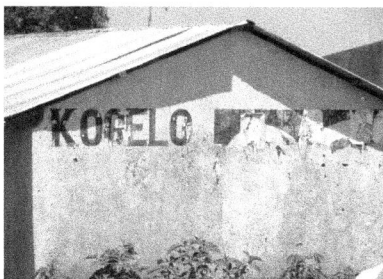

Figures 7.5 and 7.6. The main building at the Kogelo Village Resort (*left*) contrasted with a local business at the main trading center (*right*), less than two hundred meters away, in May 2013. Photographs by author.

Returning to Kogelo in May 2013, we were pleasantly surprised that the sixty-kilometer drive from Kisumu was smooth and quick. Recalling a similar journey in 2004 that took several hours on dilapidated roads, we speculated that Obama's election had stimulated tangible investments in his paternal homeland. Indeed, with the international attention showered on Kogelo since 2008, the area has received a boost in development assistance from the Kenyan government. As we experienced firsthand, the formerly tortuously bumpy road to Kogelo from the main Kisumu-Bondo highway was upgraded and paved, and electricity was connected to the small village in Siaya County for the first time. Aiming to capitalize on this fresh attention, investors trickled into Kogelo, driving up local land prices and starting a few new business ventures during the first years of the Obama presidency.[38] Also, tourists interested in the president's ancestral home made their way to Western Kenya. However, by 2013, the initial excitement of Obamamania had died down, and the rural landscape of Kogelo reflected increasing inequality. The Obama family's ties to Kogelo were not necessarily a boon to all the village's residents.[39]

Kogelo is now a community of contrast. Run-down *maduka*, small kiosk shops, and businesses visibly struggling to make ends, so typical of many rural Kenyan communities, stand at the market crossroad of the town center. However, the paved road forks at a glossy sign for the Kogelo Village Resort and the Senator Obama Kogelo Secondary School, leading ultimately to the homestead of Obama's step-grandmother, who is affectionately known as "Mama Sarah" or "Granny Sarah." The resort, which opened in 2011, features well-manicured lawns and a swimming pool (under construction) opposite the three-story building some Kogelo residents call the "White House." The resort is owned by Nicholas Rajula, a controversial former local official and self-proclaimed cousin of President Obama.[40] Financed in part by a loan of close to twenty million Kenyan shillings (KSH) from the Kenya Tourism Development Corporation and benefiting from waivers on VAT and import taxes, the property has been reported to be worth close to 80 million KSH (close to 1 million US dollars).[41] With rooms named "Michelle," "Sasha," "Malia," and "Mama Sarah," it is clear that the resort's goal is to market the president's connections to Kenya—and to Kogelo. The resort's manager reported a slow but steady growth in visitors, adding that the hotel was not yet operating at capacity (in summer 2013), and served mainly out-of-town tourists and local politicians.[42]

Traveling down the road from the hotel, one immediately passes the Senator Obama Kogelo Secondary School, which, as its name suggests, has also benefited the president's connection to the area. Since 2006, the institution, formerly Kogelo School, has seen nearly a 100 percent increase in enrollment, stimulated mainly by the speculation that scholarship opportunities abroad would be forthcoming. Donations from abroad have trickled in, including a 2009 gift of $35,000 from the Corporate Council on Africa for new classroom space.[43] Past the new construction at the resort and school, the road then winds down a few more meters to the imposing gate of the Obama homestead. No longer can visitors just arrive at Granny Sarah's doorstep as they did in 2008; a newly constructed police barracks guards the compound twenty-four hours a day. The roughly half-mile span of road between the Obama homestead and the main road reveals the full scope of recent development in Kogelo. Infrastructure has been upgraded and local health-care facilities improved. However, the profound economic benefits envisioned for all Kogelo residents in 2008 have been realized by only a select few.

The brief development boom and growing inequality in Kogelo did not translate into an increase in the village's political clout. By 2013, even

the mystique surrounding the Obama name had begun to fade. For instance, President Obama's half brother Malik launched a campaign for the
governorship of Siaya County, but the campaign failed to gain political
momentum. Without the backing of Raila Odinga's ODM party, Malik
campaigned as an independent and garnered less than 1 percent of the
total votes.[44] As one reflects back on the dreams and grand visions Kogelo
residents espoused from 2004 to 2008, two key points become clear. The
election of a "Luo" to the White House did not translate into the windfall
that residents would have expected based on their experiences of patrimonial politics at home. However, the ascendancy of Obama quite literally
put Kogelo on the map.[45] At the same time, the voices of its residents began
to be heard around the world. The next section turns to how the increasing digitization of media has enabled the *wananchi* (citizens) to speak to
global audiences about Kenya's past and present.

Debating Contested Histories and the Politics of Belonging in the Digital Age

Much of the story of Obama and Kenya has unfolded in a world of increasingly digitized media. Whether engaging with the political blogosphere in the United States or the growing digital platforms of African
news media, readers around the world who are interested in Obama and
Kenya are more likely to search for answers through Google than they
are to scan the shelves of bookstores and libraries. When we first began
this project in 2004, it would have been hard to imagine Kogelo residents
posting on Facebook or Twitter and reading Kenyan newspapers on their
mobile phones. However, in the period of Obama's ascendancy, Kenya has
witnessed a massive increase in "connectivity." With over 50 percent of
the population now online and more than thirty million mobile phone
subscriptions throughout the country, the digital spaces for Kenyans to
comment publicly on their own histories are increasing exponentially.[46]
Today's African intellectuals and amateur historians who have taken to
the Internet have the potential to reach much broader and more diverse
audiences than did their forebears whose pamphlets and vernacular newspapers we explored in chapter 3. As the explosion of discourse on Obama

and Kenya shows, digital media offer Kenyans spaces in which to shape international representations of local issues and to debate the politics of "belonging" from the local to the global.

The proliferation of mobile phone and Internet technologies throughout the country is helping Kenyans increasingly to express their political ideas online. For much of the twentieth century, Kenyans had little chance to compete with global representations of their past and present—and certainly could not do so in real time. As we learned in earlier chapters, in the colonial era, black Kenyans' opportunities to express discontent with the colonial regime and challenge the ways in which Kenyan culture and history were represented by British colonials were strongly circumscribed. Fifty years after independence, Kenyans can and do take to Twitter and Facebook to respond in real time to scathing Western news reports like those addressed in the previous chapter or exploitative cinematic portrayals such as those we learned about in chapter 1. For example, in 2012, CNN's coverage of an Al-Shabaab attack in Nairobi that framed the incident as representative of endemic violence throughout the region sparked outrage among Kenyan viewers who critiqued the network's overwrought portrayal via "#SomeoneTellCNN." The Kenyan public's tweeted responses to the report were so overwhelmingly negative that the CNN's East Africa correspondent actually apologized for misrepresenting Kenya to the network's global audience, an unprecedented move that would likely have never occurred in a slower print age.[47]

Social and digital news media offer Kenyans at home an important way to push back at the global representations of African affairs. These spaces are also key media of exchange between East Africa and the three-million-strong Kenyan diaspora, which remits over a billion dollars to Kenya annually.[48] Nonetheless, while digital fora offer a chance for Kenyans to participate in the narration of their country's past and present, the global reach of media giants like the *New York Times*, CNN, and BBC make the playing field anything but equal.

Social media also offer an increasingly important space to debate local politics of belonging and to hold political elites increasingly accountable for their actions. For example, when former vice president Kalonzo Musyoka dismissed a question at an April 2014 press conference because of the journalist's ethnicity (Musyoka made an assumption based on the journalist's surname), Kenyans took to Twitter in droves to call out Musyoka. Within just forty-eight hours after the televised press conference on Kenya's NTV, more than 11,000 tweets had responded to the hashtag #SomeoneTellKalonzoMusyoka and another 2,000 to a related hashtag, #EthnicityinKenya.[49] Comments about the politics of ethnicity in contemporary Kenya were revealing as many dismissed the former VP as a "tribalist," while others admitted that Musyoka's comments "portray what many think, but don't say."[50]

In a similar vein, from late spring 2014 into winter 2015, Gatundu South member of Parliament (MP) Moses Kuria took to Facebook and Twitter to condemn the ODM opposition led by Raila Odinga in a series of posts that accused ODM of supporting terrorist attacks in Lamu and went so far as to revive the infantilizing old charge that Luo were "boys" rather than "men" because Luo do not circumcise, which is the Kikuyu marker of adulthood. After online outrage over Kuria's comments overflowed into the Kenyan press, the country's director of public prosecutions, Keriako Tobiko, initiated a charge of hate speech against the MP.[51]

Yet, while digital media have offered Kenyans at home and abroad new avenues and ease of expression, this freedom has also worked divisively to reinforce the importance of ethnic identification and local politics of "belonging." At the most extreme ends, as we learned in the previous chapter, rumors and hate speech were spread widely through mass text messaging and vernacular radio in order to incite violence after the 2007 elections.[52] More benignly, among Luo people, debates about the political and moral definitions of "Luoness," about "claiming" Obama, and about the politics of "belonging" carried out in vernacular online forums like jaluo.com and the Luo Union Facebook group and on the vernacular radio station Ramgoi FM continue to reinforce the notions of Luo identity discussed throughout this book.[53]

At the same time that digital media, ranging from chat rooms to comment boxes to social media platforms, have provided sources and spaces for challenging misrepresentations of Kenya's past and present, easily accessible online materials have also provided fodder with which to reinforce them and spaces of comfortable anonymity and unaccountability from which to cast aspersions on Obama, which are purportedly historically based, but are in fact historically biased. For instance, one commenter on the Right-leaning website the Daily Caller coined the nickname "O'Mau Mau" to refer to the president.[54] And, as noted above, digital media–based misrepresentation has gone global as Obama's opponents have mobilized online news sources from the continent and Kenyan government sources (newly available on Google Books) to stake claims about Obama's being a "son of the soil" of Kenya. While as scholars it is tempting to dismiss these flawed readings of Kenya's past and present as outlandish prattle, it is important to keep in mind that a significant proportion of the American public takes them at face value and recycles them into popular political discourse through various media platforms where they gain deeper traction and continue to do political work, ginning up racial prejudice and reinforcing a provincial politics of belonging.

Overall, the representations of Kenya's politics and history that we have examined throughout this book point to how easily ideas of "belonging" can be manipulated to serve political ends and how seemingly static self-evident categories like "tribe" are in fact dynamic and complicated, capable of doing important political work. The African dimension of the story of the first African American to hold the presidency of the United States will undoubtedly be a continued source of scholarly debate for years to come. Indeed, the Obama and Kenya story is still evolving, and the narratives produced within a larger geopolitical context can tell us a great deal about Kenya's contested past and the ways African issues are represented more broadly. They also tell us that the past is constantly being renegotiated in the present and that history and contested historical interpretations are often an underlying source of debate on a whole host of contemporary issues. The following epilogue continues to address these themes in the context of Obama's 2015 "homecoming" in Kenya, the first visit of a sitting US president to Kenya.

Epilogue

Tuko Pamoja—We Are Together

On the evening of July 24, 2015, Air Force One touched down at Nairobi's Jomo Kenyatta International Airport, bringing Barack Obama back to his "home cubed" for the first time in nearly ten years. The president arrived in Kenya for the Global Entrepreneurship Summit (GES) in Nairobi and to meet with Kenyan president Uhuru Kenyatta. Obama then traveled to neighboring Ethiopia to meet with President Mulatu Teshome in Addis Ababa, also the headquarters of the African Union (AU). All the events were contained within a brief, three-day East African diplomatic junket.

In the almost three decades since Obama had first visited Kenya, bumping along the road to Kogelo in his sister Auma's dilapidated Volkswagen Beetle, the country had experienced tremendous transformations and crises, as we have discussed throughout this book. In the months leading up to this historic visit, speculation swirled both in Kenya and in the United States about how Obama, as the first Kenyan American president and the first sitting American president to visit Kenya, would engage with Kenya's contested domestic and international politics and with his own complicated heritage.

A whirlwind of controversy incorporating many of the tropes explored in this book encompassed the visit. As we have illustrated throughout, discourse about the Obama-Kenya connection is often rife with hyperbole, historical inaccuracies, and political misinformation. Critiques of the president's trip were no exception as alarmist voices touched on issues ranging from terrorism to tribalism to Birtherism.

Critics used blanket warnings about "terrorism" and gruesome descriptions of attacks by Al-Shabaab, the radical Somali-based Islamist terror group with links to Al-Qaeda, to question Obama's decision to visit Kenya. The US and Kenyan governments jointly announced Obama's visit on March 30.[1] Three days later, Al-Shabaab conducted a bloody assault on Garissa University College in northeast Kenya, during which 148 people were killed on a campus near a Kenyan military base where security forces waited hours to intervene. Pundits questioned the wisdom of making a trip to such a purportedly perilous country despite the fact that Garissa is far removed from Nairobi and the attack followed regional patterns of insecurity and political violence that have plagued northeast Kenya for decades.[2] Other commentators like William Bellamy, ambassador to Kenya under George W. Bush, suggested that while it was unlikely that Al-Shabaab would attack the president and his entourage directly, the group might exploit the high-profile visit to attack elsewhere in Nairobi, "embarrassing" Kenya as the world watched.[3] Recalling earlier occasions when other periods of political violence and insecurity were dismissed as evidence of persistent primordial "tribalism," Western media accounts regarded the Garissa attack through the simplistic, totalizing prism of the "global war on terrorism" (GWOT).

Most bluntly, shortly before the visit, CNN published an article by its Pentagon correspondent asserting that in traveling to Kenya, "President Barack Obama [is] not just heading to his father's homeland, but to a hotbed of terror."[4] On the same day, the network introduced a segment about precautions and measures surrounding the president's trip with the tagline "And now security concerns for President Obama on the eve of his trip to one of the most dangerous countries in the world."[5] Similar critiques followed, with one writer going so far as to suggest, "Kenya is arguably more treacherous for the president than Afghanistan."[6]

CNN also tweeted the story and Kenyans responded in kind, marshaling the power of social media and the country's increasing economic strength to contest the inflammatory, broad-brush images of their country depicted in the Western media.[7] Taking to Twitter and reviving the hashtag #SomeoneTellCNN discussed in the previous chapter, the *wanan-*

chi (citizens) mocked CNN by appropriating the term "hotbed," often with wry humor, and using it to underscore Kenya's growing economic clout, achievements, and culture: "Kenya is a hotbed of entrepreneurship ideas,"[8] "Kenya is a hotbed of champions,"[9] "Kenya is a hotbed of BBQ!"[10] As one Kenyan tweet suggested, "I think we can now safely say that Kenya should request Copyright of the term 'Hotbed of . . .'. From @CNN We actually LOVE using the term nowadays,"[11] and another observed, "The term 'hotbed' has become vernacular in Kenya."[12]

By way of an official response to the Western press's myopic view of contemporary Kenya, the Kenya Tourism Board (KTB), the government agency charged with promoting Kenya's tourist industry, suspended a million-dollar advertising deal with CNN that was intended to market Kenya to a global audience.[13] And President Kenyatta, speaking at the GES, reclaimed the "hotbed" vernacular, describing Kenya as a "hotbed of vibrant culture, national beauty, and infinite possibility."[14] Taking action that reflected the growing power of Kenya's national brand, CNN global executive director and managing director Tony Maddox even flew to Nairobi in August to apologize in person to President Uhuru Kenyatta.[15]

Objections to the trip did not focus solely on terrorism. Echoing the misconceptions about Kenyan history and ethnic politics analyzed throughout this book, critics also posed tribalism as potentially threatening to the (Luo) American president in Kenya. For example, in a widely cited article on the upcoming Kenya visit, Robert Rotberg speculated that the mere presence of Obama, particularly if he decided to visit Kogelo, would "do nothing for inter-group harmony in that volatile country."[16] He asked:

> Do President Obama and his advisors realize that the president's father was a Luo and that the Luo largely backed President Kenyatta's opponent in the 2012 Kenyan presidential election? The rift between Luo and the Kikuyu (President Kenyatta's people) dates back to at least Obama's father's era when Jomo Kenyatta, Uhuru Kenyatta's father, ruled Kenya and was opposed by Oginga Odinga. In the last presidential contest, which Uhuru Kenyatta won, his chief opponent was Raila Odinga, son of Oginga Odinga.[17]

Leaving aside that Rotberg was off by a year in regard to the date of the Kenya elections, with this query, he revives the tropes of atavistic tribalism and the notion of literally inheritable ethnic animosity we explored earlier and thus thrusts Obama into the midst of a historical-political rivalry where he does not belong. Responding to the article's ahistoricity and ethnic stereotyping, the wananchi mobilized social media, taking Rotberg to task on Twitter, chiding the author with remarks such as "LMAO. Robert Rotberg say Obama shouldn't visit Kenya coz his dad was Luo and Uhuru is Kikuyu,"[18] and "#SomeoneTellRotberg playing the tribalism card wont work."[19]

From tweets and Facebook posts to the blogosphere, Kenyans reacted forcefully to this simplistic ethnic argument. Noted blogger Dikembe Desembe, for instance, critiqued Rotberg for proposing that the trip could morph into a full-scale "Luo-Kikuyu schism," suggesting that such a view revealed Rotberg's "ignorance of 'contentious issues' in contemporary Luo-Kikuyu relations in all aspects of public life."[20] He further took Rotberg to task for not understanding how Kenyans, particularly the Kikuyu elite, regarded the visit as a boost to Kenyan global entrepreneurship rather than as an exercise in ethnic politics.[21] Responding on the popular website of the *Sahan Journal* to Rotberg's argument about the visit stoking ethnic conflict, Jamal Axmad-Guudle pointed out that Obama would be visiting Kenya first as head of state and "second as a son of Kenya," a fact clearly recognized by the wananchi.[22]

Other critiques of the trip vis-à-vis Obama's Kenyan heritage centered not on tribalism but on whether the president's personal connections were influencing US political interests. For instance, on the day Obama arrived in Kenya, Fox News host Bret Baier posted a query on his Facebook page: "Is President Obama's Kenya trip necessary, or just Obama self-indulgence?"[23] Responses from the Fox audience ranged from the expected, "Think we all could think of a better way to spend 2,000,000 dollars, rather than on a flight to visit family in Kenya. Just another way to hide from his responsibilities as President," to the absurdist "Free trip to see his brothers, and set up the wedding of his daughter, she is worth 20 goats and some chickens, and probably a meeting with the muslim brotherhood to get his terrorist award for his work at the destruction of america, its his legacy."[24]

In an interesting reversal, the wananchi trolled Fox, overwhelming the Baier thread with their comments. In addition to welcoming Obama and shining a light on Kenya's culture and achievements—"Yes it was wise for him to come and see our #magicalkenya and also get a feel of M-PESA money transfer technology"—Kenyans expressed profound dismay at Americans' racist suppositions and seemingly willful lack of knowledge about Kenya. One Kenyan commentator succinctly summed up by invoking the newly fashionable term "hotbed": "The comments here are a true hotbed of ignorance and stupidity. Period."[25]

Unsurprisingly, Birthers, whose movement we explored in chapter 4, have been very well represented in online forums pertaining to the trip like the Facebook page addressed above. Throughout this book, we have argued that Obama's relationship to Kenya has been profoundly constrained by the American Right's use of his Kenyan heritage to indict him as "foreign," as "un-American," as "untrustworthy," and as "Other." Speaking to the *New York Times* on the eve of the visit, David Axelrod, former chief strategist to the president, addressed the issue, explaining, "If you're asking me, 'Was there a political discussion as to whether it would be disadvantageous to show up in Kenya when Donald Trump was questioning his citizenship,' I don't recall ever having that discussion," adding witheringly, "But maybe no one needed to have that discussion."[26]

Discourse surrounding the trip, even some comments offered jokingly by the president himself, further bears out the contention that Far Right pressures have restricted Obama's relationship with Kenya. For instance, appearing on Fox News the day the trip was announced, John Sununu, former governor of New Hampshire and chief of staff to George H. W. Bush, argued that by visiting Kenya, Obama would be reviving the passion of Birthers. He explained, "I think his trip back to Kenya is going to create a lot of chatter and commentary amongst some of the hard right who still don't see him as having been born in the U.S. . . . I personally think he's just inciting some chatter on an issue that should have been a dead issue a long time ago."[27] Obama himself addressed the critiques with humor during his toast at the state dinner welcoming him to Kenya, saying, "I suspect some of my critics back home are suggesting that I'm back here to look for my birth certificate. . . . That's not the case,"[28] and stated in his speech to the wananchi at Safaricom Indoor Arena that he was "proud" to be "the first Kenyan-American to be President of the United States."[29]

Keeping in line with the conspiracy theories that have followed Obama since 2008, Birthers, including Fox News commentator Todd Starnes, took to social media to parse the purportedly hidden meaning of the president's remarks, suggesting that Obama was tacitly admitting to having been born in Kenya.[30] Birther narratives have continued into the 2016 US presidential campaigns, even though Obama is not legally eligible to run for reelection. A September 2015 CNN poll found that 20 percent of Americans still believe that Obama was not born in the United States, and nearly 30 percent claim that he is Muslim.[31]

Whether critiquing the trip through claims about Kenya's insecurity, the threat posed by tribalism, or Obama's personal "indulgence," commentators fail to recognize the geopolitical importance of Kenya and its significance to the US interests on the continent. In the last one and a half decades, Kenya has emerged as a key strategic partner, along with Ethiopia, in efforts to degrade Al-Shabaab in East Africa and Al-Qaeda in the Horn. Since the 2011 invasion of southern Somalia by the Kenyan Defense Forces, the United States has poured hundreds of millions into regional counterterrorism operations. As part of the African Union–backed AMISOM mission, Kenya has maintained a strong military presence in Somalia and has been a clandestine supporter of US drone strikes and counterterrorism operations in the Horn.[32]

Critics of the trip also tended to overlook Kenya's economic significance, not merely as a regional center but also as a global growth center. With an annual growth rate of close to 6 percent in 2015 (the World Bank predicted similar rising rates to continue until at least 2018), Kenya has emerged as a regional economic powerhouse.[33] In particular, the country has become a hub of manufacturing industry and technical innovation. For example, in his video promoting the GES and welcoming businesses to Kenya and "to opportunity," President Kenyatta, standing in front of a backdrop of Nairobi's high-rise skyline, described Kenya as "a land once known for its savanna, now earning international repute as a silicon savanna."[34] More specifically, the Kenyan telecom giant, Safaricom, which has more than twenty million subscribers, pioneered the mobile money transfer service M-Pesa and has recently developed M-Shwari, a mobile banking system.[35] In 2013, the company acquired branding rights to the stadium-arena complex where Obama addressed the wananchi, changing its name from Moi International Sports Centre to Safaricom Stadium and Safaricom Indoor Arena.[36]

Cementing its historic role as the regional corridor for trade and opportunity in Eastern Africa, Kenya has recently made strategic investments in infrastructure (neglected for the first forty years of independence), and these have been key drivers of the region's continued growth. A rapidly expanding partnership between China and Kenya is also reflected in the country's recent growth; trade between China and the continent was valued at 222 billion US dollars in 2014.[37] With Chinese firms winning massive contracts to build ports and new roads and railway lines in Kenya, Obama's trip provided a space to assert US economic interests and power in counterpoint to China's mounting influence. Finally, Kenya is poised to be the central corridor for South Sudan's exportation of billions of barrels of crude oil and for recently discovered commercial reserves in Uganda and Northern Kenya.

However, the economic picture in Kenya is not one of unhampered prosperity. Large-scale development projects such as the controversial new port planned for Lamu and the development of commercial oil production in Turkana have embroiled local communities, generally to their detriment, in the politics of national development. These conflicts between the state and the local have been broadly defined by the politics of belonging, where regional or ethnic markers are perceived to control access to national development schemes. Despite Kenya's recent mounting economic successes addressed above, the stratification of wealth in the country remains profound. A corner of the "silicon savanna" is occupied by Kibera, Kenya's largest informal settlement, or slum, with an estimated population of over two hundred thousand.[38] The United Nations Development Programme (UNDP) reports that Kenya suffers significant human development losses due to inequality.[39] Today, noted historian of Kenya Robert Maxon's assessment of the immediate postcolonial era still holds: "In independent Kenya, stratification by race would go, but in its place would emerge stratification by wealth."[40]

The Kenyatta regime has also come under fire from domestic and international critics for human rights abuses related to GWOT, most notably Operation Linda Usalama. Carried out in the aftermath of the September 2013 Al-Shabaab attack on the tony Westgate Shopping Mall in Nairobi, the operation entailed Kenyan security forces going door-to-door in Nairobi's Eastleigh section, known as "Little Mogadishu" due to its long-standing Somali population, and in other parts of the city with concentrated Somali populations, and sweeping up thousands of ethnic Somalis, including Kenyan citizens and refugees from Somali; many of those detained were women and children.[41] The detainees were held and many interned in Safaricom Stadium, the site of Obama's speech to the Kenyan people. The explanation of the process by then cabinet secretary Joseph ole Lenku had eerie echoes of British colonial counterinsurgency tactics used to combat Mau Mau: "We bring the arrested persons to this place, screen them, verify those who have documents and those who do not have; we take appropriate action."[42] Since 2013, the crackdown on the Kenyan Somali population has continued and has been defended with increasingly nativist approaches to regional relations.[43] Kenyan lawmakers have gone so far as to take a cue from the American Far Right and propose building an elaborate fence along the Kenya-Somali border in the wake of the horrific attack on Garissa University College.[44]

On the eve of the visit, we wrote in *Politico* about the potential and challenges presented by the Obama-Kenya connection and about our hopes that Obama, with the combined power of the US presidency and his status as Kenya's favorite "son," would be uniquely empowered to speak to key issues such as terrorism, human rights, corruption, and development. This trip, we argued, offered an unprecedented opportunity for Obama "to employ his controversial American identity with an authority no U.S. politician may ever wield again."[45] In contrast, the majority of pundits in the United States, together with the dozens of foreign journalists preparing to travel to East Africa, covered the upcoming visit with a provincial focus on contemporary America. For instance, by reading the controversy over LGBTQ rights in Kenya and on the continent more generally through the lens of gay marriage debates in the US, or treating Kenya's struggles with Al-Shabaab simply as an example of the kind of "Islamo-terrorism" that might befall the United States, global media discourse refracted Kenyan issues through primarily American perspectives and values.[46]

When Obama landed in Kenya, the expectations of the wananchi ran high as they renewed their excitement and turned their eyes to enterprise, reviving Obamamania to a degree reminiscent of the celebrations surrounding Obama's 2008 presidential victory. Local markets throughout the country were again awash in Obama paraphernalia. CNN reported, "The Obama craze has spared no sector, from mobile phone ringtones offering extracts from his speeches, to bespoke billboards highlighting products of all kinds in the light of the president's arrival."[47] Many Luo sported Obama T-shirts and hats emblazoned with the simple Dholuo phrase "Abiro dala" (I have come home).[48]

For its part, the Nairobi county government threw tremendous resources into beautifying Nairobi for the state visit, going so far as to plant grass a few days before the president's arrival and then to replace it with turf, which was widely reputed to have been taken up and returned to the vendor at the visit's conclusion.[49] After Nairobi county governor Evans Kidero made an impassioned Twitter plea for Nairobians to stick to the sidewalks and let the grass grow,[50] the wananchi, true to form, tweeted back: "Obama atapiwe googles za green while on Mombasa road #Kiberagrass" (Obama should get green googles while on Mombasa road #Kiderograss)[51] and "#KideroGrass kwani Obama atakuja na ngombe? What of Pope will he build new churches?" (#KideroGrass why is Obama going to come with a cow?).[52]

Kenyans' excitement was necessarily tempered, however, by the president's rigid schedule, which had him spending two packed days in Nairobi. To the disappointment of many in the Luo community, the visit did not include a trip to Kogelo. Obama's relatives brought the spirit of his *dala* (home) to Nairobi, gathering for a family dinner. Nevertheless, 250 miles away in Kogelo, the government of Siaya celebrated lavishly, organizing the "Obama 7s rugby tournament" and a "Grand Air Force One Welcome Party."[53]

His visit structured by bilateral talks with Kenyan leaders, a speech to the audience of the GES, and an address to the wananchi, Obama seized the opportunities to critique and celebrate Kenya. For example, ignoring warnings by Kenyan politicians that he should not bring up gay rights, and despite President Kenyatta's claim that LGBTQ rights were a "non-issue," and anti-gay demonstrations in Nairobi,[54] Obama spoke forcibly about his opposition

Figure E.1. President Obama greeting the audience at the Safaricom Indoor Arena in Nairobi, Kenya, July 26, 2015. Official White House photo by Pete Souza, https://www.whitehouse.gov/blog/2015/07/24/behind-lens-photographing-president-50-countries.

to discrimination based on sexual orientation.[55] At the other end of the spectrum, he embraced, to wide acclaim, the "Lipala," Kenya's latest dancehall craze, hitting the dance floor with President and First Lady Kenyatta and his national security adviser, Susan Rice, at the official state dinner.[56]

The trip culminated with a lengthy speech at Safaricom Indoor Arena in front of a packed, influential political audience. Obama began his forty-minute address to the Kenyan people by pointing to his own humble origins in Kenya. Aiming to connect to the Kenyan masses, he recalled how during his first visit in 1988, "instead of eating at fancy banquets with the President, we were drinking tea and eating *ugali* and *sukumawiki* (a daily Kenya staple dish)."[57] Drawing on arguments from his memoir *Dreams from My Father*, Obama connected his family's Kenyan roots to the nation's colonial past. Setting up a critical view of Kenya's fifty years of postcolonial development, he argued for the importance of understanding deep and recent histories, of linking past and present, noting:

The daily limitations—and sometimes humiliations—of colonial-ism—that's recent history. The corruption and cronyism and trib-alism that sometimes confront young nations—that's recent history. But what these stories also tell us is an arch of progress—from for-eign rule to independence; from isolation to education, and engage-ment with a wider world. It speaks of incredible progress. So we have to know the history of Kenya, just as we Americans have to know our American history.[58]

Tempering his critiques of contemporary politics and governance with a generalization about the problems of all "young nations," Obama then fo-cused on the future of Kenya and US-Kenyan relations, citing good gover-nance, development, peace, and reconciliation as key markers of success. He promised US support for all of the aforementioned issues while at the same time holding Kenyans to account, arguing, "Progress requires that you honestly confront the dark corners of your own past; extend rights and opportunities to more of your citizens; see the differences and diver-sity of this country as a strength."[59]

While mobilizing his unique political capital to speak forcefully throughout his visit about a range of contentious issues, Obama none-theless chose his words carefully. Although he spoke at length about terrorism and political violence, his criticisms remained general, not targeting particular individuals or regimes, and his calls for peace and reconciliation did not point to specific injustices or the long history of impunity among Kenya's leaders. Some commentators in Kenya read the visit as a tacit endorsement of Kenyatta and Ruto's Jubilee government; a regime marred by the International Criminal Court (ICC) indictments of its president and vice president, who had brazenly run for office under a slogan pundits deemed "the coalition of the accused" in 2013. Some critics saw the timing of the visit toward the end of Obama's presidency as awkward, offering "too little too late."[60] Others, however, suggested that the trip could mark the beginning of a more intensive engagement between the United States and Kenya, which could extend beyond the Obama presidency. For one, Kenyan political activist Boniface Mwangi expressed both the disappointment in and the continued hopes that Ken-yans hold for their favorite "son": "George W. Bush did more for Africa—

it's a fact—but now Obama has a chance to redeem himself. . . . If you look at what he's done in the last few months, he's redeemed himself to the black community in the United States and he's redeemed himself to black Africans. Have you seen the movie Django Unchained? This is Obama Unchained."[61]

In the buildup to the visit, Obama reflected on the political frustrations of engaging with Kenya as president. Responding to a question about the trip during a White House press conference in early July, he lamented, "I'll be honest with you, visiting Kenya as a private citizen is probably more meaningful to me than visiting as President."[62]

Speculation has already begun about what Obama's connection to Kenya will yield when he is no longer constrained by the duties of his office or the intransigencies of the Far Right. Obama will be only fifty-six years old when he leaves office, ideally positioned to play an active role in public life for many years to come. Indeed, as of 2015, preparations for his presidential library and foundation in Chicago were already well under way, with reports stating that the immediate fund-raising goal for his postpresidential endeavors was upward of one billion dollars.[63] Obama declared to Kenyans, "The next time I'm back I may not be wearing a suit," and he very well may bring a powerful voice and full coffers to bear on public missions in East Africa when he leaves office.[64] While speculation about Obama's personal future in 2015 is still mainly conjecture, it is clear that Kenya's contested histories and the politics of belonging will continue to inspire heated political debate about the impact of the first African American president of the United States on Kenya and throughout the African continent. The wananchi wished Obama as he departed Kenya, "Kwaheri #Potus . . . we kenyans are proud of you. tutembelee tena . . . karibu," that is, "Goodbye #Potus . . . we Kenyans are proud of you. you should visit us again . . . you're welcome."[65]

Notes

Introduction: Obama and Kenya in the Classroom

1. Matthew Carotenuto and Brett Shadle, "Toward a History of Violence in Colonial Kenya," *International Journal of African Historical Studies* 45, no. 1 (2012): 1.

2. For some useful teaching sources aimed to privilege African voices in world history, see Trevor R. Getz, ed., *African Voices of the Global Past: 1500 to the Present* (Boulder, CO: Westview, 2014); and Donald R. Wright, *The World and a Very Small Place in Africa: A History of Globalization in Niumi, the Gambia* (New York: Sharpe, 2010).

3. See Terry Barringer and Marion Wallace, eds., *African Studies in the Digital Age: DisConnects?* (Leiden: Brill, 2014).

4. For example, Gerald Horne, *Mau Mau in Harlem? The U.S. and the Liberation of Kenya* (New York: Palgrave Macmillan, 2009).

5. CNN Library, "Barack Obama Fast Facts," http://www.cnn.com/2012/12/26/us/barack-obama---fast-facts.

Chapter 1: Discovering Obama in Kenya

1. A career diplomat, William Bellamy served as US ambassador to Kenya from 2003 to 2006. A graduate of Tufts University Fletcher School of Law and Diplomacy, he is currently the Warburg Chair in International Relations at Simmons College in Boston.

2. For more on the place of Muthaiga in colonial and postcolonial elite society, see Danielle de Lame, "Grey Nairobi: Sketches of Urban Socialities," in *Nairobi Today: The Paradox of a Fragmented City*, ed. Hélène Charton-Bigot and Deyssi Rodriguez-Torres (Dar es Salaam: Mkuki na Nyota, 2010), 167–214.

3. For more on Barack Obama Sr., see Sally H. Jacob's popular account, *The Other Barack: The Bold and Reckless Life of President Obama's Father* (New York: Public Affairs, 2011).

4. Obama was projected to win easily due primarily to the scandals that plagued a series of Republican nominees; he ultimately captured 70 percent of the vote while his Republican challenger, Alan Keyes, attained 27 percent. See CNN, "Obama Projected to Gain Seat for Dems," November 2, 2004, http://www.cnn.com/2004/ALLPOLITICS/11/02/senate.illinois/index.html.

5. Daniel Branch, *Kenya: Between Hope and Despair, 1963–2011* (New Haven, CT: Yale University Press, 2011), 230.

6. Luo speakers today are considered to be the fourth-largest ethnic group in Kenya, numbering just over four million and making up just over 10 percent of the country's citizens. Republic of Kenya, *2009 Population and Housing Census Results* (Nairobi: Kenya National Bureau of Statistics, 2010).

7. The GADO (Godfrey Mwampembwa) cartoon shown in figure 1.1, depicting the "Obama Brand," is available at http://gadocartoons.com/. Also see Tejumola Olaniyan's growing "educational encyclopedia," available at http://www.africa.wisc.edu/politicalcartooninginafrica/.

8. Dane K. Kennedy, "The Imperial History Wars," *Journal of British Studies* 54, no. 1 (2015): 6.

9. Neal W. Sobania, *Culture and Customs of Kenya* (Westport, CT: Greenwood Press, 2003), 3.

10. Branch dates this pithy question back to at least 1964. See Branch, *Kenya*, 33. The "How is Kenya?" quip is often evoked in debates about Northern Kenya on the floor of Parliament. For instance, a simple Google Books search for "How is Kenya?" calls up dozens of citations of the jocular query in the official *Kenya Gazette*, which contains Kenya's parliamentary debates from the late 1960s through the early 2000s.

11. For more on the Kenyan environment, see UNEP, *Kenya: Atlas of Our Changing Environment* (Nairobi: United Nations Environment Programme, 2009), http://www.unep.org/dewa/africa/kenyaatlas/.

12. See the United Nations population projections for Kenya at http://data.un.org/Data.aspx?d=GenderStat&f=inID%3A7. For an array of demographic information, see also the World Bank's country report on Kenya at http://www.worldbank.org/en/country/kenya. For a broader analysis of urbanization in Africa, see Bill Freund, *The African City: A History* (Cambridge: Cambridge University Press, 2007).

13. UNEP, *Kenya*, 2; and Republic of Kenya, *Kenya Vision 2030* (Nairobi: Ministry of Planning and National Development, 2007), 19. For more on Ken-

ya's current development plan, popularly referred to as "Vision 2030," visit www.vision2030.go.ke.

14. For an introduction to Kenya's cultural and linguistic diversity, see Sobania, *Culture and Customs of Kenya*.

15. Abdul Sheriff, *Dhow Cultures of the Indian Ocean: Cosmopolitanism, Commerce and Islam* (New York: Columbia University Press, 2010); and John M. Mugane, *The Story of Swahili* (Athens: Ohio University Press, 2015).

16. Notions of Luo identity and its regional connections will be discussed in chapter 3. For a short introduction to this broader literature, see John R. Campbell, "Who Are the Luo? Oral Traditions and Disciplinary Practices in Anthropology and History," *Journal of African Cultural Studies* 18, no. 1 (2006): 73–87; and David William Cohen and E. S. Atieno Odhiambo, *Siaya: The Historical Anthropology of an African Landscape* (Athens: Ohio University Press, 1989).

17. For a useful critique about notions of "tribe" in Africanist discourse, see Christopher Lowe, "Talking about 'Tribe': Moving from Stereotypes to Analysis" (Washington, DC: African Policy Information Center, 1997), http://africanactivist.msu.edu/document_metadata.php?objectid=32-130-153D.

18. Frederick D. Lugard, *The Rise of Our East African Empire: Early Efforts in Nyasaland and Uganda* (Edinburgh: Blackwood, 1893), 585–87, 69–75. Excerpts of this important nineteenth-century text on British colonial ideology can be found online, along with many other useful primary sources for African history, at Fordham University's "Internet African History Sourcebook," http://www.fordham.edu/halsall/mod/1893lugard.asp. The full-text digitized version of Lugard's book is available at archive.org.

19. Ibid.

20. Robert Ruark, *Something of Value* (New York: Doubleday, 1955), 135. Cited in David M. Anderson's *Histories of the Hanged: The Dirty War in Kenya and the End of Empire* (New York: Norton, 2005), 1.

21. Binyavanga Wainana, "How to Write about Africa," *Granta* 92 (2005): 1, http://www.granta.com/Archive/92/How-to-Write-about-Africa/Page-1.

22. For useful texts on common stereotypes about Africa in popular discourse, see Chimamanda Adichie's TED lecture, "Danger of a Single Story" (presented at TEDGlobal 2009, Palm Springs, California, July 21–29, 2009), http://www.ted.com/talks/chimamanda_adichie_the_danger_of_a_single_story.html. For a broader discussion of the influence of these stereotypes in the particular context of the United States, see Curtis Keim, *Mistaking Africa: Curiosities and Inventions of the American Mind* (Boulder, CO: Westview Press, 2013).

23. Hugh R. Trevor-Roper, "The Past and the Present: History and Sociology," *Past and Present* 42 (1969): 6.

24. These works and other Western accounts of Obama's Kenya connection are discussed in greater depth in chapter 4.

25. Derek R. Peterson and Giacomo Macola, eds., *Recasting the Past: History Writing and Political Work in Modern Africa* (Athens: Ohio University Press, 2009), 7. See also Karin Barber, ed., *Africa's Hidden Histories: Everyday Literacy and Making the Self* (Bloomington: Indiana University Press, 2006).

26. The proliferation of Kenyan texts relating to Obama in this vein will be discussed in later chapters. For early Kenyan examples, see Jomo Kenyatta's *Facing Mount Kenya: The Tribal Life of the Gikuyu* (London: Secker and Warburg, 1938). Also see Paul Mboya's *Luo kitgi gi timbegi* (Nairobi: East African Standard, 1938).

27. Barack Obama, *Dreams from My Father: A Story of Race and Inheritance* (New York: Random House, 1995). Also see Barack Obama, *The Audacity of Hope: Thoughts on Reclaiming the American Dream* (New York: Crown, 2006).

28. John L. and Jean Comaroff, *Ethnicity Inc.* (Chicago: University of Chicago Press, 2009). For more on the larger debates about evolving notions of ethnicity in Africa, see Thomas Spear, "Neo-Traditionalism and the Limits of Invention in British Colonial Africa," *Journal of African History* 44, no. 1 (2003): 3–27; and Julie MacArthur, "When Did the Luyia (or Any Other Group) Become a Tribe?" *Canadian Journal of African Studies* 47, no. 3 (2013): 351–63.

29. For Kenya, see Philister Adhiambo Madiega, Tracey Chantler, Gemma Jones, and Ruth Prince, "'Our Son Obama': The US Presidential Election in Western Kenya," *Anthropology Today* 24, no. 6 (2008): 4–7; Matthew Carotenuto and Katherine Luongo, "*Dala* or Diaspora? Obama and the Luo Community of Kenya," *African Affairs* 108, no. 431 (2009): 197–219; Steve Ouma Akoth, "The Meanings of Obama in K'ogello: Culture, Ethno-Politics and the Making of Leaders in Multiparty Kenya," *Anthropology Southern Africa* 33, nos. 3–4 (2010): 114–25; Keguro Macharia, "Jambo Bwana: Kenya's Barack Obama," *Qualitative Sociology* 35, no. 2 (2012): 213–27; Karin van Bemmel, "Obama Made in Kenya: Appropriating the American Dream in Kogelo," *Africa Today* 59, no. 4 (2013): 68–90. For a broader context, see Paul Tiyambie Zeleza, *Barack Obama and African Diasporas: Dialogues and Dissensions* (Athens: Ohio University Press, 2009).

30. Stephen Ellis, "Writing Histories of Contemporary Africa," *Journal of African History* 43, no. 1 (2002): 1–26.

31. Matt Raymond, "How Tweet It Is! Library Acquires Entire Twitter Archive," *Library of Congress Blog*, April 14, 2010, http://blogs.loc.gov/loc/2010/04/how-tweet-it-is-library-acquires-entire-twitter-archive.

Chapter 2: Representations of Kenya

This chapter draws attention to the numerous open-access primary sources pertaining to African history generally and the history of Kenya available on the web and ideal for use in undergraduate classrooms.

1. The Roosevelts paid for themselves. Smithsonian, "Celebrating 100 Years: Smithsonian-Roosevelt African Expedition," http://www.mnh.si.edu/onehundredyears/expeditions/SI-Roosevelt_Expedition.html.

2. "President Roosevelt's African Trip," *Science* 28, no. 729 (December 18, 1908): 876–77.

3. Relative value is calculated at $1,320,000. Information available at http://www.measuringworth.com/uscompare/. It should be noted that these calculations are estimates and highly varied. For a useful popular account of the challenging nature of this question for historians, see Ed Crews, "How Much Is That in Today's Money?" *Colonial Williamsburg* (Summer 2002). Available at http://www.history.org/foundation/journal/summer02/money2.cfm.

4. Edward I. Steinhart, "Hunters, Poachers and Gamekeepers: Towards a Social History of Hunting in Colonial Kenya," *Journal of African History* 30, no. 2 (1989): 253.

5. Ibid.

6. For example, Ernest Hemingway, *Green Hills of Africa* (New York: Scribner, 1935). The upmarket tour provider Abercrombie and Kent until this year operated a safari in Kenya and Tanzania called "The Hemingway Safari," and currently lodges its travelers at Hemingway's, a new boutique hotel in Nairobi built to resemble British colonial style. Images are available at http://www.hemingways-nairobi.com/. For a scholarly account, see Edward M. Bruner, "The Maasai and the Lion King: Authenticity, Nationalism, and Globalization in African Tourism," *American Ethnologist* 28, no. 4 (2001): 881–908.

7. Theodore Roosevelt, *African Game Trails: An Account of the African Wanderings of an American Hunter-Naturalist* (New York: Scribner, 1910), vii–viii. Full text is available for download at https//archive.org/details/african-gametrailooroseve.

8. Barack Obama, *Dreams from My Father: A Story of Race and Inheritance* (New York: Random House, 1995), 434.

9. Will Jackson, "White Man's Country: Kenya Colony and the Making of a Myth," *Journal of Eastern African Studies* 5, no. 2 (2011): 344–68.

10. *Kenya* is a corruption of the Kikuyu word *Kirinyaga*, the original name of Mount Kenya. Land alienation and squatter farming were similar to the South African model where the Native Lands Act of 1913 effectively turned African squatter farmers into wanderers performing occasional, casual labor. This legislation was a driving force behind the development of the African National Congress. See Solomon T. Plaatje, *Native Life in South Africa* (London: King, 1914).

11. See Elspeth Huxley, *White Man's Country: Lord Delamere and the Making of Kenya* (London: Chatto and Windus, 1954).

12. Brian Herne, *White Hunters: The Golden Age of African Safaris* (New York: Holt, 1999), 6.

13. Delamere later acquired another fifty thousand acres at Soysambu. James S. Olson and Robert Shadle, eds., *Historical Dictionary of the British Empire*, vol. 1 (Westport, CT: Greenwood Press, 1996), 296. For a useful collection of primary sources on the life of early settlers, see Paul Sullivan, *Kikuyu District: The Edited Letters of Francis Hall, 1892–1901* (Dar es Salaam: Mkuti na Nyota, 2006).

14. The section heading above is inspired by Bruce Berman and John Lonsdale's definitive, two-volume political history of colonial Kenya. See Berman and Lonsdale, *State and Class*, bk. 1 of *Unhappy Valley: Conflict in Kenya and Africa* (London: James Currey, 1992); and *Violence and Ethnicity*, bk. 2 of *Unhappy Valley: Conflict in Kenya and Africa* (London: James Currey, 1992).

15. Caroline Elkins, *Imperial Reckoning: The Untold Story of Britain's Gulag in Kenya* (New York: Holt, 2005), 11. For a contemporary Kenyan reflection on this history fifty years after independence, see Morris Kiruga, "Socialite Settlers: How Sex, Drugs and Crime Built the Colony," *Daily Nation*, June 6, 2013.

16. Isak Dinesen, *Out of Africa* (London: Penguin, 1937).

17. *Out of Africa*, directed by Sydney Pollack (1985; Hollywood: Mirage Enterprises/Universal Studios). See also Beryl Markham, *West with the Night* (Boston: Houghton Mifflin, 1942). And on the most intrigue-laden scandal of the Happy Valley set, see Errol Trzebinski, *The Life and Death of Lord Erroll: The Truth behind the Happy Valley Murder* (London: Fourth Estate, 2000).

18. More recently, *Vogue* shot June 2007 cover girl Keira Knightley "on safari" in the Maasai Mara, accompanied by Maasai warriors and attired in designer clothing that echoed the Victorian era and heaped in Maasai beads. See Plum Sykes, "Keira Knightley: The Chronicles of Keira," *Vogue* 97, no. 6 (June 2007): 176–87, http://www.vogue.com/magazine/article/keira-knightley-the-chronicles-of-keira/#1.

19. Dane K. Kennedy, *Islands of White: Settler Society and Culture in Kenya and Southern Rhodesia, 1890–1939* (Durham, NC: Duke University Press, 1987).

20. For example, see Johann L. Krapf, *Travels, Researches, and Missionary Labors, during an Eighteen Years' Residence in Eastern Africa* (Boston: Ticknor and Fields, 1860).

21. The true provenance of Kilimanjaro remains a point of contention in some circles. See Patrick Wachira, "Did Queen Victoria Yank Mount Kilimanjaro from Kenya?" *Standard Digital*, August 13, 2011, http://www .standardmedia.co.ke/business/article/2000040730/did-queen-victoria-yank-mount-kilimanjaro-from-kenya?pageNo=1.

22. Berman and Lonsdale, *State Class*, bk. 1 of *Unhappy Valley*, 16.

23. John Lonsdale, "The Conquest State, 1895–1904," in *A Modern History of Kenya, 1895–1980: In Honour of B. A. Ogot*, ed. William R. Ochieng' (Nairobi: Evans, 1989), 19–20.

24. At the time of its construction, the Mombasa-Kampala railway was considered a folly, and its progress was plagued by numerous setbacks, including a pair of man-eating lions who consistently attacked the railway camps, carrying off the "coolies," laborers imported from British India. See Charles Miller, *The Lunatic Express* (New York: Macmillan, 1971). The story is told from the perspective of a military-officer-cum-white-hunter tasked with slaying the lions in the film *The Ghost and the Darkness*, starring Val Kilmer and Michael Douglas, directed by Stephen Hopkins (1996; Hollywood: Constellation Films/Paramount Pictures). Eventually shot to death, the (taxidermied) lions are now on display at Chicago's Field Museum, http://archive.fieldmuseum.org/exhibits/exhibit_sites/tsavo/maneaters.html.

25. For Lugard's vision in his own words, see Frederick D. Lugard, *The Dual Mandate in British Tropical Africa* (London: Blackwood, 1922).

26. Sara Berry, "Hegemony on a Shoestring: Indirect Rule and Access to Agricultural Land," *Africa* 62, no. 3 (1992): 327–55. "Hegemony" is an authority so taken for granted and unquestioned that it becomes natural and expected.

27. Brett L. Shadle, *"Girl Cases": Marriage and Colonialism in Gusiiland Kenya, 1890–1970* (Portsmouth, NH: Heinemann, 2006), 64.

28. Kenya National Archives (hereafter KNA), DC/MKS 1/1/3, Ulu Quarterly Report 1909, 42.

29. For a useful look at this style of colonial propaganda, see Alexander Shaw, *Men of Africa* (London: Colonial Empire Marketing Board, 1940). This film is available for streaming online at http://www.colonialfilm.org.uk/.

30. John Iliffe, *A Modern History of Tanganyika* (Cambridge: Cambridge University Press, 1979), 323–24.

31. Gabrielle Lynch, *I Say to You: Ethnic Politics and the Kalenjin in Kenya* (Chicago: University of Chicago Press, 2011); Justin Willis, *Mombasa, the Swahili, and the Making of the Mijikenda* (New York: Oxford University

Press, 1993); and Julie E. MacArthur, "When Did the Luyia (or Any Other Group) Become a Tribe?" *Canadian Journal of African Studies* 47, no. 3 (2013): 351–63.

32. For example, the *New York Times* published Jeffrey Gettleman's article, "Tribal Rivalry Boils over after Kenya Election," December 30, 2007, http://www.nytimes.com/2007/12/30/world/africa/30cnd-kenya.html?em&ex=1199250000&en=d992eb43cf06b8bd&ei=5087%0A&_r=0.

33. Paul Tiyambe Zeleza, "The Establishment of Colonial Rule, 1905–1920," in Ochieng', *Modern History of Kenya*, 43.

34. Elspeth Huxley, *White Man's Country: Lord Delamere and the Making of Kenya* (New York: Praeger, 1968), 215. Cited in Opolot Okia, *Communal Labor in Colonial Kenya: The Legitimization of Coercion, 1912–1930* (New York: Palgrave Macmillan, 2012), 35.

35. KNA, DC/MKS 1/1, Machakos District Annual Report, 1908–1909.

36. Leah Onyango, Anne Omollo, and Elizabeth Ayo, "Gender Perspectives of Property Rights in Rural Kenya," in *Essays in African Land Law*, ed. Robert Home (Pretoria: Pretoria University Press, 2011), 137.

37. This idea first appeared in a 1921 report by the South African Native Affairs Commission and was cited by Kenyan counterparts in 1926 as a preferred model for Kenya. See KNA, *Native Affairs Department Report* (1926): 55.

38. Brett L. Shadle, "Settlers, Africans, and Inter-Personal Violence in Kenya, ca. 1900–1920s," *International Journal of African Historical Studies* 45, no. 1 (2012): 61.

39. Shaw, *Men of Africa*. For other useful representations through digitized news reels and short films, see http://www.britishpathe.com/.

40. Opolot Okia, "In the Interests of Community: Archdeacon Walter Owen and the Issue of Communal Labour in Colonial Kenya, 1921–30," *Journal of Imperial and Commonwealth History* 32, no. 1 (2004): 23–24.

41. James C. Scott, *Weapons of the Weak: Everyday Forms of Peasant Resistance* (New Haven, CT: Yale University Press, 1985), xvi.

42. KNA, DC/MKS 4/1, G. H. Osborne, "Unrest in Ulu: Military Patrol," March 23, 1912, Machakos District Political Record Book, 1911–1912. See also Katherine Luongo, "Prophecy, Possession, and Politics: Negotiating the Supernatural in 20th Century Machakos, Kenya," *International Journal of African Historical Studies* 45, no. 2 (2012): 191–216.

43. KNA, DC/KSM, 1/35/5, Central Kavirondo Annual Report, 1929.

44. For a description of the workings of *githaka*, see Tabitha Kanogo, *Squatters and the Roots of Mau Mau, 1905–63* (London: James Currey, 1987), 10–11; and David M. Anderson, *Histories of the Hanged: The Dirty War in Kenya and the End of Empire* (New York: Norton, 2005), 25–28.

45. For a comprehensive explanation of Luo land tenure and related ideas of belonging, see David William Cohen and E. S. Atieno Odhiambo, *Siaya: The Historical Anthropology of an African Landscape* (Athens: Ohio University Press, 1989), 25–30.

46. For a useful collection of primary documents from early African political associations, see Wangari Muoria-Sal, Bodil F. Frederiksen, John Lonsdale, and Derek Peterson, eds., *Writing for Kenya: The Life and Works of Henry Muoria* (Leiden: Brill, 2009).

47. Public Record Office—London (hereafter PRO), CO 533/530/10, Sir Alison Russell, "Memorandum on Political Affairs in Kenya," 1943.

48. John Lonsdale has suggested that there were "multiple" Mau Maus. The term referred to the rebellion itself, to its active fighters and passive adherents, and to the oaths they took or were forced to take. See Lonsdale, "Mau Maus of the Mind: Making Mau Mau and Remaking Kenya," *Journal of African History* 31, no. 3 (1990): 393–421.

49. For a detailed, comprehensive study of the Mau Mau as a Kikuyu civil war, see Daniel Branch, *Defeating Mau Mau, Creating Kenya: Counterinsurgency, Civil War, and Decolonization* (Cambridge: Cambridge University Press, 2009).

50. Anderson writes that a conservative estimate would hold that one in four adult male Kikuyu were interned during Mau Mau. Anderson, *Histories of the Hanged*, 4, 313.

51. The prisoners, known as the "Kapenguria Six," also included Achieng Oneko, Kungu Karumba, Fred Kubai, Paul Ngei, and Bildad Kaggia. In 1993, a museum commemorating the Kapenguria Six was established as a branch of the National Museums of Kenya. Part of the project to expand the narrative of Mau Mau beyond the Kikuyu, the museum's website describes the six as "founding fathers of the Kenyan nation," http://www.museums.or.ke/content/blogcategory/15/21/.

52. Propagandist British newsreel footage is widely available on YouTube. For example, http://www.bing.com/videos/search?q=british+newsreel+mau+mau&FORM=VIRE2#view=detail&mid=B05CD2BB0C1421C456A0B-05CD2BB0C1421C456A0.

53. For example, see "Mau Mau Growing Despite Reverse; Terrorist Movement in Kenya Spreads Even as It Loses 100 Killed in One Week," *New York Times*, June 6, 1952; *Simba*, directed by Brian Desmond Hurst (1955; London: Rank Organisation); and *Safari*, directed by Terence Young (1956; London: Warwick Films/Columbia Pictures).

54. Audio of Jomo Kenyatta's thoughts on independence and cheering crowds on independence day is available via the BBC, http://www.bbc.co.uk/worldservice/africa/features/storyofafrica/14chapter8.shtml.

55. Tom Mboya, *The Challenge of Nationhood: A Collection of Speeches and Writings* (London: Heinemann, 1970), 2.

56. For an interesting summary of the case and its contemporary, see the recent BBC Storyville documentary, *Last White Man Standing*, directed by Justin Webster (2009; London: BBC).

57. See Caroline Elkins's controversial book, *Imperial Reckoning*.

58. Ibid.

59. "Mau Mau Torture Victims to Receive Compensation—Hague," BBC News UK, June 6, 2013, http://www.bbc.com/news/uk-22790037.

Chapter 3: The Obama Family

1. Barack H. Obama, *Dreams from My Father: A Story of Race and Inheritance* (New York: Random House, 1995), 369. Also see Georgiana Banita, "'Home Squared': Barack Obama's Transnational Self-Reliance," *Biography* 33, no. 1 (2010): 24–45.

2. The use of the word *homeland* here does not have the same connotations as in South Africa, where it defined the marginal, ethnically segregated rural regions to which black populations were relegated under apartheid. In Kenya, the "native reserves" discussed in the previous chapter bear the closest resemblance to the South Africa "homeland."

3. David William Cohen and E. S. Atieno Odhiambo, *Burying SM: The Politics of Knowledge and the Sociology of Power in Africa* (Portsmouth, NH: Heinemann, 1992).

4. Derek R. Peterson and Giacomo Macola, eds., *Recasting the Past: History Writing and Political Work in Modern Africa* (Athens: Ohio University Press, 2009), 5–7.

5. Suzanna Owiyo, "Kisumu 100," *Mama Africa* (West Sussex: ARC Music, 2002). Lyrics available in Luo at http://www.suzannaowiyo.net/lyrics/kisumu100.txt.

6. Obama, *Dreams from My Father*, 372.

7. Kisumu's urban population is estimated at 409,928 residents according to data from the 2009 census, available at https://www.opendata.go.ke/Population/2009-Census-Vol-1-Table-3-Rural-and-Urban-Populatie/e7c7-w67t/1. This figure indicates a remarkable expansion since the late 1960s, when the population was estimated at 32,000. See Republic of Kenya, *Kenya Population Census 1969*, Vol. 2, *Data on Urban Population* (Nairobi: Statistics Division, 1971). On urbanization in Western Kenya, see Robert Obudho, "Urbanisation and Industrialisation," in *Historical Studies and Social Change in Western Kenya: Essays in Memory of Professor Gideon S. Were*, ed. William R. Ochieng' (Nairobi: East African Educational Publishers, 2002), 194–218.

8. Lesa B. Morrison, "Banished to the Political Wilderness? The Standard Narrative and the Decline of the Luo of Kenya" (PhD diss., Duke University, 2004).

9. Bethwell A. Ogot, *A History of the Luo-Speaking Peoples of Eastern Africa* (Kisumu: Anyange Press, 2009), 485–92.

10. Charles W. Hobley, "British East Africa: Anthropological Studies in Kavirondo and Nandi," *Journal of the Royal Anthropological Institute of Great Britain and Ireland* 33 (1903): 326.

11. James Okoth, interview, Nairobi, Kenya, June 12, 2007.

12. While many scholars speak of Luo as a linguistic group that encompasses this entire larger diaspora, we use the term "Lwo" when referring to the larger Nilotic-speaking diaspora and leave "Luo" to refer only to the Kenyan Dholuo-speaking population. This is a more valid distinction, as Acholi or Padhola groups might say, for instance, that they speak Lwo/Luo but they are Acholi. Kenya's Dholuo-speaking populations are the only cultural group who commonly assert both Luo linguistic and ethnic cultural markers.

13. Lwo-speakers more generally sometimes refer to themselves collectively as Jonam/Joka-Nyanam, or "people of lakes and rivers."

14. See Bethwell A. Ogot, *History of the Southern Luo: Migration and Settlement, 1500–1900* (Nairobi: East African Publishing, 1967); David William Cohen, "The River-Lake Nilotes from the Fifteenth to the Nineteenth Century," in *Zamani*, ed. Bethwell A. Ogot (Nairobi: East African Educational Publishers, 1968), 135–49; Ralph S. Herring, David William Cohen, and Bethwell A. Ogot, "The Construction of Dominance: The Strategies of Selected Luo Groups in Uganda and Kenya," in *State Formation in Eastern Africa*, ed. Ahmed I. Salim (London: Heinemann, 1984), 126–52; David William Cohen and E. S. Atieno Odhiambo, *Siaya: The Historical Anthropology of an African Landscape* (Athens: Ohio University Press, 1989).

15. Herring, Cohen, and Ogot, "Construction of Dominance"; William R. Ochieng', *An Outline History of Nyanza up to 1914* (Nairobi: East African Literature Bureau, 1974); Bethwell A. Ogot, *Building on the Indigenous Selected Essays, 1981–1998* (Kisumu: Anyange Press, 1999), 180–81.

16. Matthew Carotenuto, "Riwruok e teko: Cultivating Identity in Colonial and Postcolonial Kenya," *Africa Today* 53, no. 2 (2006): 57.

17. Cohen and Odhiambo, *Siaya*, 31.

18. This quote comes from the English translation of Paul Mboya's 1938 text. See Jane Achieng, *Paul Mboya's "Luo kitgi gi timbegi": A Translation into English* (Nairobi: Atai Joint, 2001), vii.

19. Frederick Cooper, *On the African Waterfront: Urban Disorder and the Transformation of Work in Colonial Mombasa* (New Haven, CT: Yale Univer-

sity Press, 1987); Ralph D. Grillo, *African Railwaymen: Solidarity and Opposition in an East African Labour Force* (Cambridge: Cambridge University Press, 1973).

20. Kenya National Archives (hereafter KNA), MAA 7/589, T. J. Askwith, "Municipal African Affairs Report, Nairobi, 1948."

21. For instance, KNA, DC/KSM 1/19/106, "Law and Order-Undesirables"; KNA, CA 9/92, "Movement of Women (Mombasa), 1941–52"; and Matthew Carotenuto, "Repatriation in Colonial Kenya: African Institutions and Gendered Violence," *International Journal of African Historical Studies* 45, no. 1 (2012): 9–28.

22. "Detribalization" and urban African life were major concerns of the anthropological Rhodes-Livingston Institute. For example, see the work of its founder, Godfrey Wilson, *The Economics of Detribalization* (Manchester: Manchester University Press, 1940).

23. M. J. B. Molohan, *Detribalization* (Dar es Salaam: Government Printer, 1959), 11; Luise White, *The Comforts of Home: Prostitution in Colonial Nairobi* (Chicago: University of Chicago Press, 1990).

24. Derek R. Peterson, *Ethnic Patriotism and the East African Revival: A History of Dissent, c. 1935–1972* (Cambridge: Cambridge University Press, 2012), 133.

25. Luo were not alone in writing their own prescriptive ethnohistories as a response to the exigencies of colonial rule. Also published in 1938, Jomo Kenyatta's *Facing Mount Kenya: The Tribal Life of the Gikuyu* (London: Secker and Warburg), is the prime example of this genre of ethnohistorical writing. However, Kenyatta's text evidences the formal anthropological training he undertook with the famed Bronislaw Malinowski at the London School of Economics, and is much more explicitly political, having been produced in response to the controversy over female circumcision among the Kikuyu in the late 1920s. See also Bruce Berman, "Ethnography as Politics, Politics as Ethnography: Kenyatta, Malinowski, and the Making of *Facing Mount Kenya*," *Canadian Journal of African Studies* 30, no. 3 (1996): 313–44.

26. *Ramogi*, November 15, 1948.

27. *Ramogi*, March 17, 1951. For more on the gendered analysis of Luo discourse, see Carotenuto, "Repatriation in Colonial Kenya"; Peterson, *Ethnic Patriotism*, 127–51; and Samwel Ong'wen Okuro, "Our Women Must Return Home: Institutionalized Patriarchy in Colonial Central Nyanza District, 1945–1963," *Journal of Asian and African Studies* 45, no. 5 (2010): 522–33.

28. *Ramogi*, December 15, 1947.

29. See Carotenuto, "Riwruok e teko"; James Ogude, "The Vernacular Press and the Articulation of Luo Ethnic Citizenship: The Case of Achieng' Oneko's *Ramogi*," *Current Writing* 13, no. 2 (2001): 42–55.

30. The earliest official references to the Luo Union emerged in Nairobi. See, for instance, KNA, PC/CP 4/3/1, Annual Report for Central Province, 1938, 19.

31. KNA, PC/NZA 3/1/363, Municipal Native Affairs Officer, Nairobi, to D. C. Kericho, April 29, 1944.

32. KNA, District Commissioner, Kakamega (hereafter DC/KMG), 2/1/99, Luo Union North Kavirondo Branch to DC/KMG, November 1945.

33. A. Odera, interview, Kisumu, Kenya, October 13, 2004; Awendo, interview, Kisumu, Kenya, July 1, 2007.

34. Alogo Raila, interview, April 12, 2004. Some informants spoke of belonging to both their clan association and the Luo Union, and emphasized that the Luo Union was an umbrella under which these smaller organizations came together. Alogo Raila, interview, Bondo, Kenya, April 12, 2004.

35. KNA, DC/KMG 2/1/99, Luo Union, North Kavirondo Branch, to DC/KMG, November 1945.

36. KNA, PC/NZA 3/2/368, Walter Odede to PC/NZA, March 1945.

37. KNA, RN 13/23, Municipal Council of Nairobi Annual Report, 1949. Mboya was widely praised by colonial officials for his work as a senior chief in South Nyanza. During World War II he was even awarded the King's Medal for Patriotic Service. See KNA, *Ministry of African Affairs Summary Report, 1939–1945* (Nairobi: Government Printer, 1945). Available via microfilm through the Syracuse University's Kenya National Archive collection; microfilm number 4723, reel 63.

38. Ajuma Oginga Odinga, *Not Yet Uhuru: The Autobiography of Oginga Odinga* (London: Heinemann, 1967), 71.

39. Here we use the constructivist approach to understanding ethnic ties, which has been broadly applied to the colonial encounter.

40. Public Record Office—London (hereafter PRO), FCO 141/5927, "The Security Situation in Nyanza Province—Appreciation by the Kenya Intelligence Committee, Nyanza Province and Mau Mau," 1955.

41. Contrast these numbers with the scope of the internment of Kikuyu in Central Province described by Anderson, Branch, and Elkins, and evident throughout British colonial archives. Some scholars do, however, allege significant Luo participation in Mau Mau. See William Ochieng', "Thunder from the Islands: Mau Mau in Western Kenya," in Ochieng', *Historical Studies and Social Change in Western Kenya*, 181–93.

42. *Ramogi*, February 1952. Cited in KNA, UY 1/11, "Summary of Opinions Expressed in Press, Jan-1951 to Feb-1953."

43. KNA, DC/KMG 2/1/99, Luo Union to PC/NZA, September 1954.

44. Gilbert E. M. Ogutu, *Ker in the 21st Century Luo Social System* (Kisumu: Sundowner, 2004).

45. KNA, African Affairs Department Report, 1952.

46. Bethwell A. Ogot, "Mau Mau and Nationhood: The Untold Story," in *Mau Mau and Nationhood*, ed. E. S. Atieno Odhiambo and John Lonsdale (Athens: Ohio University Press, 2003), 21–22. For a state view of Ofafa's death, see KNA, African Affairs Department Report, 1953.

47. Remark made at a June 1954 meeting of the Luo Union Mombasa branch, reportedly attended by 250 people. PRO, CO 822/842, "African Politics in Kenya, 1954–56."

48. David M. Anderson, *Histories of the Hanged: The Dirty War in Kenya and the End of Empire* (New York: Norton, 2005), 200–212.

49. KNA, PC/NZA 4/4/63, T. C. Watts, Annual Report Central Nyanza, 1954.

50. KNA, RN 13/4, Annual Report City African Affairs, 1955–1958.

51. PRO, FCO 141/592, "African Affairs, Unrest, Nyanza Province," 1952–1957.

52. "The Strength of Luo Loyalty," *Sunday Post*, June 20, 1954.

53. KNA, PC/NZA 3/1/316, Luo Union to PC/NZA, "A Plan of Work," August 24, 1954.

54. Fund-raising for the Ofafa Memorial Hall was frequently mentioned in official Luo Union correspondence as well as in government summaries of the association's activities throughout the late 1950s. See KNA, DC/KMG 2/1/99, Luo Union North Kavirondo Branch to DC Kakamega, November 1945; and KNA, DO/VOI 1/2/4, Daily File, August, 1958.

55. KNA, PC/NZA 4/4/111, Central Nyanza Annual Report, 1961.

56. Jomo Kenyatta, "The Kenya African Union Is Not the *Mau Mau*" (speech presented at the Kenya African Union meeting at Nyeri, July 26, 1952). Available at http://www.fordham.edu/halsall/mod/1952kenyatta-kau1.html.

57. "Kenya African Leader Held: Successor to Jomo," *Glasgow Herald*, March 10, 1953.

58. Bethwell A. Ogot, "The Decisive Years," in *Decolonization and Independence in Kenya, 1940–93*, ed. Bethwell A. Ogot and William R. Ochieng' (London: James Currey, 1995), 58–61.

59. Justin Willis and George Gona, "Tradition, Tribe, and State in Kenya: The Mijikenda Union, 1945–1980," *Comparative Studies in Society and History* 55, no. 2 (2013): 463–65; Julie E. MacArthur, *Cartography and the Po-*

litical Imagination: Mapping Community in Colonial Kenya. (Athens: Ohio University Press, 2016).

60. Tom Mboya, *Freedom and After* (Boston: Little, Brown, 1963); David Goldsworthy, *Tom Mboya: The Man Kenya Wanted to Forget* (Portsmouth, NH: Heinemann, 1982).

61. See a transcript of Mboya's appearance on *Meet the Press*, vol. 3, April 12, 1959; Gerald Horne, *Mau Mau in Harlem?: The U.S. and the Liberation of Kenya* (New York: Palgrave Macmillan, 2009), 171–83; PRO, CO 822/1303, "The Activities of Tom Mboya, 1957–1959."

62. Tom Shachtman, *Airlift to America: How Barack Obama, Sr., John F. Kennedy, Tom Mboya, and 800 East African Students Changed Their World and Ours* (New York: St. Martin's, 2009).

63. Sally H. Jacobs, *The Other Barack: The Bold and Reckless Life of President Obama's Father* (New York: Public Affairs, 2011), 54–75.

64. KNA, African Affairs Department Report, 1957, 107.

65. Ochieng', "Thunder from the Islands"; and Edith A. Miguda, "Mau Mau in Nairobi: 1946–1956: The Luo Experience" (MA thesis, University of Nairobi, 1987).

66. "People Who Want Assistance," *Ramogi*, April 7, 1959.

67. Anderson, *Histories of the Hanged*, 9–53.

68. "Obama, Raila Similarities," April 4, 2007. Available at http://www.Jaluo.com. Jaluo.com, the discussion board for Luos in Kenya and in the diaspora, succinctly summed up contemporary interpretations of Luo exclusion at home and abroad.

69. Morrison, "Banished to the Political Wilderness?"

70. David Goldsworthy, "Ethnicity and Leadership in Africa: The 'Untypical' Case of Tom Mboya," *Journal of Modern African Studies* 20, no. 1 (1982): 107–26; *Time*, March 7, 1960 (cover designed by Bernard Safran).

71. Jacobs, *Other Barack*, 178–81.

72. Guy Vanthemsche, *Belgium and the Congo, 1885–1980*, trans. Alice Cameron and Stephen Windross (Cambridge: Cambridge University Press, 2012).

73. PRO, DO 213/205, Internal Report from the British High Commission, Nairobi, January 29, 1964.

74. Daniel Branch, *Kenya: Between Hope and Despair, 1963–2011* (New Haven, CT: Yale University Press, 2011), 40–44.

75. Githu Muigai, "Jomo Kenyatta and the Rise of the Ethno-Nationalist State in Kenya," in *Ethnicity and Democracy in Africa*, ed. Bruce Berman, Dickson Eyoh, and Will Kymlicka (Athens: Ohio University Press, 2004), 215.

76. William R. Ochieng', "Structural and Political Changes," in Ogot and Ochieng', *Decolonization and Independence in Kenya*, 98–103; Branch, *Kenya*, 44–66; Charles Hornsby, *Kenya: A History Since Independence* (London: Tauris, 2013), 156–220.

77. Branch, *Kenya*, 75–88.

78. Ogot and Ochieng', *Decolonization and Independence*, 98–102.

79. Peterson, *Ethnic Patriotism*, 133–34.

80. Ogot, *History of the Southern Luo*, 25.

81. See Bethwell A. Ogot, *My Footprints on the Sands of Time: An Autobiography* (Kisumu: Anyange Press, 2003)

82. Luo Union leaders and Tom Mboya met with Kenyatta on June 21, 1967, at Statehouse, Nakuru. See KNA, MAC/KEN 70/2, *Jodong luo oromo gi jaduong Jomo Kenyatta* (Nairobi: East African Institute Press, 1967).

83. David J. Parkin, *The Cultural Definition of Political Response: Lineal Destiny among the Luo* (London: Academic Press, 1978), 235. Oneko recalled the importance of this burial in a 2004 interview as a key point in reconciling the political unity of the Luo community. Achieng Oneko, interview, Kunya Beach, Kenya, October 15, 2004.

84. Patrick O. Alila, *Kenya General Elections in Bondo and Gem: The Origins of Luo Ethnic Factor in Modern Politics* (Nairobi: Institute for Development Studies, University of Nairobi, 1984).

85. Ogot, *My Footprints*, 245–63.

86. KNA, CQ 1/39, Registrar of Societies, August 1970.

87. For an example of Cheluget's engagements with Luo customary laws in the 1970s, see Paul Nyambala, "P. C. Cheluget and the Luo," *Weekly Review*, October 25, 1976; "Thus Spare the P.C.," *Weekly Review*, February 20, 1978.

88. See Paul Mboya's editorial in the *Weekly Review*, February 27, 1978. An earlier, similar editorial had also been published by Nairobi Branch official Amolo Ochieng in the *Weekly Review* on December 27, 1976.

89. Ethnic associations began to have a problem with the shifting political quality of their public images. This issue was increasingly covered in the national press throughout the 1970s. See "How Political Are Tribal Societies?" *Weekly Review*, May 19, 1975; Christopher Mullei, "Is Tribalism in Kenya Increasing, Waning?" *Weekly Review*, November 21, 1977.

90. For discussion of the Luo Union leadership controversy in the local press, see "Who's the Boss in Luo Union (EA)?" *Weekly Review*, July 7, 1978; "Luo Union End of an Era," *Weekly Review*, April 6, 1979.

91. Gabrielle Lynch, *I Say to You: Ethnic Politics and the Kalenjin in Kenya* (Chicago: University of Chicago Press, 2011), 111–41.

92. "Pressure on Tribal Unions to Wind Up," *Weekly* Review, August 8, 1980.

93. "Luo Union Disbanded," *Daily Nation*, October 19, 1980.

94. James Ger,"Editorial," *Weekly Review*, August 22, 1980.

95. It should be noted that the clan associations many Luo Union members also belonged to did not disappear after the 1980 ban. These associations continued to serve as burial cooperatives with the Umira Kager clan association, playing a large role in the famous battle to bury Luo lawyer S. M. Otieno. See David William Cohen and E. S. Atieno Odhiambo, *Burying SM: The Politics of Knowledge and the Sociology of Power in Africa* (Portsmouth, NH: Heinemann, 1992).

96. Solomon Waliaula and Joseph Basil Okong'o, "Performing Luo Identity in Kenya: Songs of Gor Mahia," in *Identity and Nation in Africa Football: Fans, Community, and Clubs*, ed. Chuka Onwumechili and Gerard Akindes (New York: Palgrave Macmillan, 2014).

97. Martin Adero, personal communication, Lela, Kenya, April 1998.

98. Daniel Branch, Nicholas Cheeseman, and Leigh Gardner, eds., *Our Turn to Eat: Politics in Kenya since 1960* (Berlin: Lit, 2009).

99. David William Cohen and E. S. Atieno Odhiambo, *The Risks of Knowledge: Investigations into the Death of the Hon. Minister John Robert Ouko in Kenya, 1990* (Athens: Ohio University Press, 2004).

100. M. Metho, interview, Lela, Kenya, April 10, 2004.

101. Gilbert E. M. Ogutu, *Ker Jaramogi Is Dead, Who Shall Lead My People? Reflections on Past, Present, and Future Luo Thought and Practice* (Kisumu: Palwa Research, 1994).

102. See Amnesty International's petition on Raila's behalf, http://www.amnesty.org/en/library/asset/AFR32/007/1991/en/8054f100-f946-11dd-92e7-c59f81373cf2/afr320071991en.pdf. Also see Babafemi A. Badejo, *Raila Odinga: An Enigma in Kenyan Politics* (Lagos: Yintab, 2006); and Raila's autobiography: *Raila Odinga: The Flame of Freedom* (Nairobi: Mountain Top, 2013).

103. A. Odhiambo, interview, Maseno, Kenya, June 26, 2007.

104. Meshack Riaga Ogallo, interview, Karachuonyo, Kenya, October 14, 2004, and July 1, 2007. Investment in "home" was promoted more broadly by Raila Odinga himself in 2008 with specific reference to Kenyans living abroad. Robert Nyasato and Kepher Otieno, "Venture out of Kenya, Raila Tells Businesses," *East African Standard Online*, August 4, 2008.

105. This conclusion is drawn from a general trend of more than thirty interviews conducted with members and supporters of the Luo Council of Elders (LCE) in 2004 and 2007. For example, Opiyo Otondi, Awendo, Kenya, July 2, 2007.

106. Excerpts from Jacobs, *Other Barack*, were published in one of Kenya's leading newspapers. See, for instance, "How Obama Father's Dream Was Ruined by Nairobi's Happy Hour and Ethnicity," *Daily Nation*, July 30, 2011.

107. David Otieno, interview, Nairobi, Kenya, June 10, 2007.

108. For an extended anthropological evaluation of how important these exchanges are in Luo society on a local level, see Parker M. Shipton, *The Nature of Entrustment: Intimacy, Exchange, and the Sacred in Africa* (New Haven, CT: Yale University Press, 2007).

Chapter 4: The Politics of Condemnation

1. Wesley Pruden, "Obama Bows, Nation Cringes," *Washington Times*, November 17, 2009.

2. We use the phrase "American Far Right" to describe the constituency for whom the condemnation of the Obama and Kenya connection resonated most. The Tea Party, Libertarians, and other conservative political groups have actively sought to frame the Obama-Kenya connection in the tradition of nativism increasingly espoused by the Republican Party more generally.

3. Peter Geschiere traces how a global array of political actors, most typically those situated far on the right of their respective political communities, have engaged languages of "belonging" in order to stake claims about rights to political power. See Geschiere, *The Perils of Belonging: Autochthony, Citizenship, and Exclusion in Africa and Europe* (Chicago: University of Chicago Press, 2009), 2–6.

4. While biographies of Barack Obama Jr., Barack Obama Sr., and the Obama family abound, no body of literature and media has emerged from the Left with the goal of actively refuting claims made by the Far Right or to offer squarely partisan histories of Kenya and the Obamas like those Rightist examples discussed here.

5. The White House released Obama's long-form birth certificate in April 2011. This action failed to quell the furor of Birthers, who contend that the long-form birth certificate is a forgery. See www.birthers.org.

6. See Jim Edwards, "Lamar, CBS, Clear Channel Ban Obama Birth Certificate Billboards," CBS Moneywatch, June 12, 2009, http://www.cbsnews.com/news/lamar-cbs-clear-channel-ban-obama-birth-certificate-billboards/.

7. Ben Smith and Byron Tau, "Birtherism: Where It All Began," *Politico*, April 24, 2011, http://www.politico.com/news/stories/0411/53563.html.

8. Birthers seem to have cheerfully abandoned this line of argument with the announcement of the presidential candidacy of Canadian-born, Far Right wunderkind Ted Cruz.

9. Martin A. Parlett, *Demonizing a President: The "Foreignization" of Barack Obama* (Santa Barbara, CA: Praeger, 2014).

10. Matthew W. Hughey, "Show Me Your Papers! Obama's Birth and the Whiteness of Belonging," *Qualitative Sociology* 35, no. 2 (2012): 171.

11. Stephanie Condon, "Poll: One in Four Americans Think Obama Was Not Born in U.S.," *CBS News*, April 21, 2011, http://www.cbsnews.com/news/poll-one-in-four-americans-think-obama-was-not-born-in-us/.

12. Benjamin R. Warner and Ryan Neville-Shepard, "Echoes of a Conspiracy: Birthers, Truthers, and the Cultivation of Extremism," *Communication Quarterly* 62, no. 1 (2014): 4. Also see Jarret T. Crawford and Anuschka Bhatia, "Birther Nation: Political Conservatism Is Associated with Explicit and Implicit Beliefs That President Barack Obama Is Foreign," *Analyses of Social Issues and Public Policy* 12, no. 1 (2012): 364–76.

13. Peter Knight, ed., *Conspiracy Nation: The Politics of Paranoia in Postwar America* (New York: New York University Press, 2002).

14. Michael Barkun, *A Culture of Conspiracy: Apocalyptic Visions in Contemporary America* (Berkeley: University of California Press, 2013).

15. "Kenyan-Born Obama All Set for U.S. Senate," *Sunday Standard*, June 27, 2004. For an example of how this is operationalized in Birther rhetoric, see John Charlton, "AP Declared Obama 'Kenyan-Born,'" InfoWars, October 16, 2009, http://www.infowars.com/ap-declared-obama-kenyan-born/; and Drew Zahn, "Shocker! Obama Still 'Kenyan-Born' in 2007," *World Net Daily*, May 18, 2012, http://www.wnd.com/2012/05/shocker-obama-was-still-kenyan-born-in-2003/.

16. "National Assembly Official Report," March 25, 2010, 31, books.google.com. For its use in Birther rhetoric, see Drew Zahn, "Kenyan Official: Obama Born Here," *World Net Daily*, April 11, 2010, http://www.wnd.com/2010/04/139481/.

17. George Lewis, "Barack Hussein Obama: The Use of History in the Creation of an 'American' President,'" *Patterns of Prejudice* 45, nos. 1–2 (2011): 43–61.

18. Autochthony, or "belonging," Geschiere points out, "needs history," and to the "protagonists of autochthony claims, it seems of little concern whether these claims rest on a highly special interpretation of history or even a downright distortion." Geschiere, *Perils*, 103, 169.

19. Jerome R. Corsi, *The Obama Nation: Leftist Politics and the Cult of Personality* (New York: Threshold, 2008).

20. The book reached #1 on August 10, 2008, and remained on the list for "Hardcover Nonfiction" until mid-October 2008, http://www.nytimes.com/best-sellers-books/.

21. John E. O'Neill and Jerome L. Corsi, *Unfit for Command: Swift Boat Veterans Speak Out against John Kerry* (Washington, DC: Regnery, 2004); G. Mitchell Reyes, "The Swift Boat Veterans for Truth, the Politics of Realism, and the Manipulation of Vietnam Remembrance in the 2004 Presidential Election," *Rhetoric and Public Affairs* 9, no. 4 (2006): 571–600.

22. Corsi's most recent book is devoted to directly challenging Obama's American "belonging." Jerome R. Corsi, *Where's the Birth Certificate? The Case That Barack Obama Is Not Eligible to Be President* (Washington, DC: WND, 2011).

23. Corsi, *Obama Nation*, 15–16.

24. Achille Mbembe and Janet Roitman, "Figures of the Subject in Times of Crisis," *Public Culture* 7, no. 2 (1995): 323–52.

25. Corsi, *Obama Nation*, 93.

26. Ibid.

27. Ibid.,101.

28. See Toyin Falola and Kwame Essien, eds., *Pan-Africanism, and the Politics of African Citizenship and Identity* (New York: Routledge, 2014).

29. Corsi, *Obama Nation*, 107. See Peter Kagwanja, "Courting Genocide: Populism, Ethno-Nationalism and the Informalisation of Violence in Kenya's 2008 Post-Election Crisis," *Journal of Contemporary African Studies* 27, no. 3 (2009): 377; Justin Willis, "What Has He Got up His Sleeve? Advertising the Kenyan Presidential Candidates in 2007," *Journal of Eastern African Studies* 2, no. 2 (2008): 264–71.

30. Corsi, *Obama Nation*, 107–9.

31. Athman Amran, "Propagandists Now Utilising Technology," *Standard*, November 11, 2007.

32. Hassan Mwakimako, "The Historical Development of Muslim Courts: The Kadhi, Mudir and Liwali Courts and the Civil Procedure Code and Criminal Procedure Ordinance, c. 1963," *Journal of Eastern African Studies* 5, no. 2 (2011): 329–43. See also Pravin Bowry, "Demystifying the Kadhi Courts," *Standard*, April 20, 2010; Yash Ghai, "Why the Constitution Should Recognise Kadhi's Courts," *Pambazuka News*, April 29, 2010; and Alphonce Shiundu, "Groups Warn Church Leaders of Kadhi Courts," *Daily Nation*, February 7, 2010.

33. Amran, "Propagandists."

34. Corsi, *Obama Nation*, 108–9.

35. Chadwick Matlin, "Obama Gets Dressed," *Slate*, February 25, 2008, http://www.slate.com/content/slate/blogs/trailhead/2008/02/25/obama_gets_dressed.html.

36. The original photograph was taken on August 27, 2006, in Wajir by an AP photographer. See ID #06082709658 on apimages.com.

37. David Plouffe's remark was widely reprinted. See, for instance, Ewen MacAskill, "Obama Camp Claims Smear Over Turban Photograph," *Guardian*, February 25, 2008.

38. Jerome Corsi, "'Muslim' Photo Raises Obama Connection Questions," *World Net Daily*, February 25, 2008, http://www.wnd.com/2008/02/57363/.

39. Corsi, *Obama Nation*, 92–95; Amran, "Propagandists."

40. Dorothy Rabinowitz, "The Alien in the White House," *Wall Street Journal*, June 9, 2010.

41. John Lonsdale, "Mau Maus of the Mind: Making Mau Mau and Remaking Kenya," *Journal of African History* 31, no. 3 (1990): 393–421.

42. Ibid., 393.

43. Barack H. Obama, *Dreams from My Father: A Story of Race and Inheritance* (New York: Random House, 1995), 416–18.

44. "Barack Obama's Grandfather 'Tortured by the British' during Kenya's Mau Mau Rebellion," *Mail Online*, December 3, 2008. We are grateful to David William Cohen for drawing this article to our attention. See also Ben Macintyre and Paul Orengoh, "Beatings and Abuse Made Barack Obama's Grandfather Loathe the British," *Sunday Times*, December 3, 2008.

45. Tim Shipman, "Barack Obama Sends Bust of Winston Churchill on Its Way Back to Britain," *Daily Telegraph*, February 14, 2009.

46. Ibid.

47. Nicholas Watt, "Special Relationship Is Over, MPs Say. Now Stop Calling Us America's Poodle," *Guardian*, March 28, 2010.

48. Carl G. Rosberg Jr. and John Nottingham, *The Myth of "Mau Mau": Nationalism in Kenya* (Nairobi: East Africa Publishing, 1966).

49. Tania Long, "British Worried by Kenya Terror," *New York Times*, October 20, 1952, 6.

50. For example, "Desecrations Laid to Kenya Terrorists," *New York Times*, September 17, 1952, 5; and Alexander Campbell, "Land of Murder and Muddle: A Report from Kenya," *Time*, March 30, 1953.

51. James Humes, "Obama Slams Churchill," *Newsmax*, March 12, 2009.

52. Macmillan resigned in October 1963 as a result of the Profumo scandal, approximately two months before Kenya achieved independence. Alexander Douglas-Home succeeded Macmillan.

53. David Anderson, interviewed by Justin Elliott in "Mike Huckabee's Crimes against History," *Salon*, March 2, 2011, http://www.salon.com/2011/03/03/huckabee_kenya_mau_mau/.

54. Dinesh D'Souza, *The Roots of Obama's Rage* (Washington, DC: Regnery, 2010), 34.

55. For a useful summary of some of this commentary, see Oliver Willis, "Highbrow Birtherism: Conservatives Attack Obama as an 'African Colonial,'" Media Matters, September 13, 2010, http://mediamatters.org/research/2010/09/13/highbrow-birtherism-conservatives-attack-obama/170555.

56. Dinesh D'Souza, "How Obama Thinks," *Forbes*, September 9, 2010, 1–5; and Robert Costa, "Gingrich: Obama's 'Kenyan, Anti-Colonial' Worldview," *National Review*, September 11, 2010.

57. See Adam Hochschild, "What Gingrich Didn't Learn in Congo," *New York Times*, December 4, 2011. Despite Gingrich's graduate training in African history, his political views seem to trump any critical appraisal of D'Souza's work. See Paul Ocobock, "Anticolonial Behavior," *Dissent*, October 29, 2010.

58. D'Souza's *Roots of Obama's Rage* debuted at number four and remained among the top thirty hardback nonfiction books until November 28, 2010. See http://www.nytimes.com/best-sellers-books/. Produced with an estimated budget of $2.5 million, the film *2016: Obama's America* was shown at more than two thousand movie theaters across the United States in the fall campaign season of 2012, grossing $33,349,949. See http://www.imdb.com/title/tt2247692/business?ref_=tt_dt_bus.

59. D'Souza, *Roots of Obama's Rage*, 34, 198.

60. *2016: Obama's America*, directed by Dinesh D'Souza and John Sullivan (2012; Los Angeles, CA: Lionsgate, 2012), DVD.

61. Barack H. Obama, "Problems Facing Our Socialism," *East Africa Journal* 2, no. 4 (1965): 26–33.

62. D'Souza, "How Obama Thinks," 2.

63. See D'Souza's discussion of the four "tenets" of anticolonialism, which (unintentionally) underscore the predatory nature of colonial regimes. D'Souza, *Roots of Obama's Rage*, 30–32.

64. Ibid., 30–34, 69–71.

65. William R. Ochieng', "Structural and Political Changes," in *Decolonization and Independence in Kenya, 1940–93*, ed. Bethwell A. Ogot and William R. Ochieng' (London: James Currey, 1995), 83.

66. Ibid., 84.

67. David William Cohen, "Perils and Pragmatics of Critique: Reading Barack Obama Sr.'s 1965 Review of Kenya's Development Plan" (paper presented at the University of KwaZulu Natal History and African Studies Seminar, March 24, 2010), 2. See also Cohen, "Perils and Pragmatics of Critique: Reading Barack Obama Sr.'s 1965 Review of Kenya's Development Plan," *African Studies* 74, no. 2 (2015): 1–23.

68. Obama, "Problems Facing Our Socialism." For more on the origins and wide influence of the *East Africa Journal* during the 1960s, see Bethwell A. Ogot, "East African Institute of Social and Cultural Affairs, Nairobi," *Journal of Modern African Studies* 3, no. 2 (1965): 283–85.

69. Obama, "Problems Facing Our Socialism," 27.

70. He states only, "Obama Sr. was an economist, and in 1965 he published an article in the *East Africa Journal* called 'Problems Facing our Socialism.'" D'Souza, "How Obama Thinks," 3.

71. Sessional Paper No. 10, quoted in Ochieng', "Structural and Political Changes," 84.

72. D'Souza, "How Obama Thinks," 3.

73. Ochieng', "Structural and Political Changes," 87–88. Swynnerton reported, "The Kenya Government embarked on a major scheme of land consolidation in the Central Province about 1956 to gather the fragments of each individual farmer into a single consolidated holding and brought in legislation providing for freehold title to such holdings and allowing of purchase, sale, mortgage and their registration. This work is nearing completion in Central Province, covering about 1½ million acres, and is spreading to other areas of Kenya." R. J. M. Swynnerton, "Agricultural Advances in Eastern Africa," *African Affairs* 61, no. 244 (1962): 204. See also Parker M. Shipton, *Mortgaging the Ancestors: Ideologies of Attachment in Africa* (New Haven, CT: Yale University Press, 2009), 143–47.

74. Obama, "Problems Facing Our Socialism," 29.

75. See also Cohen, "Perils and Pragmatics of Critique" (2015), 7–8.

76. D'Souza, "How Obama Thinks," 3.

77. Ochieng', "Structural and Political Changes," 84; Obama, "Problems Facing Our Socialism," 31.

78. Obama, "Problems Facing Our Socialism," 31.

79. Ibid.

80. For instance, Julius K. Nyerere, *Ujamaa: Essays on Socialism* (Oxford: Oxford University Press, 1968); also Cohen, "Perils and Pragmatics of Critique" (2015), 10.

81. Ajuma Oginga Odinga, *Not Yet Uhuru: The Autobiography of Oginga Odinga* (London: Heinemann, 1967).

82. Obama Sr. critiqued "Sessional Paper No. 10" for its lack of specificity in articulating African socialism within the Kenyan context. He wrote, "One would have been pleased to see African Socialism defined and how Kenya fits into this definition, and an indication of those characteristics in which Kenya is unique before one can think of the applicability of this definition to Kenya." Obama, "Problems Facing Our Socialism," 27.

83. D'Souza, "How Obama Thinks," 5.

84. D'Souza, *Roots of Obama's Rage*, 28.

85. See Edmund D. Morel, *The Black Man's Burden: The White Man in Africa from the Fifteenth Century to World War I* (New York: Monthly Review Press, 1969. Reprint of the 1920 edition). Although D'Souza borrows Morel's title, he does not cite or quote Morel's text. D'Souza, *Roots of Obama's Rage*, 17.

86. Rudyard Kipling, "The White Man's Burden," *McClure's* 12 (1899). D'Souza also uses "cagey" to describe President Obama's behavior. For example, see D'Souza, *Roots of Obama's Rage*, 42.

87. D'Souza, *Roots of Obama's Rage*, 114.

88. Ibid., 117. On British myth-making surrounding the rebellion, see Gautam Chakravarty, *The Indian Mutiny and the British Imagination* (Cambridge: Cambridge University Press, 2005).

89. David M. Anderson, *Histories of the Hanged: The Dirty War in Kenya and the End of Empire* (New York: Norton, 2005); Caroline Elkins, *Imperial Reckoning: The Untold Story of Britain's Gulag in Kenya* (New York: Holt, 2005).

90. D'Souza, *Roots of Obama's Rage*, 118.

91. Ibid., 187. See Barack Obama, *The Audacity of Hope: Thoughts on Reclaiming the American Dream* (New York: Crown, 2006), 317.

92. "Anti-Obama Author Arrested in Nairobi," *Standard*, October 7, 2008. See also Lee Glendinning, "Anti-Obama Author Deported from Kenya," *Guardian*, October 7, 2008.

93. See also Philip Ochieng, "Action on 'Obama Nation' Writer Justified," *Daily Nation*, November 11, 2008.

94. Anthony Karanja, "Kenyan Embassy Takes Swipe at Tea Party Movement with Own Tea Party in Washington, DC," Jambonewspot.com, April 21, 2010.

95. Drew Zahn, "Does Obama Really Hate America?" *World News Daily*, September 2, 2012, http://www.wnd.com/2012/09/does-obama-really-hate-america/.

96. John L. Comaroff and Jean Comaroff, *Ethnicity Inc.* (Chicago: University of Chicago Press, 2009).

Chapter 5: The Politics of Celebration

1. Walter Gor, interview, Lela, Kenya, April 13, 2004.

2. Ibid.

3. For a full transcript of Obama's address, see "Transcript: Illinois Senate Candidate Barack Obama," .

4. Monica Davey, "As Quickly as Overnight, a Democratic Star Is Born," *New York Times*, March 18, 2004.

5. Alex Johnson, "Heinz Kerry Hails America; Obama Offers 'a Brighter Day,'" July 28, 2004, http://www.nbcnews.com/id/5537294/ns/politics/t/heinz-kerry-hails-americaobama-offers-brighter-day/#.UovV9PldXzg; and Christopher Buckley, "A Show Called Hope," *New York Times*, August 1, 2004, http://www.nytimes.com/2004/08/01/opinion/a-show-called-hope.html.

6. John L. Comaroff and Jean Comaroff, *Ethnicity Inc.* (Chicago: University of Chicago Press, 2009), 24.

7. An idea commonly expressed as a question and an aspiration by Luo in Kenya and the diaspora. See "Could US Elect a Luo before Kenya?" *BBC*, January 3, 2008, http://news.bbc.co.uk/2/hi/africa/7170089.stm.

8. "Cutting Edge," *Daily Nation*, October 9, 2004; Tom Oladipo, "Kenyan Beer Stirs Obamamania," BBC News, February 21, 2008, http://news.bbc.co.uk/2/hi/africa/7251273.stm; Isaiah Andebe, "'Obama' Offers Serious Challenge to Informal Brews," *Daily Nation*, March 12, 2005; and "The Senator Story," https://www.eabl.com/downloads/The-Senator-Story.pdf.

9. Charles Onyango-Obbo, "We're All Made from the Same Genes," *Daily Nation*, November 4, 2004.

10. Rob Crilly, "A World Away, Kenyan Village Rallies for Favorite U.S. Son," *USA Today*, October 14, 2004, 15A.

11. Ibid.

12. "Moi Congratulates Bush as Kenyans Fete Obama," *Standard*, November 4, 2004.

13. John Oywa, "Village's Great Expectations after the Obama Poll Victory," *Daily Nation*, November 7, 2004.

14. Kevin J. Kelley, "Joy as Obama Romps Home," *Daily Nation*, November 4, 2004.

15. Oywa, "Village's Great Expectations."

16. Kelley, "Joy as Obama Romps Home."

17. Oywa, "Village's Great Expectations."

18. Kelley, "Joy as Obama Romps Home."

19. Patrick Nzioka, "'I'll Help If I Can,' Says Obama," *Daily Nation*, November 25, 2004.

20. Barack Obama, "An Honest Government and a Hopeful Future," University of Nairobi, August 28, 2006, http://nairobi.usembassy.gov/uploads/J3/Ch/J3ChJw8qmXwd19ok8rg8lg/Obama-speech.pdf.

21. Macharia Gaitho and Julie Gichuru, "Obama: I Speak What Is True and Say It Best," *Daily Nation*, September 1, 2006.

22. Bob Hercules and Keith Walker, *Senator Obama Goes to Africa* (2006; New York: First Run Features), DVD.

23. Bahati Amaya, "Don't Expect any Goodies from Obama," *Standard*, June 6, 2006.

24. Lesa B. Morrison, "The Nature of Decline: Distinguishing Myth from Reality in the Case of the Luo of Kenya," *Journal of Modern African Studies* 45, no. 1 (2007): 136.

25. James Howard Smith, "Snake-Driven Development: Culture, Nature and Religious Conflict in Neoliberal Kenya," *Ethnography* 7, no. 4 (2006): 430.

26. Nicholas Kristof, "Obama's Kenyan Roots," *New York Times*, February 24, 2008; Maina Waruru, "Why Are We Wary of an Obama Victory?" March 28, 2008, http://www.africanews.com/site/list_messages/16948.

27. "Will Kikuyu Americans Vote for Obama?" http://www.mashada.com/ forums/kenya-2008/68218-will-kikuyu-americans-vote-obama.html.

28. Ibid.

29. Ibid.

30. Ibid.

31. Daniel Ambunya, "Obama-Bashing Letter Writer Had His Facts Upside Down," *Daily Nation*, September 2, 2008.

32. Peter Atsiaya, "Kisumu Town Holds Mock US Voting Exercise," *Standard Online*, November 4, 2008.

33. "Senator Beer Runs Out after Obama Victory," *Daily Nation*, November 8, 2008.

34. Anthony Kariuki, "In Kenya, a Holiday, Song and Dance for Obama," *Daily Nation*, November 5, 2008; "Obama Beer Unveiled," *New Vision*, February 17, 2009, http://www.newvision.co.ug/D/8/220/671758.

35. Millicent Mwololo, "What Do You Call Child," *Daily Nation*, January 27, 2009.

36. UNESCO Convention for the Safeguarding of Intangible Cultural Heritage (2003). The convention defines "intangible cultural heritage" as the practices, representations, expressions, knowledge, skills—as well as the instruments, objects, artifacts and cultural spaces associated therewith," http://www.unesco.org/culture/.

37. "Obama's Kogelo Now a Protected Area," *Daily Nation*, September 21, 2009. See also "The National Museums and Heritage Act," in *The Laws of Kenya* (Nairobi: Government Printer, 1972), chapter 216, http://www .kenyalaw.org.

38. They write that "heritage" is a "form of cultural production in the present that has recourse to the past." See Derek R. Peterson, Kodzo Gavua, and Ciraj Rassool, eds., *The Politics of Heritage in Africa: Economies, Histories, and Infrastructures* (Cambridge: Cambridge University Press, 2015), 1–2.

39. Lucas Barasa, "Kenya Eyes Tourism Boom," *Daily Nation*, November 12, 2008; "Presidential Ancestral Home Draws Americans to Kenya," *Voice of America*, January 15, 2009, http://www1.voanews.com/english/news/a-13-2009-01-15-voa8-68763557.html.

40. Such comments were made by a number of curators and tour guides at the National Museums of Kenya branch in Kisumu, as well as staff at the Kisumu Hotel in July 2009. See also "Report: Kenyan MPs Want to Upgrade Airport for Obama," *US News & World Report*, October 17, 2008.

41. Title of a wall panel explaining Luo origins in the Kisumu Museum. See also Karega Munene, "Museums in Kenya: Spaces for Selecting, Ordering and Erasing Memories of Identity and Nationhood," *African Studies* 70, no. 2 (2011): 224–45.

42. Matthew Carotenuto, "Riwruok e teko: Cultivating Identity in Colonial and Postcolonial Kenya," *Africa Today* 53, no. 2 (2006): 61. Curators and staff at the Kisumu branch museum explained in July 2009 that international tourism had peaked with Obama's senatorial victory in 2004 and expanded even more after he was elected president. For more on the Kisumu museum, see http://www.museums.or.ke/content/blogcategory/14/20/.

43. Comaroff and Comaroff, *Ethnicity Inc.*, 83.

44. Group interview with members of the Kisumu museum staff, July 13, 2009. Museum and monumental depictions of Mau Mau have been contested and virtually absent for most of Kenya's independent history. See Lotte Hughes, "'Truth Be Told': Some Problems with Historical Revisionism in Kenya,'" *African Studies* 70, no. 2 (2011): 182–201; Daniel Branch, "The Search for the Remains of Dedan Kimathi: The Politics of Death and Memorialization in Post-Colonial Kenya," *Past and Present* 206, no. S5 (2010): 301–20.

45. Karin van Bemmel, "Obama Made in Kenya: Appropriating the American Dream in Kogelo," *Africa Today* 59, no. 4 (2013): 68–90; and Steve Ouma Akoth, "The Meanings of Obama in K'ogello: Culture, Ethno-Politics and the Making of Leaders in Multiparty Kenya," *Anthropology Southern Africa* 33, nos. 3–4 (2010): 114–25.

46. Dorcas Odege, Kogelo Culural Development Manager, interview, Kisumu, July 14, 2009.

47. Speech by minister of state for National Heritage and Culture, Hon. William Ole Ntimama, read by Stephen Mau, assistant director of Library Service, Kogelo Community Cultural Festival, January 20, 2010, http://www.nationalheritage.go.ke. See also http://www.vision2030.go.ke/.

48. National Assembly Official Report, April 14, 2010, 8, https://books.google.com/books?id=G-2_G5NnofQC&printsec=frontcover&source=gbs_ge_summary_r&cad=0#v=onepage&q&f=false.

49. Mangoa Mosota, "Sh5m Set aside for Kogelo Museum," *Standard*, November 28, 2008. Within a year, the Kenyan press reported that the official government estimate for the new Obama cultural center had grown from 5 million to 112 million Kenyan shillings (KSH). See "Obama Monument to Cost Sh112 Million," *Daily Nation*, October 31, 2009.

50. Leo Odera Omolo, "Multimillion Museum to Be Constructed in Kogelo Village by Kenyan Government Following Obama's Presidential Victory: The Boosting of Tourism in Western Kenya," *African Press International*, November 24, 2008, https://africanpress.wordpress.com/2008/11/24/multi-million-dollar-museium-to-be-constructed-in-kogelo-village-by-kenyan-government-following-obamas-presidential-victory-the-boosting-of-tourism-in-western-kenya/.

51. William Ole Ntimama, untitled speech, 3.

52. Ibid., 1.

53. Mangoa Masota, "Kogelo Village Reaps Big from Grandson's Fame," *Standard*, January 21, 2011.

54. Philip Ochieng, "The Pride of a People: Barack Obama, the Luo," *Daily Nation*, January 17, 2009.

55. Anonymous, interview, Kisumu, Kenya, July 15, 2009.

56. For his part, Corsi took the festival and the development of the cultural center as more evidence of Obama's Kenyan "belonging," asserting it lent credence to his claim that the autochthonously "Kenyan" Obama is constitutionally ineligible to be president. Jerome R. Corsi, "Intel Report: Kenyans Honor Obama's 'Birthplace,'" *World Net Daily*, May 30, 2011, http://www.wnd.com/?pageId=303165#ixzz1NtxG9jh1.

57. Samuel Opondo, interview, Kogelo, Kenya, July 14, 2009.

58. Ibid.

59. Female student from group interview with ten female and ten male form III and form IV students, Obama Kogelo Secondary School, Kogelo, Kenya, July 14, 2009.

60. Comaroff and Comaroff, *Ethnicity Inc.*, 1. See also Janet McIntosh, "Elders and 'Frauds': Commodified Expertise and Politicized Authenticity among Mijikenda," *Africa* 79, no. 1 (2009): 35–52.

61. *Kit Mikayi* means "rock of the first wife" in Dholuo. For more on Kit Mikayi as a cultural and spiritual site, see Celia Nyamweru, "Natural Cultural Sites of Kenya: Changing Contexts, Changing Meanings," *Journal of Eastern African Studies* 6, no. 2 (2012): 270–302. Also see Cynthia Hoehler-Fatton, *Women of Fire and Spirit: History, Faith, and Gender in Roho Religion in Western Kenya* (New York: Oxford University Press, 1996), 135. And for a popular retelling of the cultural significance of the site, see Gitau

Warigi, "Mystical Rock Where Many Seek Solace," *Daily Nation*, September 12, 2007.

62. Gideon Oyugi, secretary of the Luo Council of Elders (LCE) for Kisumu West District, interview, Kit Mikayi, Kenya, July 15, 2009.

63. James O. Gwada, "Brief History of the Rock," oral historical narrative with accompanying notes on LCE letterhead, July15, 2009. Personal collection of Matt Carotenuto.

64. Ibid.

65. LCE, "Report on Proposed Kit Mikayi Tourist Site," 2009.

66. H. O. Omanjo, "The Constitution of the Luo Council of Elders 21st Century and Beyond," LCE, 2001.

67. Gilbert E. M. Ogutu, *Ker in the 21st Century Luo Social System* (Kisumu: Sundowner, 2001).

68. David Kazia, "An 'Irresistible, Awful, Marvelous People': The Portrait of the Luos of East Africa," *East African*, July 11, 2008.

69. Ibid.

70. Morrison, "Nature of Decline," 135.

71. For instance, variations of this phrase were evoked by the LCE chairman Riaga Ogallo in 2004 and in discussions of Garang's 2005 death with LCE elder Opiyo Otondi in 2007.

72. Ogutu, *Ker in the 21st Century Luo Social System*. For a closer look at how Christianity influences notions of ethnogenesis, see Adrian Hastings, *The Construction of Nationhood: Ethnicity, Religion and Nationalism* (Cambridge: Cambridge University Press, 1997); and Derek R. Peterson, *Ethnic Patriotism and the East African Revival: A History of Dissent, c. 1935–1972* (Cambridge: Cambridge University Press, 2012).

73. For the colonial-era files of the Luo Language Committee, see Kenya National Archives—Nairobi (hereafter KNA), DC/KSM 1/10/60, "Cultural Languages and Dialect," 1930–1954; and KNA, PC/NZA 3/6/129, "Vernacular Education," 1944–1949. For a discussion of a similar body created to deal with the Gikuyu and Luhya vernaculars in Kenya, see Derek R. Peterson, *Creative Writing: Translation, Bookkeeping, and the Work of Imagination in Colonial Kenya* (Portsmouth, NH: Heinemann, 2004), 118–22; and Julie MacArthur, "The Making and Unmaking of African Languages: Oral Communities and Competitive Linguistic Work in Western Kenya," *Journal of African History* 53, no. 2 (2012): 151–72.

74. KNA, PC/NZA 3/6/129, Ohanga, "Report on the Linguistic Relationships of the Luo," July 25, 1946.

75. *Ramogi*, April 15, 1949. Readers praised the work of the LLC in the 1940s, with a number of editorials asking for its rules to be published in the

paper so that they could learn the language properly. One 1949 article called for unity in the "Nilotic areas" rising out of the Luo Language Committee and recommended that *Ramogi* should evolve into a common paper "to enable people in Uganda and Sudan to read news of common interest."

76. This view was consistently expressed during more than thirty interviews with LCE officials and supporters in 2004.

77. John Oywa, "Dr. Kiir: Newest Luo Elder Rose from Rebel Ranks," *Standard*, May 6, 2009.

78. Emeka-Mayaka Gekara,"Raila's New Strategy for Power," *Daily Nation*, May 30, 2010; and Jervasio Okot and Larco Lomayat,"Kenyan Luo Elders Arrived in Juba, Capital City of South Sudan," *Nile Buffalo Gazette*, May 17, 2009, http://www.nilebuffalo.com/news_detail.php?txt_id=254.

79. Ali Mazrui, "In a Nilotic Embrace: From Obote to Obama," *Monitor*, November 8, 2008.

80. Kazia, "Irresistible, Awful, Marvelous People."

81. David William Cohen and E. S. Atieno Odhiambo, "Ayany, Malo, and Ogot: Historians in Search of a Luo Nation," *Cahiers d'études africaines* 27, nos. 107–8 (1987): 274.

82. Ibid., 274–75. See also Ben G. Blount, "Agreeing to Agree on Genealogy: A Luo Sociology of Knowledge," in *Sociocultural Dimensions of Language Use*, ed. Mary Sanches and Ben G. Blount (New York: Academic Press, 1975), 117–35.

83. See East African Educational Publisher's popular series Makers of Kenya's History for a number of titles that walk a fine line between popular history and political hagiography.

84. Lila Luce, *Barack Obama: Yes, We Can!* (Nairobi: Sasa Sema, 2009), 79. For more examples of local children's literature, see Philo Ikonya, *The Kenyan Boy Who Became President of America* (Nairobi: Media Horizons Network, 2008); and Phyllis Andrews, *Who Am I? The Story of Barack Obama* (Nairobi: East African Educational Publishers, 2010).

85. Peter Firstbrook, *The Obamas: The Untold Story of an African Family* (New York: Crown, 2010).

86. Excerpts from Sally H. Jacobs, *The Other Barack: The Bold and Reckless Life of President Obama's Father* (New York: Public Affairs, 2011), were published in one of Kenya's leading newspapers. See, for instance, "How Obama Father's Dream Was Ruined by Nairobi's Happy Hour and Ethnicity," *Daily Nation*, July 30, 2011.

Chapter 6: Political Violence and History at the Ballot Box

1. President Uhuru Kenyatta, speaking at the celebration of the fiftieth anniversary of Kenyan independence, December 12, 2013. Available at http://jamhurimagazine.com/index.php/kenya-president/4534-president-uhuru-kenyatta-speech-kenya-50th-independence-day-celebration.html.

2. John Kamau, "Fifty Years On, Uhuru Confronts the Same Mountains His Father Faced," *Daily Nation*, May 21, 2014.

3. As Daniel Branch argues, due to the widespread anticolonial violence of Mau Mau and the targeted political violence of the early postcolonial era, Kenya in the 1960s should be seen as both a postconflict and postcolonial state. Branch, *Defeating Mau Mau, Creating Kenya: Counterinsurgency, Civil War, and Decolonization* (Cambridge: Cambridge University Press, 2009), 180.

4. Jomo Kenyatta, *Harambee! The Prime Minister of Kenya Speeches, 1963–1964* (London: Oxford University Press, 1964), 8.

5. Karuti Kanyinga, "The Legacy of the White Highlands: Land Rights, Ethnicity and the Post-2007 Election Violence in Kenya," *Journal of Contemporary African Studies* 27, no. 3 (2009): 325–44.

6. For a nuanced discussion of Kalenjin history and politics, see Gabrielle Lynch, *I Say to You: Ethnic Politics and the Kalenjin in Kenya* (Chicago: University of Chicago Press, 2011).

7. *Majimbo* is the Swahili word for "states" or "region." David M. Anderson, "'Yours in Struggle for Majimbo': Nationalism and the Party Politics of Decolonization in Kenya, 1955–64," *Journal of Contemporary History* 40, no. 3 (2005): 547–64. Anderson notes that majimboism was initially advocated by the opposition to the Kenya African National Union (KANU) in the early 1960s and again in the early 2000s. See also Charles Hornsby, *Kenya: A History Since Independence* (London: Tauris, 2012), 482–83.

8. Anderson, "Yours in Struggle," 564.

9. Republic of Kenya, "Record of Evidence Taken before the Judicial Commission of Inquiry into Tribal Clashes in Kenya," July 20, 1998. Hereafter cited as Akiwumi Commission. Cited in Human Rights Watch, "Violence as a Political Tool in Kenya," 2002, http://www.hrw.org/reports/2002/kenya/Kenya0502-04.htm.

10. Akiwumi Commission, 49, http://www.hrw.org/sites/default/files/related_material/Akiwumi%20Report.pdf.

11. Dave Opiyo, "Moi Incited Ethnic Cleansing in Rift Valley, Says Witness," *Daily Nation*, February 18, 2014, http://mobile.nation.co.ke/news/Moi-incited-ethnic-cleansing-in-Rift-Valley-says-witness/-/1950946/2212268/-/format/xhtml/-/10aca2bz/-/index.html.

12. Akiwumi Commission, 91.

13. Ibid., 50.

14. Binaifer Nowrojee, *Divide and Rule: State-Sponsored Ethnic Violence in Kenya* (New York: Human Rights Watch, 1993).

15. Claims to indigeneity are contested in Kenya. For instance, in the Rift, Okiek communities have often challenged Maasai or Kalenjin claims of indigeneity, while the politics of decolonization encouraged coastal communities to attempt to reclaim their political and territorial autonomy. See Gabrielle Lynch, "Becoming Indigenous in the Pursuit of Justice: The African Commission on Human and People's Rights and the Endorois," *African Affairs* 111, no. 442 (2012): 24–45; and Jeremy Prestholdt, "Politics of the Soil: Separatism, Autochthony, and Decolonization at the Kenyan Coast," *Journal of African History* 55, no. 2 (2014): 249–70.

16. International Federation for Human Rights and Kenya Human Rights Commission, *Massive Internal Displacement in Kenya Due to Politically Instigated Ethnic Clashes: Absence of Political and Humanitarian Responses*, nos. 471–72 (2007), http://www.fidh.org/IMG/pdf/Kenya_engNB.pdf.

17. Daniel Branch, *Kenya: Between Hope and Despair, 1963–2011* (New Haven, CT: Yale University Press, 2011), 221–22.

18. Lynch, *I Say to You*, 35.

19. Hornsby, *Kenya*, 555.

20. Nyayo House is now, ironically, home to Kenya's Department of Immigration Services. See Kenya National Commission on Human Rights, "The Dark Days Unforgotten—the *Nyayo* Torture Chambers," http://www.knchr.org/Thedarkdaysunforgotten.aspx. Also see Branch, *Kenya*, 167.

21. Branch, *Kenya*, 209–12. FORD-Kenya was Odinga's party. *Asili* means "original" in Swahili.

22. Hornsby, *Kenya*, 529.

23. Gilbert E. M. Ogutu, *Ker Jaramogi Is Dead, Who Shall Lead My People? Reflections on Past Present, and Future Luo Thought and Practice* (Kisumu: Palwa Research, 1994).

24. Hornsby, *Kenya*, 592.

25. Branch, *Kenya*, 227–28, 246–47.

26. Raila Amolo Odinga, *Raila Odinga: The Flame of Freedom* (Nairobi: Mountain Top, 2013).

27. "Victory Is Not Enough," *Africa Confidential* 44, no. 7 (April 4, 2003): 5, http://www.africa-confidential.com/article-preview/id/226/Victory_is_not_enough.

28. Branch, *Kenya*, 240.

29. For footage of Raila's speech at the National Rainbow Coalition (NARC) rally on October 14, 2002, at Uhuru Park, see https://www.you-

tube.com/watch?v=my_PLdbNCic. Harambee was the name given to Kenyatta's national self-development project that was the precursor to Moi's Nyayo.

30. Hear Gidi Gidi Maji Maji perform "Unbwogable" at http://www.youtube.com/watch?v=kT5orKxAGwc. See also Joyce Nyairo and James Ogude, "Popular Music, Popular Politics: *Unbwogable* and the Idioms of Freedom in Kenyan Popular Music," *African Affairs* 104, no. 415 (2005): 225–49.

31. See the Kenya Broadcasting Company (KBC) coverage of the swearing-in at http://www.youtube.com/watch?v=zP2VPzgguC8.

32. "President Kibaki's Speech to the Nation on His Inauguration as Kenya's 3rd President," December 30, 2002, http://www.statehousekenya.go.ke/speeches/kibaki/2002301201.htm.

33. Kenya ranked 129th out of 146 nations, Finland being the least corrupt and Haiti and Bangladesh tied for being the most corrupt. See the 2004 Corruption Perceptions Index, http://archive.transparency.org/policy_research/surveys_indices/cpi/2004. In 1998, Kenya ranked 74th out of the 85 countries for which there was sufficient data available to rank. See the 1998 Corruption Perceptions Index, http://archive.transparency.org/policy_research/surveys_indices/cpi/previous_cpi/1998.

34. See Michela Wrong's detailed analysis of the scandal. Wrong, *It's Our Turn to Eat: The Story of a Kenyan Whistle-Blower* (New York: Harper, 2009).

35. Branch, *Kenya*, 255.

36. Jeevan Vasagar, "Kenyan President Faces Rebellion on Sleaze," *Guardian*, February 23, 2005, http://www.theguardian.com/world/2005/feb/24/kenya.jeevanvasagar.

37. Lucas Barasa, "United Stand in Vote against 2005 Constitution Gave Birth to Orange," *DailyNationMobile*, February 26, 2014, http://mobile.nation.co.ke/news/Orange-Democratic-Movement/-/1950946/2223566/-/format/xhtml/-/rppvte/-/index.html.

38. Branch, *Kenya*, 259.

39. Hornsby, *Kenya*, 755.

40. Daniel Branch, "At the Polling Station in Kibera," *London Review of Books* 30, no. 2 (January 28, 2008), http://www.lrb.co.uk/v30/n02/daniel-branch/at-the-polling-station-in-kibera.

41. For a breakdown of seats, see Makau Mutua, *Kenya's Quest for Democracy: Taming Leviathan* (Boulder, CO: Rienner, 2008), 245.

42. Branch, *Kenya*, 270.

43. Hornsby, *Kenya*, 759.

44. "Kenya: Violence Erupts as Kibaki Sworn In," *Citizen*, December 31, 2007, http://allafrica.com/stories/200712310859.html.

45. David Mugoyoni, "Kenya: Raila also Declared President," *Daily Nation*, December 31, 2007. Available at http://allafrica.com/stories/200712310012.html.

46. Human Rights Watch, "The Immediate and Underlying Causes and Consequences of Flawed Democracy in Kenya," United States Senate Committee on Foreign Relations, Subcommittee on African Affairs, February 7, 2008, http://www.hrw.org/news/2008/02/06/hearing-immediate-and-underlying-causes-and-consequences-flawed-democracy-kenya.

47. Republic of Kenya, *Report of the Commission of Inquiry into the Post Election Violence* (Nairobi: Government Printer, 2008), 173–74. Hereafter cited as "Waki Commission." Available at http://reliefweb.int/sites/reliefweb.int/files/resources/15A00F569813F4D549257607001F459D-Full_Report.pdf.

48. Commonwealth Secretariat, *Kenya General Election, Report of the Commonwealth Observer Group*, December 27, 2007, 6, http://secretariat.thecommonwealth.org/document/34293/35144/174418/report_of_the_commonwealth_observer_group_for_the.htm.

49. For detailed accounts of the postelection violence, see the special issue "Election Fever: Kenya's Crisis," *Journal of Eastern African Studies* 2, no. 2 (2008); Human Rights Watch, "Ballots to Bullets: Organized Political Violence and Kenya's Crises of Governance" (New York: Human Rights Watch, 2008), http://hrw.org/reports/2008/kenya0308/kenya0308webwcover.pdf; Jerome Lafargue, ed., *The General Elections in Kenya, 2007* (Dar es Salaam: Mkuki na Nyota, 2009); and Peter Kagwanja and Roger Southall, eds., Special Issue: "Kenya's Uncertain Democracy: The Electoral Crisis of 2008," *Journal of Contemporary African Studies* 27, no. 3 (2009).

50. Akiwumi Commission, 2.

51. Ibid., 11. *Madoadoa* is a derisive vernacular term for "foreigner" literally meaning "spots." Terms like this have been used in election rhetoric to speak of "outsiders," along with other words such as *viroboto* (fleas). See Republic of Kenya, *Report of the Truth, Justice and Reconciliation Commission*, vol. 2 (Nairobi: Truth, Justice and Reconciliation Commission, 2013), 506. This six-volume report is available for download at http://www.tjrckenya.org/.

52. Waki Commission, 54.

53. Human Rights Watch, "Ballots to Bullets," 43–52.

54. Michael Chege, "Kenya: Back from the Brink?" *Journal of Democracy* 19, no. 4 (2008): 125–39.

55. "Key Points: Kenya's Power-Sharing Deal," *BBC News*, February 28, 2008, http://news.bbc.co.uk/2/hi/africa/7269476.stm.

56. Jeffrey Gettleman, "Disputed Vote Plunges Kenya into Bloodshed," *New York Times*, December 31, 2007, http://www.nytimes.com/2007/12/31/world/africa/31kenya.html?pagewanted=all.

57. "Could Kenya Become Rwanda?" BBC, January 30, 2008, http://news.bbc.co.uk/2/hi/africa/7217462.stm.

58. Thilo Thielke, "Chaos in Africa: Tribal Massacres Echo Rwandan Genocide," *Spiegel Online International*, January 2, 2008, http://www.spiegel.de/international/world/chaos-in-kenya-tribal-massacres-echo-rwandan-genocide-a-526129.html.

59. For a depiction of the violence devoid of historical context, see the photographic essay "Kenyan Tribes Wage a War with Bows and Arrows," *Time*, March 18, 2008. Subtext included language describing the violence as part of "codified age-old traditions," and so on. Available at http://www.time.com/time/photogallery/0,29307,1722198,00.html.

60. Kimani Njogu, ed., *Healing the Wound: Personal Narratives about the 2007 Post-Election Violence in Kenya* (Nairobi: Twaweza, 2009), 274.

61. Ibid., 289.

62. "Odinga Says Obama Is His Cousin," BBC, January 8, 2008, http://news.bbc.co.uk/2/hi/africa/7176683.stm.

63. Jerome R. Corsi, *Obama Nation: Leftist Politics and the Cult of Personality* (New York: Threshold, 2008), 103–4.

64. Ibid.

65. For well-substantiated analyses of the electoral controversy and its historical underpinnings, see Thomas P. Wolf, "'Poll Poison'? Politicians and Polling in the 2007 Kenya Election," *Journal of Contemporary African Studies* 27, no. 3 (2009): 279–304; Daniel Branch, Nicholas Cheeseman, and Leigh Gardner, eds., *Our Turn to Eat: Politics in Kenya since 1950* (Berlin: LIT, 2010); David Anderson, "Vigilantes, Violence and the Politics of Public Order in Kenya," *African Affairs* 101, no. 405 (2002): 531–55.

66. Corsi, *Obama Nation*, 105.

67. Ibid.

68. Ibid., 104.

69. Ibid.

70. Barack Obama interviewed by Capital FM Kenya, January 29, 2008. Transcript available at http://www.pambazuka.org/en/category/comment/45744/print.

71. Waki Commission, 5–9; Human Rights Watch, "Ballots to Bullets"; and Susanne D. Mueller, "Kenya and the International Criminal Court (ICC): Politics, the Election and the Law," *Journal of Eastern African Studies* 8, no. 1 (2014): 25–42.

72. Waki Commission, 472.

73. David William Cohen and E. S. Atieno Odhiambo, *Risks of Knowledge: Investigations into the Death of the Hon. Minister John Robert Ouko in Kenya, 1990* (Athens: Ohio University Press, 2004), 43–45.

74. "Don't Be Vague, Let's Go to the Hague," *Africa Confidential*, December 17, 2010, http://www.africa-confidential.com/article preview/id/3783/Don't_be_vague%2c_let's_go_to_the_Hague.

75. The original six were: Mohammed Hussein Ali (Commissioner of Police); Henry Kiprono Kosgey (Chairman of the Orange Democratic Movement—ODM); Francis Kirimi Muthaura (Head of the Public Service and Secretary to the Cabinet); Joseph Sang (Head of Operations at Kalenjin-language radio station Kass FM); William Samoei Ruto (member of Parliament for Eldoret North); and Uhuru Muigai Kenyatta (member of Parliament for Gatundu South). See the ICC's website: http://www.icc-cpi.int/.

76. Barack Obama, "Statement by President Obama on the International Criminal Court Announcement," December 15, 2010, http://www.whitehouse.gov/the-press-office/2010/12/15/statement-president-obama-international-criminal-court-announcement. The United States is not a signatory to the Rome Statute (1998) that established the ICC.

77. Oliver Mathenge, "Kenya: 'Yes' Wins with Over 6 Million Votes," *Daily Nation*, August 5, 2010.

78. For more on Kenya's Truth Commission, see Lydiah Kemunto Bosire and Gabrielle Lynch, "Kenya's Search for Truth and Justice: The Role of Civil Society," *International Journal of Transitional Justice* 8, no. 2 (2014): 256–76.

79. See the CORD website: http://www.cordkenya.org/.

80. Gabrielle Lynch, "Electing the 'Alliance of the Accused': The Success of the Jubilee Alliance in Kenya's Rift Valley," *Journal of Eastern African Studies* 8, no. 1 (2014): 93–114.

81. Republic of Kenya, "National Assembly Official Report," December 22, 2010, 69.

82. Kenya-based IPSOS Public Affairs noted a drop in overall Kenyan approval of the ICC process from a height of 68 percent in October 2010 to 56 percent by July 2011. During the same period, support for the ICC dropped from 73 percent to 36 percent in Kenyatta's Central Province stronghold and from 61 percent to 37 percent in Ruto's Rift Valley. See Synovate Research, "Countdown for ICC support Declines," August 11, 2011, http://www.ipsos.co.ke/.

83. Barack Obama, "Statement by President Obama on the International Criminal Court Announcement," December 15, 2010, http://www.whitehouse.gov/the-press-office/2010/12/15/statement-president-obama-international-criminal-court-announcement.

84. Barack Obama, "President Obama's Message to the People of Kenya," February 5, 2013, http://www.whitehouse.gov/blog/2013/02/05/president-obamas-message-people-kenya.

85. Grant T. Harris, Special Assistant to the President and Senior Director for African Affairs, "President Obama's Message to the People of Kenya," February 5, 2013, http://www.whitehouse.gov/blog/2013/02/05/president-obamas-message-people-kenya.

86. Kevin Kelley, "'Choices Have Consequences,' US Tells Kenyan Voters," *Daily Nation*, February 7, 2013.

87. Jason Straziuso and Tom Odula, "Kenya's Tribal 'O' Factor: Obama, Ocampo, Odinga," *Huffington Post*, April 15, 2011, http://www.huffingtonpost.com/2011/04/18/kenya-obama-ocampo-odinga_n_849914.html. The article was also posted on popular blog sites like thegrio.com and on the *Boston Globe's* public site, Boston.com.

88. Jerome Corsi, "Obama Funded Foreign Thug Who Promised Islamic State," *World News Daily*, October 19, 2008, http://www.wnd.com/2008/10/78324/; Jerome Corsi, "Democrat Firm Advising Obama's Communist Kenyan Pal," *World News Daily*, December 19, 2011, http://www.wnd.com/2011/12/377429/.

89. "Obama's Kenyan Pal Target of Tell-All Book," *World News Daily*, February 22, 2012, http://www.wnd.com/2012/02/obamas-kenyan-pal-target-of-tell-all-book/#Zq4Woxs22OVlS9kA.99. Also see Bernard Namunane, "Miguna Sends Book on Raila to Controversial US Publisher," *Daily Nation*, February 26, 2012; and Miguna Miguna, *Peeling Back the Mask: A Quest for Justice in Kenya* (London: Gilgamesh, 2012).

90. "Raila's Fightback Plan amid Miguna Storm," *Daily Nation*, July 14, 2012.

91. Jeffery Gettleman, "Neighbors Kill Neighbors as Kenyan Vote Stirs Old Feuds," *New York Times*, February 23, 2013.

92. Nima Elbagir, "Armed as Kenyan Vote Nears," CNN, February 28, 2014, http://www.cnn.com/video/#/video/international/2013/02/28/elbagir-kenya-armed.cnn?iref=allsearch.

93. Michael Holman, "Foreign Reporters Armed and Ready to Attack Kenya," *Daily Nation*, March 2, 2013.

94. Ibid.

95. Mkoma wa Ngugi, "Kenya Vote: How the West Was Wrong," *Guardian*, March 12, 2013, http://www.theguardian.com/world/2013/mar/12/kenya-elections-west-wrong.

96. For instance, Lance Kipngetich, "Politicians Should Rise above Tribalism, Parochialism," *Standard*, November 18, 2012; and Mutuma Mathiu, "Elections: What We Must Do Right to Prevent a 2008-Style Meltdown," *Daily Nation*, February 13, 2013.

97. Nicholas Cheeseman, Gabrielle Lynch, and Justin Willis, "Democracy and Its Discontents: Understanding Kenya's 2013 Elections," *Journal of Eastern*

African Studies 8, no. 1 (2014): 2–24. For official vote tallies, visit the Independent Electoral and Boundaries Commission of Kenya's website: http://www.iebc.or.ke/.

98. Stephen Brown and Rosalind Raddatz, "Dire Consequences or Empty Threats? Western Pressure for Peace, Justice and Democracy in Kenya," *Journal of Eastern African Studies* 8, no. 1 (2014): 43–62; and Mueller, "Kenya and the International Criminal Court."

Chapter 7: Obama for Africa or Africa for Obama?

1. Vice President and Minister for Home Affairs Kalonzo Musyoka, "National Assembly Official Report," January 20, 2009, during a debate in Parliament on a motion to congratulate the people of the United States.

2. The popular news website allafrica.com even had a special section devoted to the 2008 US elections, compiling articles and viewpoints from media sources across the continent. See also Robert E. Washington, "Obama and Africa," *Research in Race and Ethnic Relations* 16 (2010): 3–26.

3. In 2008 allafrica.com posted 1,816 articles evoking Obama from dozens of African newspapers and media outlets across the continent and throughout the diaspora. In the month of November alone, 726 articles were posted.

4. Kilemi Mwiria, "The Freshness of Obama Candidacy Can Also Be Replicated in Kenya," *Standard*, August 30, 2008.

5. Sam N. Fonkem, "Snapshot—Had Barack Obama Been Born Cameroonian," *Post (Buea)*, August 29, 2008, http://allafrica.com/stories/200809010109.html.

6. Alfredo T. Hengari, "Obama's Triumph Provides a Moral Lesson about Democracy," *Namibian (Windhoek)*, July 11, 2008, http://allafrica.com/stories/200807110730.html; and Boco Edet, "Nigeria: The Obama Phenomenon," *Daily Trust (Abuja)*, July 29, 2008, http://allafrica.com/stories/200807290235.html.

7. Tendai Biti, MDC Secretary-General, "World Leaders Congratulate Obama," November 5, 2008, http://politicalticker.blogs.cnn.com/2008/11/05/world-leaders-congratulate-obama/.

8. Kihura Nkuba, "Uganda: Great Black Men Who Dominated the World," *New Vision*, January 3, 2009, http://allafrica.com/stories/200901050104.html.

9. Washington, "Obama and Africa," 5; W. Hassan Marsh, "Africa: Obama 'Reframes the Black Question,'" June 27, 2008, http://allafrica.com/stories/200806271195.html?viewall=1.

10. Achille Mbembe, "Obama and the Continent of Africa," *Pambazuka News*, August 11, 2008, http://www.pambazuka.org/en/category/comment/50075.

11. Barack Obama, "Renewing American Leadership," *Foreign Affairs*, July 1, 2007, http://www.foreignaffairs.com/articles/62636/barack-obama/renewing-american-leadership.

12. Witney W. Schneidman, "Africa: Obama's Three Objectives for Continent," September 29, 2008, http://allafrica.com/stories/200809291346.html.

13. References to Africa were confined mainly to a discussion of peacekeeping operations in Darfur, with Obama evoking Kenya during the first presidential debate in relation to immigration and educational opportunity. For full transcripts and video, see http://elections.nytimes.com/2008/president/debates/presidential-debates.html.

14. Nicolas Van de Walle, "US Policy towards Africa: The Bush Legacy and the Obama Administration," *African Affairs* 109, no. 434 (2010): 1–21; Bereket Habte Selassie, "Can We Expect More Than Symbolic Support? *African Studies Review* 53, no. 2 (2010): 6–11.

15. Barack Obama, "On a New Beginning," Cairo University, Cairo, Egypt, June 4, 2009, http://www.whitehouse.gov/the-press-office/remarks-president-cairo-university-6-04-09.

16. For more on the activities of civil rights luminaries such as W. E. B. Dubois, Richard Wright, and Malcom X in Ghana, see Kevin K. Gaines, *American Africans in Ghana: Black Expatriates and the Civil Rights Era* (Chapel Hill: University of North Carolina Press, 2006).

17. Barack Obama, "Remarks by the President to the Ghanaian Parliament," July 11, 2009, http://www.whitehouse.gov/the-press-office/remarks-president-ghanaian-parliament.html.

18. Donna R. Jackson, Jimmy *Carter and the Horn of Africa: Cold War Policy in Ethiopia and Somalia* (Jefferson, NC: McFarland, 2007), 33–38; and Mashudu G. Ramuhala, "Continuity or Change in U.S. Foreign Policy in Africa," in *National Security under the Obama Administration*, ed. Bahram M. Rajaee and Mark J. Miller (New York: Palgrave Macmillan, 2012), 143–59.

19. Farouk Chothia, "What Does Gaddafi's Death Mean for Africa?" BBC Africa, October 21, 2011, http://www.bbc.com/news/world-africa-15392189.

20. Kepher Otieno, "Gaddafi Gift Sparks Row in Council of Elders," *Standard*, March 14, 2010; "Kenya Elders Crown Gaddafi 'King of Africa,'" K24TV, January 4, 2011, https://www.youtube.com/watch?v=8Qw_oAUhjhc.

21. Denver Kisting, "Africa Expects Better: Obama Disappoints Africa in First Term," *Namibian*, November 8, 2012, http://allafrica.com/stories/201211080257.html.

22. Abdi Ismail Samatar, "Africa: Beware of Obama's Second Term," *African Studies Review* 56, no. 2 (2013): 179–83; Paul Tiyambe Zeleza, "Obama's Africa Policy: The Limits of Symbolic Power," *African Studies Review* 56, no. 2

(2013): 165–78; Jeremy Prestholdt, "Kenya, the United States, and Counterterrorism," *Africa Today* 57, no. 4 (2011): 2–27.

23. Geoffrey York, "Africans Pleased with Obama Victory, but Less Enthusiastic Than in 2008," *Globe and Mail*, November 7, 2012.

24. David Makali, "Kenya: Obama Has Earned World's Admiration," *Star*, November 9, 2012, http://allafrica.com/stories/201211100141.html; Mboneko Munyaga, "Africa: Obama Victory—Time for Enhanced African-American Ties," *Tanzanian Daily News*, November 9, 2012, http://allafrica.com/stories/201211100388.html?viewall=1.

25. Cintia Taylor, "Africa: Kenyan Photographer Reflects on Obamamania '08," Radio Netherlands Worldwide, November 7, 2012, http://allafrica.com/stories/201211071181.html.

26. Murithi Mutiga, "The View from Nairobi," *New York Times*, November 5, 2012.

27. Ibid.

28. "America's Global Image Remains More Positive Than China's" (Washington, DC: Pew Research Center, 2013), http://www.pewglobal.org/files/2013/07/Pew-Research-Global-Attitudes-Project-Balance-of-Power-Report-FINAL-July-18-2013.pdf.

29. Data for 2012 from "Africa," Office of the United States Trade Representative, http://www.ustr.gov/countries-regions/africa.

30. Official coverage of "2013 Africa Trip: June 27–July 2," available at http://www.whitehouse.gov/africa-trip-2013.

31. "Obama Speaks Out on Review Process," *Daily Nation*, June 4, 2010, http://www.nation.co.ke/Kenya-Referendum/Obama-speaks-out-on-review-process/-/926046/932356/-/6wcut2z/-/index.html; Rachael Nakitare and Barack Obama, Washington, DC, United States, June 1, 2010, http://vimeo.com/12268122.

32. Kevin J. Kelley, "Obama Could Visit Kenya Soon," *Daily Nation*, January 25, 2013, http://www.nation.co.ke/news/politics/Obama-could-visit-Kenya-soon/-/1064/1675512/-/orka5yz/-/index.html.

33. "Obama Snub May Be Linked to ICC, but It Has Consequences for Kenya," *Daily Nation*, May 22, 2013.

34. Barack Obama, "Remarks by President Obama at Young African Leaders Initiative Town Hall," Johannesburg, South Africa, June 28, 2013, http://www.whitehouse.gov/the-press-office/2013/06/29/remarks-president-obama-young-african-leaders-initiative-town-hall.

35. Simon Ndonga, "Kenya Not Bothered by Obama's Snub—Ruto," Capital FM (Nairobi), June 30, 2012, http://allafrica.com/stories/201307020002.html. See also Kwamchetsi Makokha, "Obama Refusal to Visit Kenya

Will Have Consequences," *Daily Nation*, June 28, 2013, http://www.nation .co.ke/oped/Opinion/Obama-refusal-to-visit-Kenya-will-have-consequences /-/440808/1898286/-/ax3nrwz/-/index.html.

36. Francis Otieno, interview, Kisumu, Kenya, May 27, 2013.

37. Joel Lawi, "Kenya: Mixed Feelings over Obama's Kenya Snub," *Tanzanian Daily News*, June 28, 2013, http://allafrica.com/stories/201306280108. html.

38. "Strange Reversal in Kogelo," *East African*, January 23, 2009; Patrick Mayoyo, "Kogelo Big Attraction for Land Buyers and Business Owners," *Daily Nation*, November 17, 2008.

39. Karin van Bemmel, "Obama Made in Kenya: Appropriating the American Dream in Kogelo," *Africa Today* 59, no. 4 (2013): 81–85.

40. Manager of Kogelo Village Resort, Kogelo, Kenya, May 28, 2013. The Obama family has disputed Rajula's claims of familial ties. See Eric Oloo, "Obama Kin Disown Ex-Councillor," *Star,* January 24, 2013, http://www.the-star.co.ke/news/2013/01/24/obama-kin-disown-ex-councillor_c729753.

41. Harold Ayodo, "The American Face of Nyangoma Kogelo," *Standard*, July 7, 2011; and Ayodo, "Real Estate Spurs Kisumu's Tourism Growth," *Standard*, May 31, 2012.

42. Manager of Kogelo Village Resort, May 28, 2013.

43. Samuel Opondo, interview, Kogelo, Kenya, July 14, 2009. See also Corporate Council on Africa, "Barack Obama Secondary School in Kenya to Receive $35,000 in Proceeds from January 20 Africa-themed Inaugural Ball in Washington," January 28, 2009, http://allafrica.com/stories/200901280724. html.

44. According to Kenya's electoral and boundaries commission in charge of the 2013 election, Malik Obama received 2,816 out of the 281,663 votes cast. Independent Electoral Boundaries Commission, "Summary of Results for Governor. March 3, 2013 General Election," 5, http://www.iebc.or.ke/.

45. In January 2009, Kogelo found its way onto Google Maps. See "Mapping Barack Obama's hometown of Kogelo," http://google-africa.blogspot. com/2009/01/mapping-barack-obamas-hometown-of.html.

46. Communications Commission of Kenya, "Quarterly Sector Statistics Report Second Quarter of the Financial Year 2013/14 (Oct–Dec)," http://www. cck.go.ke/resc/downloads/Sector_Statistics_Report_Q2_201314.pdf.

47. See Melissa Tully and Brian Ekdale, "Sites of Playful Engagement: Twitter Hashtags as Spaces of Leisure and Development in Kenya," *Information Technologies and International Development* 10, no. 3 (2014): 67–82.

48. Republic of Kenya, "Draft Diaspora Policy of Kenya" (Nairobi: Ministry of Foreign Affairs, 2011), http://www.kenyaembassy.com/pdfs/Draft

DiasporaPolicyof Kenya.pdf. Central Bank of Kenya, "Diaspora Remittances," https://www.centralbank.go/ke/index.php.

49. Data acquired via topsy.com in April 2014. Topsy was purchased by Apple in 2015 and no longer exists.

50. "Last Name Politics Light Up Twitter," *Al Jazeera*, April 24, 2014, http://stream.aljazeera.com/story/201404241950-0023671; Aggrey Mutambo, "Kalonzo Musyoka 'Ethnic Slur' Draws Fury," *Daily Nation*, April 24, 2014, http://www.nation.co.ke/news/politics/Kalonzo-Musyoka-Cord-Press-Conference/-/1064/2292484/-/138c1yk/-/index.html.

51. See Vincent Agoya, "Moses Kuria Charged with Hate Speech," *Daily Nation*, June 26, 2014; Agoya, "Outrage as Moses Kuria Makes Another Hate Remark," *Daily Nation*, January 13, 2015.

52. Michelle Osborn, "Fuelling the Flames: Rumour and Politics in Kibera," *Journal of Eastern African Studies* 2, no. 2 (2008): 315–27; Maurice N. Amutabi, "Media Boom in Kenya and Celebrity Galore," *Journal of African Cultural Studies* 25, no. 1 (2013): 14–29.

53. Jaluo.com, http://blog.jaluo.com/; "Luo Union Organizations," https://www.facebook.com/groups/luounion/; and Shepherd Mpofu, "Social Media and the Politics of Ethnicity in Zimbabwe," *Ecquid Novi: African Journalism Studies* 34, no. 1 (2013): 115–22.

54. Comments chiding the US president as "O'Mau Mau" appeared in a number of articles far removed from any foreign policy debates linked to Kenya. See, for instance, the comments attached to the following article: Brian Joondeph, "New Regulations Force Doctors to Choose between Expensive Medicine and More Visits," Daily Caller, July 11, 2014, http://dailycaller.com/2014/07/11/new-regulations-force-doctors-to-choose-between-expensive-medicine-and-more-visits/2/.

Epilogue: *Tuko Pamoja*: We Are Together

The words in the epilogue title were spoken by Auma Obama as she introduced her brother Barack Obama before his speech at Kasarani Stadium in Nairobi on July 26, 2015. The speech is available at https://www.youtube.com/watch?v=tPQWGow7VjY.

1. Rawlings Otini, "President Obama to Visit Nairobi in July," *Daily Nation*, March 30, 2015.

2. Matthew Carotenuto, "Terrorism and Violence in Kenya: Balancing a Global vs Local View," *African Studies Association Blog*, April 3, 2015, http://www.africanstudiesassociation.org/blog/128-april-2015/528-terrorism-and-violence-in-kenya-balancing-a-global-vs-local-view; and "How to Make Sense of the #GarissaAttack in Kenya (You May Want to Switch Off Television

News)," Africa Is a Country, April 4, 2015, http://africasacountry.com/2015/04/how-to-make-sense-of-the-garissaattack-in-kenya/.

3. Edward-Isaac Dovere, "Obama's Most Dangerous Trip Yet," *Politico*, July 25, 2015, http://www.politico.com/story/2015/07/obama-kenya-visit-security-120586.

4. Barbara Starr, "Obama's Trip Raises Security Concerns," CNN.Com, July 23, 2015, http://edition.cnn.com/2015/07/22/politics/obama-kenya-visit-al-shabaab-threat/.

5. See *Erin Burnett OutFront*, CNN, July 23, 2015, https://archive.org/details/CNNW_20150722_230000_Erin_Burnett_OutFront.

6. Dovere, "Obama's Most Dangerous Trip Yet."

7. Ishaan Tharoor, "Kenyans Ridicule CNN Report Calling Their Country a Terror Hotbed," *Washington Post*, July 23, 2015, https://www.washingtonpost.com/news/worldviews/wp/2015/07/23/kenyans-ridicule-cnn-report-calling-their-country-a-terror-hotbed/.

8. Nandwa Dan, Twitter post, July 26, 2015, 10:12 a.m., https://twitter.com/dan_nayo.

9. Irua Mwongera, Twitter post, August 30, 2015, 1:38 p.m., https://twitter.com/IruraMwongera.

10. Mkuu_wa_Itifaki, Twitter post, July 27, 2015, 11:53 p.m., https://twitter.com/pheloval.

11. Creatives Ambassadors, Twitter post, August 31, 2015, 3:12 a.m., https://twitter.com/davidmuriithi.

12. Shamit Patel, Twitter post, September 2, 2015, 12:17 p.m., https://twitter.com/just_sham_it.

13. Stellar Murumba, "Kenya Promotion Deal with CNN Still Suspended Despite Apology," *Business Daily*, August 16, 2015, http://www.businessdailyafrica.com/Corporate-News/No-advertising-deal-with-CNN-despite-apology--KTB-boss-says/-/539550/2834914/-/c254iaz/-/index.html.

14. "Kenya Is a Hotbed of Vibrant Culture, Says Uhuru," July 25, 2015. Available at http://www.kbc.co.ke/kenya-is-a-hotbed-of-vibrant-culture-says-uhuru/.

15. Murithi Mutiga, "CNN Executive Flies to Kenya to Apologise for 'Hotbed of Terror' Claim," *Guardian*, August 14, 2015, http://www.theguardian.com/world/2015/aug/14/cnn-kenya-apologise-obama.

16. Robert I. Rotberg, "Going to Kenya Is a Dumb Idea, Mr. President," *Politico*, May 7, 2015, http://www.politico.com/magazine/story/2015/05/going-to-kenya-is-a-dumb-idea-mr-president-117737.

17. Ibid.

18. Siddartha Mitter, Twitter post, May 8, 2015, 1:33 p.m., https://twitter.com/siddhmi/status/596775058988761088.

19. Robert, Twitter post, May 8, 2015, 7:47 a.m., https://twitter.com/Robert_ Lunalo/status/596687967579721728.

20. Dikembe Disembe, "President Obama's Coming to Kenya Is Indeed a Dumb Idea," *Kenya Today*, May 9, 2015, http://www.kenya-today.com/ opinion/dikembe-president-obama-coming-to-kenya-is-indeed-dumb-idea.

21. Ibid.

22. Jamal Axmad-Guudle, "Obama Come to Kenya, Rotberg Take a Hike," *Sahan Journal*, May 10, 2015, http://sahanjournal.com/obama-come-kenya-rotberg-take-hike/#.VfG1C87_ZkE.

23. Bret Baier, Facebook post, July 24, 2015, https://www.facebook.com/Bret-BaierSR/photos/a.141818502540709.41221.141513472571212/848672905188595/.

24. Ibid.

25. Ibid. Also, "How Kenyans Invaded Facebook to Troll Fox News," *Jambo Newspot*, July 26, 2015, http://www.jambonewspot.com/how-kenyans-on-facebook-invaded-fox-news-troll-question-on-obamas-visit-to-kenya/.

26. Peter Baker, "Kenya Trip Takes Obama Back to a Complex Part of Himself," *New York Times*, July 22, 2015, http://www.nytimes.com/2015/07/23/ world/africa/africa-trip-takes-obama-back-to-a-complex-part-of-himself. html?_r=0.

27. "Sununu Uses Obama's Kenya Trip to Restart Birther Talk," Fox News Radio, March 30, 2015, http://radio.foxnews.com/2015/03/30/sununu-uses-obamas-kenya-trip-to-restart-birther-talk/.

28. Elizabeth Chuck, "President Barack Obama Makes Birth Certificate Joke on Kenya Trip," NBCNews.com, July 25, 2015.

29. Barack Obama. "Remarks by President Obama to the People of Kenya," Office of the Press Secretary, July 26, 2015, https://www.whitehouse.gov/the-press-office/2015/07/26/remarks-president-obama-kenyan-people.

30. Scott Eric Kaufman, "'What Does That Mean?' Birthers Confused by Obama's Masterful Trolling of Them in Kenya," *Salon*, July 26, 2015, http:// www.salon.com/2015/07/26/what_does_that_mean_birthers_confused_by_ obamas_masterful_trolling_of_them_in_kenya/.

31. Jennifer Agiesta, "Misperceptions Persist about Obama's Faith, but Aren't So Widespread," CNN, September 14, 2015, http://www.cnn.com/2015/09/13/ politics/barack-obama-religion-christian-misperceptions/index.html.

32. David M. Anderson and Jacob McKnight, "Kenya at War: Al-Shabaab and Its Enemies in Eastern Africa," *African Affairs* 114, no. 454 (2015): 1–27. Also see Paul D. Williams, *Enhancing U.S. Support for Peace Operations in Africa*, council special report no. 73 (Washington, DC: Council on Foreign Relations, 2015).

33. "Kenya among the Fastest Growing Economies in Africa," World Bank, March 5, 2015, http://www.worldbank.org/en/news/press-release/2015/03/05/kenya-among-the-fastest-growing-economies-in-africa.

34. Uhuru Kenyatta, "Choose Kenya," http://www.choosekenya.go.ke/.

35. See Safaricom, http://www.safaricom.co.ke/about-us.

36. "Safaricom Awarded Kasarani Naming Rights," *Daily Nation Online*, November 29, 2013, http://www.nation.co.ke/news/Safaricom-Kasarani-Stadium-Naming-Rights/-/1056/2092920/-/itjdqr/-/index.html.

37. Marc Santora, "Obama to Push U.S. Trade in Kenya as China's Role Grows," *New York Times*, July 24, 2015, http://www.nytimes.com/2015/07/25/world/africa/obama-trip-to-kenya-offers-rare-chance-to-shore-up-economic-ties.html?_r=0.

38. Map Kibera, "Map Kibera Project—Maps and Statistics," http://mapkiberaproject.yolasite.com/maps-and-statistics.php. Kibera is a central location in the Netflix Original Series *Sense8*.

39. UNDP, "Human Development Indicators: Kenya," http://hdr.undp.org/en/countries/profiles/KEN.

40. Robert M. Maxon, "Social and Cultural Changes," in *Decolonization and Independence in Kenya*, ed. Bethwell A. Ogot and Robert Ochieng' (London: James Currey, 1995), 115.

41. John Githongo, "Kenya: Insecurity, the 'War Against Terror' Jubilee Version," *Star*, April 19, 2014, http://allafrica.com/stories/201404210264.html.

42. Isma'il KushKush, "Kenya's Wide Net against Terror Sweeps Up Refugees," April 17, 2014, http://www.nytimes.com/2014/04/18/world/africa/kenyas-answer-to-terrorism-sweeping-roundups-of-somalis.html.

43. Abdi Latif Ega, "What It Is Like to Be Somali in Kenya," Africa Is a Country, April 9, 2014, http://africasacountry.com/2014/04/whats-it-like-to-be-somali-in-kenya/. And Abraham Leno, "Kenya Must Respect the Human Rights of Somali Refugees," *Al Jazeera*, June 6, 2015, http://www.aljazeera.com/indepth/opinion/2015/06/kenya-respect-human-rights-somali-refugees-150605082231426.html.

44. Isma'il Kushkush, "Kenya Envisions a Border Wall That Keeps Shabab Violence Out," *New York Times*, April 21, 2015, http://www.nytimes.com/2015/04/22/world/africa/kenya-plans-to-build-a-border-wall-that-keeps-shabab-violence-out.html?_r=0.

45. Matthew Carotenuto and Katherine Luongo, "Where the Kenyan Heritage of Barack Obama Is an Asset," *Politico*, July 21, 2015, http://www.politico.com/magazine/story/2015/07/where-obamas-heritage-is-an-advantage-120422.

46. See, for instance, Adam Taylor, "Kenyan Lawmakers Say Obama Shouldn't Be Allowed to Talk about Gay Rights During His Visit," *Washington Post*, July 6, 2015, https://www.washingtonpost.com/news/worldviews/wp/2015/07/06/kenyan-lawmakers-say-obama-shouldnt-be-allowed-to-talk-about-gay-rights-during-his-visit/.

47. Jacopo Prisco, "Obamamania Sweeps Kenya as Resourceful Businesses Cash in on His Visit," CNN.com, July 24, 2015, http://www.cnn.com/2015/07/23/africa/kenya-visit-barack-obama/.

48. Anita Chepkoech, "Brisk Business Ahead of Obama Arrival in Kenya," *Business Daily*, July 6, 2015, http://www.businessdailyafrica.com/Brisk-business-ahead-of-Obama-arrival-in-Kenya/-/1248928/2777492/-/gc4ytp/-/index.html.

49. "Kenyan Governor Kidero Denies Grass Removed after Obama," BBC.com, July 30, 2015, http://www.bbc.com/news/world-africa-33719845.

50. Evans Kidero, Twitter post, July 21, 2015, 5:36 a.m., https://twitter.com/KideroEvans/status/623471623790727168.

51. Joy Chelagat, "These Are the Funniest Tweets about 'Kidero's Grass,'" *Citizen Digital*, July 21, 2015, http://citizentv.co.ke/lifestyle/these-are-the-funniest-tweets-about-kideros-grass-95593/.

52. "KOTs Burn Kidero's Grass into Ashes under the Hashtag #KideroGrass," HekaHeka.com, July 21, 2015, http://www.hekaheka.com/kot-burn-kideros-grass-into-ashes-under-the-hashtag-kiderograss/.

53. Moses Odhiambo, "Siaya Draws Sh52m Budget to Welcome Barack Obama," *Daily Nation*, July 16, 2015, http://www.nation.co.ke/news/Siaya-County-draws-Sh52m-budget-to-welcome-Barack-Obama/-/1056/2791460/-/view/printVersion/-/p2th71z/-/index.html.

54. Sarah Wheaton, "Obama Faces Gay Rights Challenge in Kenya," *Politico*, July 23, 2015, http://www.politico.com/story/2015/07/your-obama-seen-as-promoting-lgbt-rights-in-anti-gay-kenya-120511.

55. Barack Obama, "Remarks by President Obama and President Kenyatta of Kenya in a Press Conference," Kenyan State House, July 25, 2015, https://www.whitehouse.gov/the-press-office/2015/07/25/remarks-president-obama-and-president-kenyatta-kenya-press-conference.

56. Amanda Stone, "President Obama Travels to Kenya and Ethiopia," *Whitehouse Blog*, July 26, 2015, https://www.whitehouse.gov/blog/2015/07/26/president-obama-travels-kenya-and-ethiopia.

57. Obama, "Remarks by President Obama to the People of Kenya."

58. Ibid.

59. Ibid.

60. Murithi Mutiga, "Obama's Strong Words for Kenya Are Welcome. But It's Too Little, Too Late," *Guardian*, July 28, 2015, http://www.theguardian.com/commentisfree/2015/jul/28/obama-kenya-us-africa.

61. Boniface Mwangi, quoted in David Smith, "Obama Faces Political Minefield During Kenyan 'Homecoming,'" *Guardian*, July 23, 2015, http://www.theguardian.com/world/2015/jul/23/obama-kenya-visit-political-minefield.

62. Barack Obama, "Press Conference by the President," White House East Room, July 15, 2015, https://www.whitehouse.gov/the-press-office/2015/07/15/press-conference-president.

63. Michael D. Shear and Gardiner Harris, "With High-Profile Help, Obama Plots Life after Presidency," *New York Times*, August 16, 2015, http://www.nytimes.com/2015/08/17/us/politics/with-high-profile-help-obama-plots-life-after-presidency.html.

64. Margaret Talev, David Malingha Doya, and Mike Dorning, "Obama Says Kenya Visit Is Down Payment on Post-Presidential Era," *Bloomberg Politics*, July 25, 2015, http://www.bloomberg.com/politics/articles/2015-07-25/obama-says-kenya-visit-is-down-payment-on-post-presidential-era.

65. See https://www.facebook.com/BBCSwahili/photos/a.174737689211571.40310.160894643929209/1025156267503038/.

Glossary

bwana	Man/Mr./Sir—often used in colonial times as a title for white settlers to reinforce racial hierarchies
chang'aa	Home-brewed alcohol
dala	Luo homestead
Dholuo	Luo language
futa	Cloth wrap
githaka	Kikuyu system of land tenure
gweng'	Collection of lineages bound by marriage or defensive alliances
harambee	Fund-raisers
Jaluo/Joluo	Luo person/people; Nilotic Kavirondo
Jonam	/Joka-Nyanam People of lakes and rivers
kabaka	Luganda term meaning "king"
kanzu	Long robe
Kavirondo	Colonial term used to refer to the Winam Gulf of Lake Victoria as well as to the Joluo (Nilotic Kavirondo) and Abaluhya (Bantu Kavirondo) populations of its shores
ker	"Defender of norms and values"/ Luo Union president
keyo	One's extended patrilineage
kipande	Colonial identity card for Africans
Kisumu Ndogo	Little Kisumu; urban Luo neighborhood
kofia	Cap
maduka	Small kiosk shops

majimboism	The strategy of dividing Kenya into provinces with equal political power
mama	Mrs.—implies motherhood/respect
mashambani	Kiswahili term commonly used to refer to rural areas
matatu	Common public transport vehicle used in East Africa
mzee	Wise old man (a term of respect)
nyumba	House
oganda	Multiclan territorial conglomerates (also called *piny*)
panga	Machete
piny	Multiclan territorial conglomerates (also called *oganda*)
riwruok	Union/ unity
rungu	Club
shamba	Garden/farm
ugali	Staple dish of boiled maize meal
ujamaa	Familyhood/community
wananchi	Citizen

Bibliography

Archival Sources
Kenya National Archives—Nairobi (KNA)
District Commissioner, Kakamega (DC/KMG)
District Commissioner, Kisumu (DC/KSM)
District Commissioner, Machakos (DC/MKS)
Ministry of Native/African Affairs (MAA)
Mombasa Municipal Council (UY)
Murumbi Africana Collection (KEN)
Nairobi Extra-Provincial District (RN)
Provincial Commissioner, Central Province (PC/CP)
Provincial Commissioner, Coast Province (CA)
Provincial Commissioner, Nyanza (PC/NZA)
Public Record   Office, Kew Gardens, Great Britain (PRO)
Kenya, original correspondence (CO/533)
Records of the Foreign and Commonwealth Office and Predecessors (FCO/141)
Records of the Imperial Economic Committee and Commonwealth Economic
    Committee (DO/213)
Syracuse University Kenya National Archives collection, microfilm number
    4723, reel 63

Newspapers, Periodicals, Media Outlets, and Blogs/Discussion Boards
Africasacountry.com
Al Jazeera
AllAfrica.com
blog.jaluo.com
Bloomberg

Business Daily
Capital FM (Nairobi)
Citizen
CNN
Daily Nation
Daily Telegraph
Daily Trust (Abuja)
dissentmagazine.org
East African
Forbes
Fox News
Globe and Mail
Guardian
Mashada.com
Namibian
New Vision (Kampala)
New York Times
Nile Buffalo Gazette
Politico
Post (Beau)
Radio Netherlands Worldwide
Ramogi
Salon
Spiegel Online International
Standard (Nairobi)
Star (Nairobi)
Sunday Post
Sunday Times
Tanzanian Daily News
Time
Trust
USA Today
Vanguard (Lagos)
Washington Post
Weekly Review
Weekly Standard
Whitehouse.gov
World Net Daily

Books and Articles

Achieng, Jane. *Paul Mboya's "Luo kitgi gi timbegi": A Translation into English.* Nairobi: Atai Joint, 2001.

Adichie, Chimamanda. "Danger of a Single Story." Presented at TEDGlobal 2009, Palm Springs, California, July 21–29, 2009. http://www.ted.com/talks/chimamanda_adichie_the_danger_of_a_single_story.html.

Akoth, Steve Ouma. "The Meanings of Obama in K'ogello: Culture, Ethno-Politics and the Making of Leaders in Multiparty Kenya." *Anthropology Southern Africa* 33, nos. 3–4 (2010): 114–25.

Alila, Patrick O. *Kenya General Elections in Bondo and Gem: The Origins of Luo Ethnic Factor in Modern Politics.* Nairobi: University of Nairobi Institute for Development Studies, 1984.

Amin, Shahid. *Event, Metaphor, Memory: Chauri Chaura, 1922–1992.* Berkeley: University of California Press, 1995.

Amutabi, Maurice N. "Media Boom in Kenya and Celebrity Galore." *Journal of African Cultural Studies* 25, no. 1 (2013): 14–29.

Anderson, David M. *Histories of the Hanged: The Dirty War in Kenya and the End of Empire.* New York: Norton, 2005.

———. "Vigilantes, Violence and the Politics of Public Order in Kenya." *African Affairs* 101, no. 405 (2002): 531–55.

———. "'Yours in Struggle for Majimbo': Nationalism and the Party Politics of Decolonization in Kenya, 1955–64." *Journal of Contemporary History* 40, no. 3 (2005): 547–64.

Anderson, David M., and Jacob McKnight. "Kenya at War: Al-Shabaab and Its Enemies in Eastern Africa." *African Affairs* 114, no. 454 (2015): 1–27.

Andrews, Phyllis. *Who Am I? The Story of Barack Obama.* Nairobi: East African Educational Publishers, 2010.

Anyany, Samuel. *Kar Chakruok Mar Luo.* Kisumu: Equatorial Publishers, 1952.

Badejo, Babafemi A. *Raila Odinga: An Enigma in Kenyan Politics.* Lagos: Yintab, 2006.

Banita, Georgiana. "'Home Squared': Barack Obama's Transnational Self-Reliance." *Biography* 33, no. 1 (2010): 24–45.

Barber, Karin, ed. *Africa's Hidden Histories: Everyday Literacy and Making the Self.* Bloomington: Indiana University Press, 2006.

Barkun, Michael. *A Culture of Conspiracy: Apocalyptic Visions in Contemporary America.* Berkeley: University of California Press, 2013.

Barringer, Terry, and Marion Wallace, eds. *African Studies in the Digital Age: DisConnects?* Leiden: Brill, 2014.

Berman, Bruce. "Ethnography as Politics, Politics as Ethnography: Kenyatta, Malinowski, and the Making of *Facing Mount Kenya.*" *Canadian Journal of African Studies* 30, no. 3 (1996): 313–44.

Berman, Bruce, and John Lonsdale. *State and Class*. Bk. 1 of *Unhappy Valley: Conflict in Kenya and Africa*. London: James Currey, 1992.

———. *Violence and Ethnicity*. Bk. 2 of *Unhappy Valley: Conflict in Kenya and Africa*. London: James Currey, 1992.

Berry, Sara. "Hegemony on a Shoestring: Indirect Rule and Access to Agricultural Land." *Africa* 62, no. 3 (1992): 327–55.

Blount, Ben G. "Agreeing to Agree on Genealogy: A Luo Sociology of Knowledge." In *Sociocultural Dimensions of Language Use*, edited by Mary Sanches and Ben G. Blount, 117–35. New York: Academic Press, 1975.

Bosire, Lydiah Kemunto, and Gabrielle Lynch. "Kenya's Search for Truth and Justice: The Role of Civil Society." *International Journal of Transitional Justice* 8, no. 2 (2014): 256–76.

Branch, Daniel. "At the Polling Station in Kibera." *London Review of Books* 30, no. 2 (2008): 26–27.

———. *Defeating Mau Mau, Creating Kenya: Counterinsurgency, Civil War, and Decolonization*. Cambridge: Cambridge University Press, 2009.

———. *Kenya: Between Hope and Despair, 1963–2011*. New Haven, CT: Yale University Press, 2011.

———. "The Search for the Remains of Dedan Kimathi: The Politics of Death and Memorialization in Post-Colonial Kenya." *Past and Present* 206, no. S5 (2010): 301–20.

Branch, Daniel, Nicholas Cheeseman, and Leigh Gardner, eds. *Our Turn to Eat: Politics in Kenya since 1950*. Berlin: LIT, 2010.

Brown, Stephen, and Rosalind Raddatz. "Dire Consequences or Empty Threats? Western Pressure for Peace, Justice and Democracy in Kenya." *Journal of Eastern African Studies* 8, no. 1 (2014): 43–62.

Bruner, Edward M. "The Maasai and the Lion King: Authenticity, Nationalism, and Globalization in African Tourism." *American Ethnologist* 28, no. 4 (2001): 881–908.

Campbell, John R. "Who Are the Luo? Oral Tradition and Disciplinary Practices in Anthropology and History." *Journal of African Cultural Studies* 18, no. 1 (2006): 73–87.

Carotenuto, Matthew. "Repatriation in Colonial Kenya: African Institutions and Gendered Violence." *International Journal of African Historical Studies* 45, no. 1 (2012): 9–28.

———. "Riwruok e teko: Cultivating Identity in Colonial and Postcolonial Kenya." *Africa Today* 53, no. 2 (2006): 53–73.

Carotenuto, Matthew, and Katherine Luongo. "*Dala* or Diaspora? Obama and the Luo Community of Kenya." *African Affairs* 108, no. 431 (2009): 197–219.

Carotenuto, Matthew, and Brett Shadle. "Toward a History of Violence in Colonial Kenya." *International Journal of African Historical Studies* 45, no. 1 (2012): 1–7.

Chakravarty, Gautam. *The Indian Mutiny and the British Imagination.* Cambridge: Cambridge University Press, 2005.

Charton-Bigot, Hélène, and Deyssi Rodriguez-Torres, eds. *Nairobi Today: The Paradox of a Fragmented City.* Dar es Salaam: Mkuki na Nyota, 2010.

Cheeseman, Nicholas, Gabrielle Lynch, and Justin Willis. "Democracy and Its Discontents: Understanding Kenya's 2013 Elections." *Journal of Eastern African Studies* 8, no. 1 (2014): 2–24.

Chege, Michael. "Kenya: Back from the Brink?" *Journal of Democracy* 19, no. 4 (2008): 125–39.

Cohen, David William. "Perils and Pragmatics of Critique: Reading Barack Obama Sr.'s 1965 Review of Kenya's Development Plan." Paper presented at the University of KwaZulu Natal History and African Studies Seminar, March 24, 2010.

———. "Perils and Pragmatics of Critique: Reading Barack Obama Sr.'s 1965 Review of Kenya's Development Plan." *African Studies* 74, no. 3 (2015): 1–23.

———. "The River-Lake Nilotes from the Fifteenth to the Nineteenth Century." In *Zamani: A Survey of East African History*, edited by Bethwell A. Ogot, 135–49. Nairobi: East African Educational Publishers, 1968.

Cohen, David William, and E. S. Atieno Odhiambo. "Ayany, Malo, and Ogot: Historians in Search of a Luo Nation." *Cahiers d'études africaines* 27, nos. 107–8 (1987): 269–86.

———. *Burying SM: The Politics of Knowledge and the Sociology of Power in Africa.* Portsmouth, NH: Heinemann, 1992.

———. *The Risks of Knowledge: Investigations into the Death of the Hon. Minister John Robert Ouko in Kenya, 1990.* Athens: Ohio University Press, 2004.

———. *Siaya: The Historical Anthropology of an African Landscape.* Athens: Ohio University Press, 1989.

Comaroff, John L., and Jean Comaroff. *Ethnicity Inc.* Chicago: University of Chicago Press, 2009.

Communications Commission of Kenya, "Quarterly Sector Statistics Report Second Quarter of the Financial Year 2013/14 (Oct–Dec 2013)." http://216.154.209.114/resc/downloads/Sector_Statistics_Report_Q2_201314.pdf.

Cooper, Frederick. *On the African Waterfront: Urban Disorder and the Transformation of Work in Colonial Mombasa.* New Haven, CT: Yale University Press, 1987.

Corsi, Jerome R. *The Obama Nation: Leftist Politics and the Cult of Personality.* New York: Threshold, 2008.

———. *Where's the Birth Certificate? The Case That Barack Obama Is Not Eligible to Be President.* Washington, DC: WND, 2011.

Crawford, Jarret T., and Anuschka Bhatia. "Birther Nation: Political Conservatism Is Associated with Explicit and Implicit Beliefs That President Barack Obama Is Foreign." *Analyses of Social Issues and Public Policy* 12, no. 1 (2012): 364–76.

Crazzolara, Joseph P. *The Lwoo. Part I: Lwoo Migrations.* Verona: Editrice Nigrizia, 1950.

———. *The Lwoo. Part II: Lwoo Traditions.* Verona: Editrice Nigrizia, 1951.

———. *The Lwoo. Part III: Lwoo Clans.* Verona: Editrice Nigrizia, 1954.

Dahya, B. W. "Some Characteristics of Tribal Associations in Kampala." In *Proceedings of the East African Institute for Social Research Conference, Jan 1963.* Kampala: Makerere University East African Institute for Social Research, 1963.

Dinesen, Isak. *Out of Africa.* London: Penguin, 1937.

D'Souza, Dinesh. *The Roots of Obama's Rage.* Washington, DC: Regnery, 2010.

Elkins, Caroline. *Imperial Reckoning: The Untold Story of Britain's Gulag in Kenya.* New York: Holt, 2005.

Ellis, Stephen. "Writing Histories of Contemporary Africa." *Journal of African History* 43, no. 1 (2002): 1–26.

Evans-Pritchard, E. E. "Luo Tribes and Clans." *Rhodes Livingston Journal* 7 (1949): 24–40.

Falola, Toyin, and Kwame Essien, eds. *Pan-Africanism, and the Politics of African Citizenship and Identity.* New York: Routledge, 2014.

Firstbrook, Peter. *The Obamas: The Untold Story of an African Family.* New York: Crown, 2010.

Freund, Bill. *The African City: A History.* Cambridge: Cambridge University Press, 2007.

Gadsden, Fay. "The African Press in Kenya, 1945–1952." *Journal of African History* 21, no. 4 (1980): 515–35.

Gaines, Kevin K. *American Africans in Ghana: Black Expatriates and the Civil Rights Era.* Chapel Hill: University of North Carolina Press, 2006.

Geissler, Paul W., and Ruth J. Prince. *The Land Is Dying: Contingency, Creativity and Conflict in Western Kenya.* New York: Berghahn Books, 2010.

Geschiere, Peter. *The Perils of Belonging: Autochthony, Citizenship, and Exclusion in Africa and Europe.* Chicago: University of Chicago Press, 2009.

Getz, Trevor R., ed. *African Voices of the Global Past: 1500 to the Present.* Boulder, CO: Westview, 2014.

Goldsworthy, David. "Ethnicity and Leadership in Africa: The 'Untypical' Case of Tom Mboya." *Journal of Modern African Studies* 20, no. 1 (1982): 107–26.
———. *Tom Mboya: The Man Kenya Wanted to Forget.* Portsmouth, NH: Heinemann, 1982.
Grillo, Ralph D. *African Railwaymen: Solidarity and Opposition in an East African Labour Force.* Cambridge: Cambridge University Press, 1973.
Hastings, Adrian. *The Construction of Nationhood: Ethnicity, Religion and Nationalism.* Cambridge: Cambridge University Press, 1997.
Hemingway, Ernest. *Green Hills of Africa.* New York: Scribner, 1935.
Hercules, Bob, and Keith Walker. *Senator Obama Goes to Africa.* New York: First Run Features, 2006, DVD.
Herne, Brian. *White Hunters: The Golden Age of African Safaris.* New York: Holt, 1999.
Herring, Ralph S., David William Cohen, and Bethwell A. Ogot. "The Construction of Dominance: The Strategies of Selected Luo Groups in Uganda and Kenya." In *State Formation in Eastern Africa*, edited by Ahmed I. Salim, 126–52. London: Heinemann, 1984.
Hobley, Charles W. "British East Africa: Anthropological Studies in Kavirondo and Nandi." *Journal of the Royal Anthropological Institute of Great Britain and Ireland* 33 (1903): 325–36.
———. "Nilotic Tribes of Kavirondo." In *Eastern Uganda: An Ethnological Survey*, 26–35. Occasional Papers, No. 1. London: Royal Anthropological Institute of Great Britain and Ireland, 1902.
Hoehler-Fatton, Cynthia. *Women of Fire and Spirit: History, Faith, and Gender in Roho Religion in Western Kenya.* New York: Oxford University Press, 1996.
Horne, Gerald. *Mau Mau in Harlem? The U.S. and the Liberation of Kenya.* New York: Palgrave Macmillan, 2009.
Hornsby, Charles. *Kenya: A History since Independence.* London: Tauris, 2012.
Hughes, Lotte. "'Truth Be Told': Some Problems with Historical Revisionism in Kenya." *African Studies* 70, no. 2 (2011): 182–201.
Hughey, Matthew W. "Show Me Your Papers! Obama's Birth and the Whiteness of Belonging." *Qualitative Sociology* 35, no. 2 (2012): 163–81.
Hughey, Matthew W., and Jessie Daniels. "Racist Comments at Online News Sites: A Methodological Dilemma for Discourse Analysis." *Media, Culture and Society* 35, no. 3 (2013): 332–47.
Human Rights Watch. "Violence as a Political Tool in Kenya: The Case of the Coast." In *Playing with Fire: Weapons Proliferation, Political Violence, and Human Rights in Kenya.* New York: Human Rights Watch, 2002.
Huxley, Elspeth. *White Man's Country: Lord Delamere and the Making of Kenya.* London: Chatto and Windus, 1954; New York: Praeger, 1968.

Ikonya, Philo. *The Kenyan Boy Who Became President of America*. Nairobi: Media Horizons Network, 2008.

Iliffe, John. *A Modern History of Tanganyika*. Cambridge: Cambridge University Press, 1979.

International Federation for Human Rights and Kenya Human Rights Commission. *Massive Internal Displacement in Kenya Due to Politically Instigated Ethnic Clashes: Absence of Political and Humanitarian Responses*. Nos. 471–72 (2007).

Jackson, Donna R. *Jimmy Carter and the Horn of Africa: Cold War Policy in Ethiopia and Somalia*. Jefferson, NC: McFarland, 2007.

Jackson, Will. "White Man's Country: Kenya Colony and the Making of a Myth." *Journal of Eastern African Studies* 5, no. 2 (2011): 344–68.

Jacobs, Sally H. *The Other Barack: The Bold and Reckless Life of President Obama's Father*. New York: Public Affairs, 2011.

Jerven, Morten. *Africa: Why Economists Get It Wrong*. London: Zed Books, 2015.

Kagwanja, Peter. "Courting Genocide: Populism, Ethno-Nationalism and the Informalisation of Violence in Kenya's 2008 Post-Election Crisis." *Journal of Contemporary African Studies* 27, no. 3 (2009): 365–87.

Kanogo, Tabitha. *Squatters and the Roots of Mau Mau, 1905–63*. London: James Currey, 1987.

Kanyinga, Karuti. "The Legacy of the White Highlands: Land Rights, Ethnicity and the Post-2007 Election Violence in Kenya." *Journal of Contemporary African Studies* 27, no. 3 (2009): 325–44.

Keim, Curtis A. *Mistaking Africa: Curiosities and Inventions of the American Mind*. Boulder, CO: Westview, 2013.

Kennedy, Dane K. "The Imperial History Wars." *Journal of British Studies* 54, no. 1 (2015): 5–22.

———. *Islands of White: Settler Society and Culture in Kenya and Southern Rhodesia, 1890–1939*. Durham, NC: Duke University Press, 1987.

Kenyatta, Jomo. *Facing Mount Kenya: The Tribal Life of the Gikuyu*. London: Secker and Warburg, 1938.

———. *Harambee! The Prime Minister of Kenya's Speeches, 1963–1964*. London: Oxford University Press, 1964.

———. "The Kenya African Union Is Not the Mau Mau." Speech presented at the Kenya Africa Union Meeting at Nyeri, July 26, 1952. http://www.fordham.edu/halsall/mod/1952kenyatta-kau1.html.

Klopp, Jacqueline M. "Pilfering the Public: The Problem of Land Grabbing in Contemporary Kenya." *Africa Today* 47, no. 1 (2000): 7–26.

Knight, Peter, ed. *Conspiracy Nation: The Politics of Paranoia in Postwar America*. New York: New York University Press, 2002.

Krapf, Johann L. *Travels, Researches, and Missionary Labors, during an Eighteen Years' Residence in Eastern Africa.* Boston: Ticknor and Fields, 1860.

Lafargue, Jerome, ed. *The General Elections in Kenya, 2007.* Dar es Salaam: Mkuki na Nyota, 2009.

Lame, Danielle de. "Grey Nairobi: Sketches of Urban Socialities." In Charton-Bigot and Rodriguez-Torres, *Nairobi Today*, 167–214.

Lewis, George. "Barack Hussein Obama: The Use of History in the Creation of an 'American' President." *Patterns of Prejudice* 45, nos. 1–2 (2011): 43–61.

Lonsdale, John. "The Conquest State, 1895–1904." In Ochieng', *Modern History of Kenya*, 6–35.

———. "Mau Maus of the Mind: Making Mau Mau and Remaking Kenya." *Journal of African History* 31, no. 3 (1990): 393–421.

Luce, Lila. *Barack Obama: Yes, We Can!* Nairobi: Sasa Sema, 2009.

Lugard, Frederick D. *The Dual Mandate in British Tropical Africa.* London: Blackwood, 1922.

———. *The Rise of Our East African Empire: Early Efforts in Nyasaland and Uganda.* Edinburgh: Blackwood, 1893.

Luo Council of Elders. "Report on Proposed Kit Mikayi Tourist Site." Unpublished report, 2009.

Luongo, Katherine. "Prophecy, Possession, and Politics: Negotiating the Supernatural in 20th Century Machakos, Kenya." *International Journal of African Historical Studies* 45, no. 2 (2012): 191–216.

Lynch, Gabrielle. "Becoming Indigenous in the Pursuit of Justice: The African Commission on Human and People's Rights and the Endorois." *African Affairs* 111, no. 442 (2012): 24–45.

———. "Electing the 'Alliance of the Accused': The Success of the Jubilee Alliance in Kenya's Rift Valley." *Journal of Eastern African Studies* 8, no. 1 (2014): 93–114.

———. *I Say to You: Ethnic Politics and the Kalenjin in Kenya.* Chicago: University of Chicago Press, 2011.

Maathai, Wangari. *Unbowed: A Memoir.* New York: Anchor, 2007.

MacArthur, Julie E. *Cartography and the Political Imagination: Mapping Community in Colonial Kenya.* Athens: Ohio University Press, 2016.

———. "The Making and Unmaking of African Languages: Oral Communities and Competitive Linguistic Work in Western Kenya." *Journal of African History* 53, no. 2 (2012): 151–72.

———. "When Did the Luyia (or Any Other Group) Become a Tribe?" *Canadian Journal of African Studies* 47, no. 3 (2013): 351–63.

Macharia, Keguro. "Jambo Bwana: Kenya's Barack Obama." *Qualitative Sociology* 35, no. 2 (2012): 213–27.

Madiega, Philister Adhiambo, Tracey Chantler, Gemma Jones, and Ruth Prince. "'Our Son Obama': The US Presidential Election in Western Kenya." *Anthropology Today* 24, no. 6 (2008): 4–7.

Malo, Shadrack. *Dhoudi Mag Central Nyanza*. Nairobi: Eagle Press, 1953.

Mamdani, Mahmood. *When Victims Become Killers: Colonialism, Nativism, and the Genocide in Rwanda*. Princeton, NJ: Princeton University Press, 2002.

Markham, Beryl. *West with the Night*. Boston: Houghton Mifflin, 1942.

Maxon, Robert M. "Social and Cultural Changes." In Ogot and Ochieng', *Decolonization and Independence in Kenya*, 110–47.

Mbembe, Achille, and Janet Roitman. "Figures of the Subject in Times of Crisis." *Public Culture* 7, no. 2 (1995): 323–52.

Mboya, Paul. *Luo kitigi gi timbegi*. Nairobi: East African Standard, 1938.

Mboya, Tom. *The Challenge of Nationhood: A Collection of Speeches and Writings*. London: Heinemann, 1970.

———. *Freedom and After*. Boston: Little, Brown, 1963.

McIntosh, Janet. "Elders and 'Frauds': Commodified Expertise and Politicized Authenticity among Mijikenda." *Africa* 79, no. 1 (2009): 35–52.

Miguda, Edith A. "Mau Mau in Nairobi,1946–1956: The Luo Experience." MA thesis, University of Nairobi, 1987.

Miguna, Miguna. *Peeling Back the Mask: A Quest for Justice in Kenya*. London: Gilgamesh, 2012.

Miller, Charles. *The Lunatic Express*. New York: Macmillan, 1971.

Molohan, M. J. B. *Detribalization*. Dar es Salaam: Government Printer, 1959.

Morel, Edmund D. *The Black Man's Burden: The White Man in Africa from the Fifteenth Century to World War I*. New York: Monthly Review Press, 1969. Reprint of the 1920 edition.

Morrison, Lesa B. "Banished to the Political Wilderness? The Standard Narrative and the Decline of the Luo of Kenya." PhD diss., Duke University, 2004.

———. "The Nature of Decline: Distinguishing Myth from Reality in the Case of the Luo of Kenya." *Journal of Modern African Studies* 45, no. 1 (2007): 117–42.

Mpofu, Shepherd. "Social Media and the Politics of Ethnicity in Zimbabwe." *Ecquid Novi: African Journalism Studies* 34, no. 1 (2013): 115–22.

Mueller, Susanne D. "Kenya and the International Criminal Court (ICC): Politics, the Election and the Law." *Journal of Eastern African Studies* 8, no. 1 (2014): 25–42.

Mugane, John M. *The Story of Swahili*. Athens: Ohio University Press, 2015.

Muigai, Githu. "Jomo Kenyatta and the Rise of the Ethno-Nationalist State in Kenya." In *Ethnicity and Democracy in Africa*, edited by Bruce Berman, Dickson Eyoh, and Will Kymlicka, 200–217. Athens: Ohio University Press, 2004.

Munene, Karega. "Museums in Kenya: Spaces for Selecting, Ordering and Erasing Memories of Identity and Nationhood." *African Studies* 70, no. 2 (2011): 224–45.

Muoria-Sal, Wangari, Bodil F. Frederiksen, John Lonsdale, and Derek Peterson, eds. *Writing for Kenya: The Life and Works of Henry Muoria*. Leiden: Brill, 2009.

Mutua, Makau. *Kenya's Quest for Democracy: Taming Leviathan*. Boulder, CO: Rienner, 2008.

Mwakimako, Hassan. "The Historical Development of Muslim Courts: The Kadhi, Mudir and Liwali Courts and the Civil Procedure Code and Criminal Procedure Ordinance, c. 1963." *Journal of Eastern African Studies* 5, no. 2 (2011): 329–43.

Njogu, Kimani, ed. *Healing the Wound: Personal Narratives about the 2007 Post-Election Violence in Kenya*. Nairobi: Twaweza, 2009.

Nowrojee, Binaifer. *Divide and Rule: State-Sponsored Ethnic Violence in Kenya*. New York: Human Rights Watch, 1993.

Nyairo, Joyce, and James Ogude. "Popular Music, Popular Politics: *Unbwogable* and the Idioms of Freedom in Kenyan Popular Music." *African Affairs* 104, no. 415 (2005): 225–49.

Nyamweru, Celia. "Natural Cultural Sites of Kenya: Changing Contexts, Changing Meanings." *Journal of Eastern African Studies* 6, no. 2 (2012): 270–302.

Nyerere, Julius K. *Ujamaa: Essays on Socialism*. Oxford: Oxford University Press, 1968.

Obama, Barack H. *The Audacity of Hope: Thoughts on Reclaiming the American Dream*. New York: Crown, 2006.

———. *Dreams from My Father: A Story of Race and Inheritance*. New York: Random House, 1995.

Obama, Barack H. "Problems Facing Our Socialism." *East Africa Journal* 2, no. 4 (1965): 26–33.

Obudho, Robert. "Urbanisation and Industrialisation." In Ochieng', *Historical Studies and Social Change in Western Kenya*, 194–218.

Ochieng', William R., ed. *Historical Studies and Social Change in Western Kenya: Essays in Memory of Professor Gideon S. Were*. Nairobi: East African Educational Publishers, 2002.

———, ed. *A Modern History of Kenya, 1895–1980: In Honour of B. A. Ogot*. Nairobi: Evans, 1989.

———. *An Outline History of Nyanza Up to 1914*. Nairobi: East African Literature Bureau, 1974.

———. "Structural and Political Changes." In Ogot and Ochieng', *Decolonization and Independence in Kenya*, 83–109.

Odhiambo, E. S. Atieno. "'Seek Ye First the Economic Kingdom': A History of the Luo Thrift and Trading Corporation (LUATATCO), 1945–56." In *Hadith 5: Economic and Social History of East Africa*, edited by Bethwell A. Ogot, 218–56. Nairobi: East African Literature Bureau, 1975.

Odhiambo, E. S. Atieno, and John Lonsdale, eds. *Mau Mau and Nationhood: Arms, Authority and Narration*. Athens: Ohio University Press, 2003.

Odinga, Ajuma Oginga. *Not Yet Uhuru: The Autobiography of Oginga Odinga*. London: Heinemann, 1967.

Odinga, Raila Amolo. *Raila Odinga: The Flame of Freedom*. Nairobi: Mountain Top, 2013.

Ogot, Bethwell A. *Building on the Indigenous Selected Essays, 1981–1998*. Kisumu: Anyange Press, 1999.

———. "East African Institute of Social and Cultural Affairs, Nairobi." *Journal of Modern African Studies* 3, no. 2 (1965): 283–85.

———. *A History of the Luo-Speaking Peoples of Eastern Africa*. Kisumu: Anyange Press, 2009.

———. *History of the Southern Luo: Migration and Settlement, 1500–1900*. Nairobi: East African Publishing, 1967.

———. "Mau Mau and Nationhood: The Untold Story." In Odhiambo and Lonsdale, *Mau Mau and Nationhood*, 8–36.

———. *My Footprints on the Sands of Time: An Autobiography*. Kisumu: Anyange Press, 2003.

Ogot, Bethwell A., and William R. Ochieng', eds. *Decolonization and Independence in Kenya, 1940–93*. London: James Currey, 1995.

Ogude, James. "The Vernacular Press and the Articulation of Luo Ethnic Citizenship: The Case of Achieng' Oneko's *Ramogi*." *Current Writing* 13, no. 2 (2001): 42–55.

Ogutu, Gilbert E. M. *Ker in the 21st Century Luo Social System*. Kisumu: Sundowner, 2004.

———. *Ker Jaramogi Is Dead, Who Shall Lead My People? Reflections on Past, Present, and Future Luo Thought and Practice*. Kisumu: Palwa Research, 1994.

Okia, Opolot. *Communal Labor in Colonial Kenya: The Legitimization of Coercion, 1912–1930*. New York: Palgrave Macmillan, 2012.

———. "In the Interests of Community: Archdeacon Walter Owen and the Issue of Communal Labour in Colonial Kenya, 1921–30." *Journal of Imperial and Commonwealth History* 32, no. 1 (2004): 19–40.

Olson, James S., and Robert Shadle, eds. *Historical Dictionary of the British Empire*. Vol. 1. Westport, CT: Greenwood Press, 1996.

Omanjo, H. O. "The Constitution of the Luo Council of Elders 21st Century and Beyond." Luo Council of Elders. Unpublished paper, 2001.

O'Neill, John E., and Jerome L. Corsi. *Unfit for Command: Swift Boat Veterans Speak Out against John Kerry*. Washington, DC: Regnery, 2004.

Ong'wen Okuro, Samwel. "Our Women Must Return Home: Institutionalized Patriarchy in Colonial Central Nyanza District, 1945–1963." *Journal of Asian and African Studies* 45, no. 5 (2010): 522–33.

Onyango, Leah, Anne Omollo, and Elizabeth Ayo. "Gender Perspectives of Property Rights in Rural Kenya." In *Essays in African Land Law*, edited by Robert Home, 135–53. Pretoria: Pretoria University Press, 2011.

Osborn, Michelle. "Fuelling the Flames: Rumour and Politics in Kibera." *Journal of Eastern African Studies* 2, no. 2 (2008): 315–27.

Owen, W. E. "Food Production and Kindred Matters amongst the Luo." *Journal of the East Africa and Uganda Natural History Society* 11 (1933): 235–49.

Parker, Mary. *Political and Social Aspects of the Development of Municipal Government in Kenya with Special Reference to Nairobi*. Nairobi: Government Printer, 1949.

Parkin, David J. *The Cultural Definition of Political Response: Lineal Destiny among the Luo*. London: Academic Press, 1978.

Parlett, Martin A. *Demonizing a President: The "Foreignization" of Barack Obama*. Santa Barbara, CA: Praeger, 2014.

Peterson, Derek R. *Creative Writing: Translation, Bookkeeping, and the Work of Imagination in Colonial Kenya*. Portsmouth, NH: Heinemann, 2004.

———. *Ethnic Patriotism and the East African Revival: A History of Dissent, c. 1935–1972*. Cambridge: Cambridge University Press, 2012.

Peterson, Derek R., Kodzo Gavua, and Ciraj Rassool, eds. *The Politics of Heritage in Africa: Economies, Histories, and Infrastructures*. Cambridge: Cambridge University Press, 2015.

Peterson, Derek R., and Giacomo Macola, eds. *Recasting the Past: History Writing and Political Work in Modern Africa*. Athens: Ohio University Press, 2009.

Plaatje, Solomon T. *Native Life in South Africa*. London: King, 1914.

Prestholdt, Jeremy. "Kenya, the United States, and Counterterrorism." *Africa Today* 57, no. 4 (2011): 2–27.

———. "Politics of the Soil: Separatism, Autochthony, and Decolonization at the Kenyan Coast." *Journal of African History* 55, no. 2 (2014): 249–70.

Ramuhala, Mashudu G. "Continuity or Change in U.S. Foreign Policy in Africa." In *National Security under the Obama Administration*, edited by Bahram M. Rajaee and Mark J. Miller, 143–59. New York: Palgrave Macmillan, 2012.

Republic of Kenya. *Constitution of Kenya*. Nairobi: Government Printer, 2010.

———. *Kenya National Assembly Official Record*. Kenyan parliamentary debates. books.google.com.

———. *Kenya Population Census 1969*. Vol. 2, *Data on Urban Population*. Nairobi: Statistics Division, 1971.

———. *Kenya: Vision 2030*. Nairobi: Ministry of Planning and National Development, 2007. www.vision2030.go.ke.

———. *The Laws of Kenya*. Nairobi: Government Printer, 1972. http://www.kenyalaw.org.

———. "Record of Evidence Taken before the Judicial Commission of Inquiry into Tribal Clashes in Kenya." July 20, 1998. Cited in Human Rights Watch, "Violence as a Political Tool in Kenya," 2002. http://www.hrw.org/reports/2002/kenya/Kenya0502-04.htm.

———. *Report of the Commission of Inquiry into the Post Election Violence*. Nairobi: Government Printer, 2008.

———. *Report of the Truth, Justice and Reconciliation Commission*. Nairobi: Truth, Justice and Reconciliation Commission, 2013.

———. *2009 Population and Housing Census Results*. Nairobi: Kenya National Bureau of Statistics, 2010.

Reyes, G. Mitchell. "The Swift Boat Veterans for Truth, the Politics of Realism, and the Manipulation of Vietnam Remembrance in the 2004 Presidential Election." *Rhetoric and Public Affairs* 9, no. 4 (2006): 571–600.

Roosevelt, Theodore. *African Game Trails: An Account of the African Wanderings of an American Hunter-Naturalist*. New York: Scribner, 1910.

Rosberg, Carl G., Jr., and John Nottingham. *The Myth of "Mau Mau": Nationalism in Kenya*. Nairobi: East Africa Publishing, 1966.

Ruark, Robert. *Something of Value*. New York: Doubleday, 1955.

Samatar, Abdi Ismail. "Africa: Beware of Obama's Second Term." *African Studies Review* 56, no. 2 (2013): 179–83.

Science. "President Roosevelt's African Trip." Vol. 28, no. 729 (December 18, 1908): 876–77.

Scott, James C. *Weapons of the Weak: Everyday Forms of Peasant Resistance*. New Haven, CT: Yale University Press, 1985.

Scotton, James F. "Growth of the Vernacular Press in Colonial East Africa." PhD diss., University of Wisconsin, 1971.

Selassie, Bereket Habte. "Can We Expect More Than Symbolic Support?" *African Studies Review* 53, no. 2 (2010): 6–11.

Shachtman, Tom. *Airlift to America: How Barack Obama, Sr., John F. Kennedy, Tom Mboya, and 800 East African Students Changed Their World and Ours*. New York: St. Martin's, 2009.

Shadle, Brett L. *"Girl Cases": Marriage and Colonialism in Gusiiland, Kenya, 1890–1970*. Portsmouth, NH: Heinemann, 2006.

———. "Settlers, Africans, and Inter-Personal Violence in Kenya, ca. 1900–1920s." *International Journal of African Historical Studies* 45, no. 1 (2012): 57–80.

Shaw, Alexander. *Men of Africa.* London: Colonial Empire Marketing Board, 1940. This film is available for streaming online at http://www.colonialfilm. org.uk/.

Sheriff, Abdul. *Dhow Cultures of the Indian Ocean: Cosmopolitanism, Commerce and Islam.* New York: Columbia University Press, 2010.

Shipton, Parker M. *Mortgaging the Ancestors: Ideologies of Attachment in Africa.* New Haven, CT: Yale University Press, 2009.

———. *The Nature of Entrustment: Intimacy, Exchange, and the Sacred in Africa.* New Haven, CT: Yale University Press, 2007.

Smith, James Howard. "Snake-Driven Development: Culture, Nature and Religious Conflict in Neoliberal Kenya." *Ethnography* 7, no. 4 (2006): 423–59.

Sobania, Neal W. *Culture and Customs of Kenya.* Westport, CT: Greenwood Press, 2003.

Spear, Thomas. "Neo-Traditionalism and the Limits of Invention in British Colonial Africa." *Journal of African History* 44, no. 1 (2003): 3–27.

Steinhart, Edward I. "Hunters, Poachers and Gamekeepers: Towards a Social History of Hunting in Colonial Kenya." *Journal of African History* 30, no. 2 (1989): 247–64.

Sullivan, Paul. *Kikuyu District: The Edited Letters of Francis Hall, 1892–1901.* Dar es Salaam: Mkuti na Nyota, 2006.

Sundiata, Ibrahim. "Obama, African Americans, and Africans: The Double Vision." In *African Americans in U.S. Foreign Policy: From the Era of Frederick Douglass to the Age of Obama*, edited by Linda Heywood, Allison Blakely, Charles Stith, and Joshua C. Yesnowitz, 200–212. Urbana: University of Illinois Press, 2015.

Swynnerton, R. J. M. "Agricultural Advances in Eastern Africa." *African Affairs* 61, no. 244 (1962): 201–15.

Throup, David, and Charles Hornsby. *Multi-Party Politics in Kenya: The Kenyatta and Moi States and the Triumph of the System in the 1992 Election.* Athens: Ohio University Press, 1998.

Trevor-Roper, Hugh R. "The Past and the Present: History and Sociology." *Past and Present* 42 (1969): 3–17.

Trzebinski, Errol. *The Life and Death of Lord Erroll: The Truth behind the Happy Valley Murder.* London: Fourth Estate, 2000.

Tully, Melissa, and Brian Ekdale. "Sites of Playful Engagement: Twitter Hashtags as Spaces of Leisure and Development in Kenya." *Information Technologies and International Development* 10, no. 3 (2014): 67–82.

United Nations Environment Programme. *Kenya: Atlas of Our Changing Environment*. Nairobi: UNEP, 2009. http://www.unep.org/dewa/africa/kenyaatlas/.

Van Bemmel, Karin. "Obama Made in Kenya: Appropriating the American Dream in Kogelo." *Africa Today* 59, no. 4 (2013): 68–90.

Van de Walle, Nicolas. "US Policy towards Africa: The Bush legacy and the Obama Administration." *African Affairs* 109, no. 434 (2010): 1–21.

Vanthemsche, Guy. *Belgium and the Congo, 1885–1980*. Translated by Alice Cameron and Stephen Windross. Cambridge: Cambridge University Press, 2012.

Wainana, Binyavanga. "How to Write about Africa." *Granta* 92 (2005).

Waliaula, Solomon, and Joseph Basil Okong'o. "Performing Luo Identity in Kenya: Songs of Gor Mahia." In *Identity and Nation in African Football: Fans, Community, and Clubs*, edited by Chuka Onwumechili and Gerard Akindes, 83–96. New York: Palgrave Macmillan, 2014.

Warner, Benjamin R., and Ryan Neville-Shepard. "Echoes of a Conspiracy: Birthers, Truthers, and the Cultivation of Extremism." *Communication Quarterly* 62, no. 1 (2014): 1–17.

Washington, Robert E. "Obama and Africa." *Research in Race and Ethnic Relations* 16 (2010): 3–26.

White, Luise. *The Comforts of Home: Prostitution in Colonial Nairobi*. Chicago: University of Chicago Press, 1990.

White, Luise, Stephan F. Miescher, and David William Cohen, eds. *African Words, African Voices: Critical Practices in Oral History*. Bloomington: Indiana University Press, 2001.

Williams, Paul D. *Enhancing U.S. Support for Peace Operations in Africa*. Council special report no. 73. Washington, DC: Council on Foreign Relations, 2015.

Willis, Justin. *Mombasa, the Swahili, and the Making of the Mijikenda*. New York: Oxford University Press, 1993.

———. "What Has He Got up His Sleeve? Advertising the Kenyan Presidential Candidates in 2007." *Journal of Eastern African Studies* 2, no. 2 (2008): 264–71.

Willis, Justin, and George Gona. "Tradition, Tribe, and State in Kenya: The Mijikenda Union, 1945–1980." *Comparative Studies in Society and History* 55, no. 2 (2013): 448–73.

Wilson, Godfrey. *The Economics of Detribalization in Northern Rhodesia*. Manchester: Manchester University Press, 1940.

Wilson, Gordon M. *Luo Customary Law and Marriage Laws Customs*. Nairobi: Government Printer, 1961.

Wolf, Thomas P. "'Poll Poison'? Politicians and Polling in the 2007 Kenya Election." *Journal of Contemporary African Studies* 27, no. 3 (2009): 279–304.

Wright, Donald R. *The World and a Very Small Place in Africa: A History of Globalization in Niumi, the Gambia*. New York: Sharpe, 2010.

Wrigley, C. C. "The Problem of the Lwo." *History in Africa* 8 (1981): 219–46.

Wrong, Michela. *It's Our Turn to Eat: The Story of a Kenyan Whistle-Blower*. New York: Harper, 2009.

Zeleza, Paul Tiyambie. *Barack Obama and African Diasporas: Dialogues and Dissensions*. Athens: Ohio University Press, 2009.

———. "The Establishment of Colonial Rule, 1905–1920." In Ochieng', *Modern History of Kenya*, 35–71.

———. "Obama's Africa Policy: The Limits of Symbolic Power." *African Studies Review* 56, no. 2 (2013): 165–78.

Interviews

Interviews cited took place from 2004 to 2013. All interviews were conducted by the authors in Kenya. Translation assistance was provided for some interviews by Henry Adera, Amos Odhiambo, and Martin Adero Metho. Transcriptions and notes remain in the authors' possession.

Gor, Walter, Lela, April 13, 2004
Members of the Kisumu Museum Staff, Kisumu, July 13, 2009
Members of the Luo Council of Elders, Maseno West Branch, Kit Mikayi, July 15, 2009
Metho, M., Lela, April 10, 2004
Oboge, Magdalene, Kisumu, June 27, 2007
Odege, Dorcas, Kisumu, July 14, 2009
Odhiambo, A. Maseno, June 26, 2007
Ogallo, Meshack Riaga, Karachuonyo, October 14, 2004, and July 1, 2007
Okoth, James, Nairobi, June 12, 2007
Oneko, Achieng, Kunya Beach, October 15, 2004
Onyango, Grace, Kisumu, June 27, 2007
Opondo, Samuel, Kogelo, July 14, 2009
Osawa, Adera, Kisumu and Awendo, October, 13, 2004, and July 1, 2007
Otieno, David, Nairobi, June 10, 2007
Otieno, Francis, Kisumu, May 27, 2013
Otondi, Opiyo, Awendo, July 2, 2007
Oyugi, Gideon, Kit Mikayi, July 15, 2009
Raila, Alogo, Bondo, April 12, 2004
Students at Senator Obama Kogelo Secondary School, Kogelo, July 14, 2009

Index

pacification, 32
patrimonialism, 60, 61, 66, 69, 99, 100, 122, 131, 140, 153

Ramogi, 45–46, 53, 60, 62, 69, 104, 110, 114, 123–24; Ramogi Institute of Advanced Technology (RIAT), 63; *Ramogi* newspaper, 46, 49–50, 53, 59, 69, 111
resistance, 18, 20–22, 29, 32, 36–37, 39–42, 48
Rift Valley, 16, 63, 118–20, 129, 133
Roosevelt, Teddy, 26–29
Ruto, William, 120, 135–37, 140, 150, 167

Siaya, 11–12, 47, 68, 96, 151, 153
social media, 3, 25, 69, 118, 154–56, 158, 160, 162
"Son of the Soil," 14, 45, 69, 74, 78, 121, 124, 132–34, 140, 143, 148, 156
South Sudan, 13, 16, 19, 45–46, 105, 109–13, 142, 163
Sudan, 2, 19, 27, 62, 109–13

Tea Party, 76, 87, 94
terrorism, 13, 39–40, 79, 82–84, 86–87, 145–47, 149, 158–60, 162, 167
terrorism in Kenya: Al-Qaeda bombing of US embassy in Nairobi (1998), 13; Al-Shabaab attack at Garissa University, 158, 164; Al-Shabaab attack at Westgate Mall, 154, 158, 162, 164
trade, 13, 18, 32, 163
tribalism, 2, 6, 19, 22, 24, 65–66, 74, 79–81, 88, 92, 100, 116–18, 122, 130–32, 138–40, 155, 158–60, 167
tribe, 19, 22–23, 30, 31–34, 38–39, 40, 44, 47–49, 52–55, 58, 61, 65, 122
Trump, Donald, 76, 161
Twitter, 153–55, 158, 160, 165

Uganda, 13, 18–19, 27, 32, 45, 46, 51–52, 110–11, 113, 163
United Nations, 106, 130, 163

Waki Commission, 128, 129, 135
World Net Daily (WND), 75, 77–78, 81–82, 83, 94, 138